HIGH CAMP

MARLENE DIETRICH (1901–1992), German-born actress in one of her 1930s Hollywood publicity photos. "If she had nothing but her voice, she could break your heart with it. But she also has that beautiful body and the timeless loveliness of her face." —Ernest Hemingway.

HIGH CAMP

*A Gay Guide to Camp
and Cult Films*

Volume 1

PAUL ROEN

LEYLAND PUBLICATIONS
San Francisco

Dedication:

for THE RANDSTER

1st edition 1994

Front cover: Publicity photo of Carmen Miranda from the film *Doll Face* (20th Century Fox 1945).
Cover layout by Rupert Kinnard

ISBN 0–943595–45–2 (hardcover)
ISBN 0–943595–42–8 (paperback)

Library of Congress Catalog Card Number: 93–80253

Leyland Publications
P.O. Box 410690
San Francisco, CA 94141
Complete catalogue of available books: $1 ppd.

CONTENTS

Titles marked with an asterisk are available on video.

*The Adventures of Captain
   Marvel 21
*Affair in Trinidad 25
*Ali Baba and the
   Forty Thieves 23
*All About Eve 25
*All This, and Heaven Too . . 27
Andy Warhol's Dracula 27
The Anniversary 28
Another Man's Poison 29
*Autumn Leaves 30
*Baby Face 32
*Beach Blanket Bingo 35
*Ben-Hur 35
*Beyond the Forest 37
*Black Lizard 38
*Blonde Venus 39
*Bloody Pit of Horror 40
*The Boys in the Band 42
*Breakfast at Tiffany's 43
The Bride and the Beast 44
*Bullwhip 45
*Can't Stop the Music 47
Cobra Woman 49
College Confidential 51
*Colossus and the
   Amazon Queen 53
*Conquest 54
*Cry-Baby 55
*The Damned 56
Damon and Pythias 57
*Dead Ringer 58
*Desperate Living 59
*Dishonored 60
*Doctor of Doom 60
*Doll Face 61
*Dragstrip Girl 62
*Drum 64
Duel of the Titans 65
*Eyes of Texas 66
*Fellini Satyricon 67

*Female Trouble 67
*The 5,000 Fingers of Dr. T . . 69
*Flamingo Road 70
*Flash Gordon 72
*Flesh 72
*Flying Down to Rio 73
*Frankenstein's Daughter 73
The Gang's All Here 74
*Gentlemen Prefer Blondes . . 75
*The Giant of Marathon 76
*The Giants of Thessaly 78
*Gilda 79
*Girls in Prison 80
*Gladiators of Rome 84
*Glen or Glenda? 81
*Goliath and the Barbarians . . 85
*Hairspray 87
*Heat 88
*Hercules 89
*Hercules Against
   the Moon Men 89
*Hercules and the Captive
   Women 91
*Hercules Unchained 92
*Hero of Rome 93
*High School Caesar 94
*High School Confidential! . . 96
Hot Rod Gang 95
*Hush . . . Hush, Sweet
   Charlotte 98
*I Could Go on Singing 98
*I, Mobster 99
*I'm No Angel 101
*The Importance of Being
   Earnest 102
*In This Our Life 103
*Jail Bait 104
*Jezebel 105
*Johnny Guitar 106
*Jubilee Trail 109
Jungle Woman 110

*La Cage aux Folles 111
*Ladies of the Chorus 112
*Laura 114
*Law of Desire 115
*The Little Foxes..........116
*The Lost City............116
*Lost Horizon 119
*The Loves of Hercules 120
*Lust in the Dust 121
*Madam Satan...........123
*The Magic Christian 124
*The Maltese Falcon 126
*Mandingo 127
*The Mark of Zorro 129
Mask of the Musketeers ...131
*Mata Hari 132
*Maurice 134
*Mildred Pierce 133
*Mr. Skeffington 136
*Mommie Dearest 136
*Mondo Trasho...........138
*Morocco 139
*Motorcycle Gang 140
*Multiple Maniacs........141
*The Music Lovers 141
*My Little Chickadee 142
*Myra Breckinridge 143
The Nanny..............145
A Night in Paradise 146
*Now, Voyager 147
Old Acquaintance 148
*The Old Maid 148
*The Outlaw 150
*Outrageous! 151
*Paris Is Burning 152
*Pink Flamingos 153
*Please Don't Touch Me! ...154
*Polyester................155
*The Private Lives of
    Elizabeth and Essex.....157
*The Prodigal 158
*Queen Christina.........159
*Queen of Outer Space 161
*The Queen of Sheba 165
*Querelle 165
*Rain and *Miss Sadie
    Thompson 166

*Rebel Without a Cause 167
*Reform School Girls 169
*Risky Business 169
*The Rocky Horror Picture
    Show 170
*The Roman Spring of
    Mrs. Stone...........171
*Salome 174
*Salome, Where She Danced ..174
*Samson Against the Sheik ..175
*Samson and Delilah 177
*Samson and the Seven
    Miracles of the World ...177
*Samson vs. the Vampire
    Woman 178
*The Scarlet Empress 179
*The Seven Year Itch......180
*Sextette 183
*Shanghai Express.........184
*She Done Him Wrong 185
*The Silver Chalice 186
*Sincerely Yours 187
*The Sinister Urge 189
*The Sisters 192
Sitting Pretty 190
Slander 193
*Some Like It Hot 195
*Son of Samson 197
*The Son of the Sheik 198
*Springtime in the Rockies ..198
*Spy Smasher.............199
Staircase 202
*The Star 203
*A Star Is Born 204
*A Stolen Life 205
Storm Center 206
Strange Fascination 207
*A Streetcar Named Desire ..208
*Suddenly, Last Summer 209
*Sunset Boulevard 212
*Superargo and the Faceless
    Giants 211
*Tarzan and the Trappers ...214
Tarzan's Hidden Jungle 216
Tarzan's Magic Fountain ...216
*Taxi Zum Klo 217
*The Ten Commandments ..218

*The Terror of Rome Against
   the Son of Hercules 219
*The Thief of Bagdad 220
*The Third Sex 221
Thirteen Women 224
*Thor and the Amazon
   Women 224
*Thoroughbreds Don't Cry . . 225
*Till the End of Time 226
*Torch Song Trilogy 227
*Trash 229
Trog 230
*The Tyrant of Lydia Against
   the Son of Hercules 231
Untamed Youth 232
*Victor / Victoria 233
*What Ever Happened to
   Baby Jane? 234

*Wicked Stepmother 235
*Wild Mustang 236
*The Wild One 236
*The Wild, Wild World
   of Jayne Mansfield 238
Will Success Spoil
   Rock Hunter? 237
*The Witch's Curse 240
*The Wizard of Oz 241
*A Woman's Face 242
*The Women 243
*Women on the Verge of a
   Nervous Breakdown 244
*The Wrestling Women vs.
   the Aztec Mummy 245
*Young Frankenstein 245
*Ziegfeld Girl 246
*Zorro's Fighting Legion 248

Index of Principal Performers 249

Front cover: Publicity photo of Carmen Miranda from the film *Doll Face*
          (20th Century Fox 1945).

Two of the many sources from which videos can be obtained:

FACETS MULTIMEDIA
1517 West Fullerton Ave.
Chicago, Illinois 60614
1-800-331-6197
[purchase and rental]

MOVIES UNLIMITED
6736 Castor Avenue
Philadelphia, Pennsylvania 19149
1-800-523-0823
[purchase only]

Invitation to Readers

We intend to publish a second volume of *High Camp* and invite those readers knowledgeable about gay camp / cult films to send in their detailed suggestions for films eligible for inclusion. Please expand on the reasons why you think the films in question are gay camp. And please remember that camp films *per se* are not eligible; they must have gay content or have gay icon stars, or be gay cult films. If we accept your suggestion, you will receive a complimentary copy of volume 2 when published. Please send letters with s.a.s.e. to:

Paul Roen
c/o Leyland Publications
PO Box 410690
San Francisco, CA 94141

MAE WEST (1892–1980), mistress of the camp quip onscreen and off: "It's not the men in my life, it's the life in my men that counts." MAE to a young man in one of her films: "How tall are you, son?" YOUTH: "M'am, I'm six feet seven inches." MAE: "Let's forget the six feet and talk about the seven inches!" Shown here in a 1930s publicity photo.

INTRODUCTION

Camp, Cult, and Cinema

Remember Mrs. Miller? Her name was Elva Miller, as I recall, but she was billed simply as Mrs. Miller. During the mid-Sixties, the heyday of camp, she enjoyed a very brief popularity for her fabulously awful soprano renditions of then-current pop songs. I remember that, shortly before her appearance on the Ed Sullivan show, a reporter asked her if she knew what the word "camp" meant. Her outraged reply: "I don't allow that kind of language in my house!"

In those days, camp could be construed as a dirty word. More than a quarter century later, camp still is largely associated with homosexuals and homosexuality, mainly because the concept originated in the homosexual subculture and is still most thoroughly appreciated there. However, despite its potential for sexual subversiveness, the idea of camp has also crossed over into the mainstream and been absorbed by it. In terms of film, camp has come to mean any brazen triumph of theatrical artifice over dramatic substance. Camp is a phoniness that glories in itself. More essential still, camp is funny. The humor derives from a certain ironic discrepancy between results and intentions.

There are those who claim that an appreciation of camp is strictly a function of the gay sensibility. I do not agree. An enormous amount of camp has been perpetrated by heterosexuals, as we all well know. And, if they are able to create it (however unintentionally), why should they not be able to enjoy it? Conversely, I've encountered a dreary assortment of gay men who are unable to comprehend the very concept of camp. They are afflicted with an excess of what is commonly known as "good" taste. ("The chief enemy of creativity is 'good' taste."—Pablo Picasso.) The truly cultivated are the fortunate few who are able to perceive and savor the virtues of "bad" taste as well as "good."

Because of the penetration of camp into general culture, it is necessary to make a distinction between gay camp and the non-gay variety. It is possible to designate many, many films as being camp, but only those of intrinsic interest to homosexuals can qualify as

9

gay camp.

A more confusing, but no less important distinction is that which separates the camp film from the cult film. A cult film is any movie which has built up a sizable and obsessive—even fanatical—following. Such films are seen over and over again by their fans, even to the point where much of the dialogue is learned by heart. Of course, there are cult films which have both a straight following and a gay following. *The Maltese Falcon* is one example.

Other cult films owe their reputation almost entirely to gays. A majority of these gay cult films are also gay camp films. *All About Eve* and *Some Like It Hot*, for example, are rightly recognized as masterworks by both the mainstream and the gay underground. But, though indisputably fine movies, both possess certain garishly theatrical qualities which definitely fall under the heading of camp. In *All About Eve*, camp resides in the brilliant flamboyance of a star performance by Bette Davis. In *Some Like It Hot*, camp forms the very essence of the plot: men dressing up as women. And even a heterosexual should have sense enough to see that, in both cases, the homosexual camp component is also the component to which the movie principally owes its success. In other words, just because a film is camp doesn't necessarily mean that it's a bad film, even by the heterosexist standards of the mainstream. Likewise, even if a film isn't camp, it may still have the potential to be a gay cult film (e.g. *Maurice*). I've included a scattering of examples in this book. A cult film, however, is often more difficult to recognize than a camp film: by definition a camp film *must* contain camp elements, whereas a cult is something which attaches itself to a film some time after it's been made.

Now, perhaps, is a good time to clarify what this book is *not*. It is not a book about serious gay-themed films such as *Parting Glances*. Nor is it a book about gay and lesbian experimental films (which, however campy, are often inaccessible). This is strictly a book about gay camp and cult films and the (often) intermingling of the two.

*   *   *

The meaning of gay camp varies somewhat according to cinematic genre. With that in mind, let's take a look at some genres and how the quality of camp specifically functions within each one.

Gay Camp and the Melodrama

This particular genre is known as melodrama, which should give us a clue as to its camp properties. Male homosexuals have always been devoted fans of the melodrama (sometimes called, with semi-sexist overtones, the "women's picture"), because of the opportunities it provides for identification with the heroine. There's also an S&M component.

The camp quality usually lurks in the highly improbable, extravagant dilemmas which comprise the plots of these films, and in the heroine's histrionic response to her various and assorted troubles. Generally speaking, the more turgid, trite, and overwrought her travails, the better.

The one leading lady most closely and consistently associated with this sort of drama is, of course, the incomparable Joan Crawford. This serves to explain her huge and devoted gay following. Crawford unfailingly valued her fans, both gay and straight. Such was sadly not the case with Bette Davis, who tended to specialize in the same type of film, and get the same type of fan. When the two combined forces in *Whatever Happened to Baby Jane?*, their straight fans may not have been pleased (the film was not what's classically considered a woman's picture), but their gay fans were delighted; the film indubitably qualifies as gay camp.

We cannot leave this genre without consideration of two exotics: Marlene Dietrich and Greta Garbo, both of whom made women's pictures which qualify as gay camp. Dietrich's were mostly for a single director: Josef von Sternberg, whose perversely romantic sensibility produced delirious, decadent visions that homosexuals especially appreciate. Garbo's films were more varied; her best-known films transcend both camp and genre. Movies such as *Ninotchka* and *Anna Karenina* fall outside the domain of this book. On occasion, however, her splendid hauteur was enlisted in the service of outright melodrama. These are the moments that the camp fancier relishes.

Gay Camp and the Musical

The Hollywood musical is a genre which, by definition, exudes camp. Any film in which people intermittently burst into song is obviously theatrical, stylized, and patently unreal. Add to this the fact that musicals tend to be all awash with glitter, tinsel, and garish artifice, and you begin to see why people associate camp with this genre more than any other. As a rule, musicals invariably have to include camp elements. It's also true that this is the film genre which gays most often gravitate toward. Because of the way this kind of film is unavoidably permeated with camp, it is difficult to pinpoint which musicals specifically qualify as being gay camp. It's safe to say that anything starring Carmen Miranda is a sure bet. Same goes for Judy Garland. As movie stars go, Garland seems to have become the ultimate gay camp icon, partly because of her androgyny (she often performed in boyish costumes), but mainly because of her painful vulnerability, her victimhood.

Gay Camp and the Action Adventure

This is the genre most pervaded with gay male sexuality. Think of the many action adventures which transpire in sultry tropical and Mediterranean locales! Think of the many action heroes partial to skimpy costumes! Tarzan is merely the most obvious example; there are numerous others.

For sheer, unmitigated gay camp, however, there's one particular kind of adventure film that constitutes a virtual mother lode. This subgenre is known by many names: Hercules movies, gladiator movies, sword-and-sandal movies, etc. Technically, this kind of film should be called by an Italian name—the peplum—since it is, in fact, an Italian species of film. Atrociously dubbed into English, these movies actually seem to have been specifically tailored to suit the demands of a male homosexual audience.

Theoretically, these are stories drawn from history and the ancient myths. In fact, however, they are sex films. The gay camp element derives from the tension between wholesome, healthy, innocuous boy-oh-boy storylines on the one hand, contrasting, on the other, with a not-so-innocent sexual subtext which often becomes explicit and which, furthermore, is frequently laden with sadism. The hero is always a bodybuilder, his muscles utterly voluptuous. Steve Reeves and Gordon Scott, both of them American, are the fellows most commonly associated with the peplum form, but many other well-constructed men toiled in this field.

For a while, in the early Sixties, the film studios of Rome were Mecca for bodybuilders (and their admirers) all over the globe.

During that all-too-brief span of time, literally hundreds of these films were produced. (This book includes a generous assortment, including all the most notorious examples.) Of course, each movie had its damsel in distress, but she was usually just a token heroine. The dramatic emphasis was always on rippling muscles, masculine camaraderie, and killing the bad guy (often as well-built as the good guy, and just as scantily clad). The homoeroticism was dealt with symbolically, but also explicitly—and was always, I think, intentional. The sexual element was, in fact, so explicit and clearly premeditated that some of these movies go beyond gay camp, into the realm of softcore erotica.

Gay Camp and the Horror Film

Can't go far wrong here. The campiest horror film, however, is generally the cheapest—the one that asks the viewer to suspend disbelief, but can't afford the special effects to keep its own end of the bargain. For example, a film that features Cadillac hubcaps masquerading as flying saucers *(Plan 9 from Outer Space)*, or a giantess who's so obviously a double exposure that we can literally see right through her *(Attack of the 50 Foot Woman)*.

To qualify as gay camp, however, it's not enough that a horror film should have a rock-bottom budget. Something more is required. The best definition of a horror film that I have ever heard is simply this: an exercise in "controlled bad taste." That may suffice in the camp horror film; in the gay camp horror film, however, it's imperative that the bad taste be seriously out of control. To appeal to gays, in other words, a camp horror film should be not only cheap, but also sleazy and vulgar. The plot should transgress the bounds of bourgeois decency. A bizarre and grotesque sexuality should pervade the proceedings (either homo- or hetero-; it makes no difference). These are the sort of films that appall the oppressive middle-class mind. In other words, what we're talking about here is the kind of horror flick which, thirty or forty years ago, used to play in fleapit theatres on 42nd Street in New York. At that time they were regarded as little better than a social disease. In those days before the era of porno chic, scuzzy and lurid horror flicks (without stars, without production values) tested the limits of how far a film could go. Which is precisely why they now deserve—and get —a new cult following.

Gay Camp and the Comedy Film

At this point we find ourselves faced with a paradox: if a camp film is one that's so bad it's unintentionally funny, how can a comedy —which, by definition, is good if it's funny and bad if it's not funny—possibly qualify as camp?! I must confess I don't really know the answer to that one. At the same time, I know of several films that have nonetheless managed to turn the trick. The significant components in the gay camp comedy tend to be actresses who (a) are gay cult figures, (b) are blatantly sexual, and (c) draw upon their sexuality as the source and basis of their humor.

Three stars immediately come to mind when we think of gay camp comedy. Each, significantly, is a favorite of female impersonators. The first is Mae West, a self-created personality who wrote her own material and who also can rightly be designated a pioneer in the field of sexual expression. Gays have always adored her films. Her camp quality resides in the tension between her aggressively masculine sexuality and her opulently feminine face, figure, and screen persona. Truly, she is like a gay man trapped in a woman's body.

The appeal of the other two great gay camp comediennes is more complicated: Marilyn Monroe and Jayne Mansfield both made some very funny, very campy movies, yet both of these women are rightly regarded as tragic figures, victimized by straight male patriarchal attitudes which, at the time these performers flourished, were operating at their highest pitch and in a most destructive capacity. Mansfield, admittedly, was a willing victim, conspiring in her own degradation every step of the way. And yet it is this very grotesqueness, this obviousness, this cartoonishness in her sex appeal which ultimately won her a legion of gay male fans. Gay men also love Marilyn Monroe, the unwilling victim, whose sex appeal was just as openly displayed, but whose breathy voice and dizzy manner made it all seem so innocent, so entirely unconscious.

Gay Camp and the Western

Here is a heading that will give many gay men pause. What can there possibly be for *us* in the genre that John Wayne made his own?

Well, quite a lot, as a matter of fact. Gay camp westerns are of three general types:

(a) Westerns which invert sexual expectations by featuring a woman in the principal tough guy role. Any western which gives an actress top billing, or which features a cast in which the women outnumber the men, is very probably gay camp material.

(b) Westerns in which all the dramatic emphasis is placed on the "buddy" relationship between two cowboys. You know what I mean. I'll grant you that hundreds and hundreds of horse operas answering to this description have been made. The gay camp ones are, obviously, the ones in which the hero and his buddy seem unusually close.

(c) The juvenile B-grade westerns of the Thirties, Forties, and early Fifties. These oatburners are a world unto themselves. Designed to satisfy the baser instincts of rowdy little boys unalterably opposed to "mush" and cinematic "love stuff," these films literally could not help but transpire in a world of dream-like homoeroticism. Enhancing the camp effect is the fact that the hero is almost always played by some winsome, wholesome male crooner, the classic examples being Roy Rogers and Gene Autry. This subgenre passed out of existence when its principal exponents migrated to television and/or Nashville. Presently obscure, these films have little or no gay following. However, I'm hoping this will change.

Gay Camp and the Cliffhanger Serial

While we're on the subject of naughty little boys and their anti-social cravings, we should take a look at the chapterplay format, which, in small town and neighborhood cinemas all across America, once enjoyed a phenomenal popularity as part of each Saturday's matinee double bill. Like the B-westerns (which often shared the same marquee), the serials were geared to amuse and entertain the sort of prepubescent males who dislike and resent the female sex. These mindless, seemingly "innocent" adventures have, over the intervening decades, taken on quite a different aura than they originally possessed. Not only are they "politically incorrect"; they are also teeming with wildly homoerotic plots and imagery.

Often the central protagonist is a superhero of some sort, clad in a clinging fairy-suit as revealing as it is outlandish. Occasionally he will have a young boy mascot (all perfectly innocent and everything aboveboard, mind you) with whom the youthful audience members are presumably intended to identify. The hero's adversary is usually some kind of masked marauder whose identity is revealed in the final episode. The superman will always have an alternate identity, also. This subtext of hidden identities automatically makes the proceedings of interest to gays, particularly closeted gays attempting to bluff their way through a hostile, homophobic environment.

Serials often take place in exotic locales. Decors are delirious; there is usually more than a touch of the surreal. Plots are violent, "action-packed," and tend to flirt with incoherence. Due to the unique demands of sitting through a narrative consisting of a dozen or so 20-minute episodes, even the most classic serials have failed to find a cult of present-day devotees. That they qualify as camp, however, should be beyond question. And their gay appeal is equally self-evident.

Gay Camp and the J.D. Film

Films about troubled youth have been a cinematic staple since the silent era. In the Fifties, however, a particularly kinky subspecies arose. These movies went by many different names (hot rod epics, teen spleen dramas, etc.). I will simply call them juvenile delinquency films. The central protagonist is typically a surly young man whose hair is artfully arranged in a meticulously combed and coiffed ducktail pompadour. Black leather jacket is optional. His personality is customarily a provocative mixture of the brutal and the sensitive—though the sensitivity is invariably inarticulate.

Already we perceive a source of homosexual fascination. In these films, the landscape is dotted with lusty adolescent males, each of them brimming with vital animal juices. The camp quality, meanwhile, is found in the low-budget production values, amateurish acting, tin-eared rock-'n'-roll music scores, and, above all, in the hopelessly outdated fashions, mannerisms, attitudes, and slang expressions. No particular star is associated with the juvenile delinquency films of the Fifties; lasting fame eluded the boys who participated in them (James Dean is an exception). We all have partialities, however: James Darren, James Dean, Russ Tamblyn, and Edd "Kookie" Byrnes each have their adherents; my own favorite "dreamboat" of the period is John Ashley.

Gay Camp and Film Noir

"Film noir" is an artsy French term referring to the many downbeat, hard-boiled suspense, detective, and crime films produced during the

Forties and Fifties with the camera used to create special effects of light and chiaroscuro. (For a more detailed and elaborate definition, read *Film Noir: An Encyclopedic Reference to the American Style* [Overlook Press, 3rd ed. 1992], or one of the other books devoted to the genre.) Camp—especially gay camp—is seldom found in the film noir format. I have a theory as to why this is so. Film noir, you see, is the only genre in which homosexuals and homosexuality are dealt with in a more or less overt fashion (though there's always a certain amount of coding in order to get around the censor). Examples in the present book include *Laura, Gilda, Affair in Trinidad, Beyond the Forest,* and *The Maltese Falcon.* Noir films are often homophobic to one extent or another. If the cast of characters includes a homosexual, you can safely bet that he'll be either a villain or a namby-pamby. In all fairness, however, it should be noted that the film noir genre takes a pessimistic view of the human race in general. These movies are down on everybody, gay or straight.

I should also mention that Joan Crawford made a number of movies which were half film noir and half women's picture. These films do indeed qualify as camp. At least some of them—*Mildred Pierce,* for example—should be termed gay camp. The first movie my parents ever took me to as a child was a Joan Crawford film noir called *Sudden Fear,* which also starred Jack Palance and Gloria Grahame. I was ruined for life.

A Trio of Camp Oddities

There are at least three truly important camp personalities whose works fall outside the usual film genre boundaries. One of these was a director (also a screenwriter and sometime actor). Edward D. Wood was an alcoholic transvestite who made outrageously inept movies on pathetically miniscule budgets. His best-known work is *Plan 9 from Outer Space,* mentioned above. Critics concur that *Plan 9* is probably the worst movie ever made. Indeed, its ill fame has increased to the point that the film has now passed into the mainstream and is therefore outside the scope of this book. Wood, however, made numerous other films, some of them quite unclassifiable, and all of them bearing the imprint of a man who liked to wear lace panties.

The other two were actresses, though perhaps I'm stretching it a bit when I call Maria Montez an actress. Her specialty was lushly romantic Arabian Nights fantasy. (Indeed, *Arabian Nights* was the title of one of her biggest hits.) She usually played a princess and got to wear all kinds of gorgeous costumes. Her dialogue, ridiculous to begin with, was rendered still funnier by her thick accent and her ludicrously unconvincing demeanor. ("Geef me zuh cobra yools!") Her films were briefly popular during the World War II years. All floss and no substance, they have since made her a camp legend. Furthermore, her movies are not without gay appeal: she was exotic; her clothes and settings were exotic; therefore, her studio (Universal) never failed to surround her with fascinatingly exotic-looking men, or adolescents (for example, Sabu).

Vera Hruba Ralston's studio was Republic. She never worked anywhere else. The fact that she was married to Herbert J. Yates, the head of Republic Pictures, may have had something to do with this. Indeed, there are unkind souls who claim that, without Yates, she might never have become a star. She worked in all genres, usually to indifferent effect. Like Maria Montez, she spoke with a thick accent. Unlike Maria, she was at least an adequate actress. One of her directors, however, complained that she wanted to play everything from children to giants, and Yates was always there to back her up. Sometimes she photographed very nicely. Other times she didn't. Even at the best of times, she was not "the screen's most beautiful woman," though Yates billed her that way in *Jubilee Trail*, her campiest film. I find her mediocrity adorable, and I'm sure a lot of gays would feel the same way, if only they were acquainted with her movies.

*　　*　　*

It may seem strange that this introductory essay contains more references to actresses than to actors. I mean, aren't gay men supposed to prefer guys? In fact, however, I think there are a lot of gay men who watch old movies because they like to look at women. I know I do. Furthermore, the great camp actresses seem to have become a fixed and immutable part of gay culture, whereas actors, on the other hand, come and go, fade, diminish, and are eventually forgotten. Women such as Bette Davis and Mae West, to give but two examples, have become gay traditions, their memory lovingly handed down from one generation to the next. Individual men, on

18

the other hand, are notoriously a matter of taste. We each have our preference; tastes vary tremendously.

A Hidden Agenda

The reviews contained in this book are, first of all, intended as entertainment. There is also, however, a wealth of information to be found within these pages. Among younger gays, I find an alarming ignorance regarding many of the films and personalities so vital to what should be our precious shared heritage of gay camp. I've therefore written this book as a handy guide to the best (or should I, perhaps, say the worst?) that gay camp has to offer.

I also have an underlying motive which is, if anything, even more urgent and compelling. Gay camp is not only funny; it can also be extremely sexy. This book will sensitize the reader to the latent gay content lurking in every sort of movie: all the genres described in this introduction, and more besides. After reading this assortment of my reviews, it is hoped that the gay man will be able to turn on his local late-night movie and discover, all on his own, the wealth of homoerotica that is waiting for him there. We need every safe sex resource we can find nowadays.

*   *   *

Putting together a book of this kind would not have been possible without the help of several people. I wish to take this opportunity to thank Dennis Kelly for loaning me several tapes, Kevin Holz for suggesting the title, and especially Timothy Frick for his time, effort, and generous assistance in providing tapes. I also wish to thank publisher Winston Leyland for his constant advice, encouragement and suggestions for films to be added to the text.

Tom Tyler (1903–1954) star of the classic camp serial, *Adventures of Captain Marvel* (Republic Pictures 1941).

The Adventures of Captain Marvel* (U.S. 1941 B&W)

The Adventures of Captain Marvel, a classic serial from the golden age of chapterplays, is essentially a romance of the polymorphous perverse. A relentless homoeroticism, utterly charming in its juvenile naiveté, underlies the plot's central premise: an effeminate wimp (Frank Coghlan, Jr.), through the simple expedient of saying the word "Shazam," is able to transform himself into a studly, macho dude (Tom Tyler), draped in the inevitable superhero drag (cape, tights; the usual fairy suit).

Captain Marvel, as the virile alter ego is known, is definitely the strong, silent type. On the other hand, the Coghlan character (known as Billy Batson) talks entirely too much—in a quavering, adenoidal adolescent whine. He's the teenage mascot and general flunky of an expedition deep in the mysterious East, consigned to doing "woman's work" like dusting ancient pottery. And, because he's too gutless to enter the sacred tomb which is being defiled, the grateful gods of the Orient magically endow him with the balls of a superman. Said endowments are put on rather prominent display, thanks to the clinging fabric of Tyler's union suit.

Stylistically, this bizarre pageant is distinguished by its wonderfully loopy mise-en-scène, redolent of a bygone, innocent America poised on the brink of World War II. After the hustle and bustle of the opening episode, the scene shifts to L.A., which comes across as a realm of palmy—but indubitably sinister—affluence. Everybody seems to reside in a rambling hacienda. As indicated above, callow and ridiculously self-important teenage faggots here hold positions of undreamt-of authority. (And furthermore seem inordinately fond of patting one another on the tummy.) Sliding panels proliferate, while cars and trucks demonstrate an astonishing ability to stay on the road even when there's no one behind the wheel. On some occa-

---

*Films in this book which have an asterisk after the title are available for purchase on video. See also the table of contents on pp. 5–7 following which is given information on companies where such videos can be purchased by mail. Film studios constantly add or delete titles, so the information provided here (while it will mostly remain valid) is open to correction.

sions, cars are even able to leap across chasms. In short, every plot development requires a vast suspension of disbelief.

The cast includes Peter George Lynn, an actor worthy of note if only because he runs with the dainty, languid gracefulness of a girl. And I'm not the only one who thinks so: "I'm beginning to wonder about him," says leading lady Louise Currie, after watching him jog to his car.

"Me, too!" Billy concurs (no doubt salivating slightly).

Later in the narrative, another somewhat questionable character (George Pembroke) has his way with Billy by gassing him unconscious, then kidnapping him to parts unknown. Such subterfuge strikes us as being not only unfair, but also unnecessary. Billy, after all, seems basically pliable. On the other hand, one of the more remarkable things about Captain Marvel, his so-called heroic alternate self, is the fact that he shows no compunction at all about killing defenseless bad guys in cold blood. (I noticed he grabs one dastard by the crotch before lifting him up and flinging him off a cliff into a lake.) Also he gets himself into some oddly erotic scrapes: chased by a tidal wave of molten rock down a long and narrow tunnel, he's like some stray particle of foreign matter in a cum shot.

Pornography is said to be inherently reactionary. The same holds true for boy-oh-boy adventure shows like this one. Yet both can undeniably be of interest to male homosexuals. Are all superheroes Fascists at heart? And do most homosexuals have a secret Fascist lurking deep inside, screaming to get out? Nietzsche neatly summarized this unfortunate tendency in his doctrine of the ruthless will triumphant: the urge to be greater and more powerful than the common herd of mortals, to subordinate the whole human race, and, most important, to render men supine. The gay boys who flock to our modern-day gymnasia all want the same outer garment of muscles, so readily symbolized by cape, tights, and a cardboard lightning bolt on a rugged, manly chest. Anyone who's taken a good look at the uniforms worn by Nazi military officers knows that they all must have been butch drag queens at heart, secretly longing to turn into Captain Marvel. Shazam, indeed!

Ali Baba and the Forty Thieves* (U.S. 1944 C)

Ali Baba and the Forty Thieves is lush and lavish, splashy and trashy. Although the story is universally known, the producers have somehow managed to turn it ass-backwards. Although they approach the tale's conventions with simpleminded slowness, they still can't quite get the details right. This time around, the thieves are the good guys. While rampaging merrily across the desert wastes, they sing in three-part harmony. Ali Baba is now the caliph's son who leads them in a fierce revolt against the oppressive Mongol hordes.

The script is sublimely ridiculous and the cast is even funnier. The stars of this movie are Maria Montez, Jon Hall, and Turhan Bey. All three are icons of camp and cult. Hall is perhaps the least charismatic link; he looks like George Brent trying to pass himself off as a swashbuckler. Maria Montez, on the other hand, is a sacred legend revered by legions of effeminate homosexuals. (Gore Vidal immortalized her by making her a major character in *Myron*, his fantastic, phantasmagoric sequel to *Myra Breckinridge*.) As the princess of Baghdad she flounces and struts with imperious petulance and haughty aplomb.

Turhan Bey, the second male lead, is a tantalizing enigma: a lacquered, lustrous, luminous presence with cool, dark, eerie eyes. In this opus he seems even more romantically devoted to Hall's Ali Baba than is Montez. Indeed, these three have the makings of a truly kinky Oriental ménage a trois.

The comic relief is broad and low, even by Forties standards. Co-stars Andy Devine and Fortunio Bonanova are two of the unlikeliest Arabs you'd ever care to come across. The Technicolor is gorgeously gaudy, while the sex appeal is sufficiently charming to meet the criteria of any period. When Maria takes a dip, her auburn hair is steeped in cerulean water. She is later surprised in her tub by Turhan. Ignoring the objections of her scandalized handmaidens, she confers with him in a slinky black bathrobe, while Ramsay Ames, as a treacherous slave-girl in the enemy's employ, stays to spy from behind a shimmering beaded curtain. Hollywood no longer makes confections like this one, and more's the pity.

©D-8066-32

RITA HAYWORTH (1918–1987) followed up the success of her famous *Gilda* with the 1952 film *Affair in Trinidad* (Columbia Pictures Corp.). She is shown here in a dance from the latter film. Photo by Lippman.

Affair in Trinidad* (U.S. 1952 B&W)

Affair in Trinidad is a largely unsuccessful attempt to recapture the magic of *Gilda*. The result is a camp version of Hitchcock's *Notorious*. Steven Geray, the men's room attendant in *Gilda*, is moving up in the world; now he gets to run the whole night club. His star attraction is Rita Hayworth, doing lurid dances and driving husbands to suicide (or worse). For much of its length, this is rather polite and civilized film noir. But then along comes Glenn Ford, the gauche and blustering hero, and hard on his heels are a raft of neurotic loudmouth crooks who might as well have wandered in from another picture. Little does anyone suspect that Rita is actually a spy for Uncle Sam. On the night of the big party at the mansion, while all of the other guests are dutifully watching a tedious native dance, Rita sneaks off to the guest house, where the secret rocket plans are stored. She hides behind a screen just in time to overhear the Commies crow about the missile base they hope to build, so near American coastal waters . . .

You get the idea? In other words, this is just further evidence of how badly the McCarthy era screwed up the business of making pictures.

All About Eve* (U.S. 1950 B&W)

All About Eve is the story of a certified Broadway legend—with the splendiferously glamorous name of Margo Channing, she could scarcely be anything else—who makes the mistake of taking a fan (named Eve and portrayed by Anne Baxter) into her home as a kind of secretary/confidante. The younger woman systematically sets about stealing her benefactor's boyfriend and career. By flattering her way into the drawing rooms of the rich and famous, she is able to cut loose like a fox in a chicken coop. Miss Baxter acts very well in the role of this consummate actress, oozing mellifluous deceit.

Some of the characters may be "read" as gay, though plot content designates them heterosexual. This is true of Eve herself; it's even more true of Addison De Witt, the waspish drama critic portrayed by George Sanders (at one point the script refers to him as a "fish-wife"). As for Margo Channing, she could pass for The Mother of Us All; the role is apparently modeled on Tallulah Bankhead, but the way Bette Davis plays it is pure, unadulterated drag queen.

This is, above all, a Bette Davis picture. One could easily dismiss her performance as being an endless series of grand theatrical gestures, yet, when she turns catty and bitchy, when, as Joseph L. Mankiewicz's screenplay puts it, she becomes "an hysterical, scream-ing harpy," in vain would we try to look away. We are transfixed by her beautiful face, which seems to be decaying right before our very eyes. This is a woman obsessed with the fear that her age will cost her the younger man she loves. Is it any wonder that this film is an all-time favorite of male homosexuals who often silently yearn for the very men they can never have? In its own way, *All About Eve* is as much a horror film as *What Ever Happened to Baby Jane?*: here we have a middle-aged woman who, upon perceiving that her world is crumbling all about her, expresses alarm and is promptly told that she's merely being paranoid. Bette's angst is ably seconded by the sickly sweet post-romanticism of Alfred Newman's music score. Ah, those poisoned strings!

The film's most famous line of dialogue—delivered by Miss Davis, of course—could almost serve as an introductory comment on the entire movie: "Fasten your seat belts! It's going to be a bumpy night." I once saw a gay porno picture (*Kiss Today Goodbye* starring George Payne) in which one of the participants actually quoted this line. That, I think, is perhaps the highest honor that could possibly be paid a gay cult film.

But *All About Eve* has lesbian elements, as well. True, the female characters betray one another left and right, but, in order to do so, they must first be placed in positions of relative intimacy. The plot mechanism depends on Margo making Eve a part of her household. In the course of the excruciatingly uncomfortable party scene (the "bumpy night" referred to above), Margo publicly humiliates Eve by inviting her to help her prepare for bed. As soon as Eve has been tricked into demonstrating a willingness to provide such help, it is immediately and contemptuously rejected. Later on, when Eve has begun her manipulation of the *men* in the film, another crypto-lesbian relationship is revealed: Eve enlists the aid of a girlfriend to make lying phone calls on her behalf. Just in case we should miss the point, the girl embraces Eve right after hanging up the receiver. Finally we see Eve falling for the very same ploy that she herself relied upon earlier: discovering a youthful female fan who's sneaked into her hotel room, Eve foolishly invites the girl to stay the night. Is Eve being willfully self-destructive? Has she learned nothing from Margo's misfortune? It's fair to say that this film has a lesbian subtext which the straight audience would prefer to ignore.

All This, and Heaven Too* (U.S. 1940 B&W)

All This, and Heaven Too is sort of like an overlong Gothic romance, with Bette Davis in the kind of role more typically associated with Joan Fontaine. Davis is cast as the meek little governess hired by a French nobleman in 1840s Paris (Charles Boyer) to tend his kids. It's fun to watch her labor under such constraints. The campiness, however, mainly resides in the crazed performance of Barbara O'Neil who, as Boyer's wife, is, to put it mildly, neurotic. She's a hard-luck, bad-ass, rotten-egg woman, who gives new meaning to the phrase "hard to live with." Her funniest moment is probably the startled look that crosses her face when she realizes that she's finally gone too far and Boyer is closing in for the kill. She's surprised, but we aren't. This is one murder that's long overdue.

The narrative has a framing device: Davis is a schoolteacher giving her pupils the low-down on her checkered past. Toward the end, one girl sobs, "Oh, *please*, Mademoiselle! Don't go on!" I could readily sympathize.

Andy Warhol's Dracula* (Italy 1974 C)

Vampire pictures are a sexy and extraordinarily campy genre. *Andy Warhol's Dracula* was made in clear recognition of this fact. The style is as Gothic as ever, but, this time out, the farcical aspects are intentional. Dracula is Udo Kier with a heavy central European accent. Only the blood of "wirgins" can satisfy his thirst, so he packs up his coffin and heads for sunny Italy, where the influence of "holy mother church" will, he hopes, assure an abundance of unsullied maidens.

Times have changed, however (the action transpires in the Roaring Twenties). Dracula unfortunately finds himself in a household where the girls are all either lesbians or nymphos. The gimmick—and it's a gory one—is simply that, when Dracula happens to drink unsuitable blood, he promptly barfs it all over the place, in full view of the camera.

The film gets off to a solemn, stately, dignified start (Udo applying make-up before a mirror), but, before too long, a bawdy, rollicking tone is set. The script may designate Kier as straight, but his screen performance is totally gay. Same goes for Arno Juerging as his assistant. Joe Dallesandro is cast as the gardener. There are no virgins to be found when he's around.

Kier and Dallesandro also starred in a companion piece titled *Andy Warhol's Frankenstein** (1974). In that opus, the gore is enhanced with 3-D effects.

The Anniversary   (G.B. 1968 C)

The Anniversary may be little more than a British cheapie, but leading lady Bette Davis is given a true superstar entrance. Hostessing a little family gathering at her mansion, she doesn't deign to appear till her eldest son (James Cossins) puts on a recording of "The Anniversary Waltz." Then she comes sweeping down the grand staircase, all dolled up in a pink party dress with matching eye-patch. She stumbles slightly on the last step. "Bloody hell!" she mutters. It's her first line in the film.

Her three grown children (all male) are clearly terrified of her, and have brought along suitable gifts as a precaution to propitiate her. The gift she likes best is presented by the youngest (Christian Roberts; with his Sixties "mod" haircut, he is evidently the rebel of the clan). It's a statue of Cupid that takes a leak when you squeeze the little rubber bulb in the back. Utterly tasteless, of course, but Bette is vastly amused. With its penile emphasis, the statue is clearly the perfect gift for the queen of castrating moms.

28

Not that her three offspring don't have quirks of their own. Cossins likes to dress up in ladies' undies. He often gets the urge to swipe used ones, which makes for moments of public embarrassment. The other two have surprises to spring: Roberts is planning to use the family get-together as a pretext to introduce Mom to his fiancée (Elaine Taylor), who, inconveniently, has a baby on the way. As for the weakling middle son (Jack Hedley), he's plotting to cut those apron strings and make off to Canada with his wife and kids. But you can't fool Mom; she'll get her way come what may, and have fun doing it. Some of her stratagems are a mite coarse (she temporarily neutralizes the fiancée by telling her she has body odor), but why waste subtlety on youngsters as thickheaded as these? Not that deviousness is outside her repertoire: during the course of the evening, it comes out that she's been paying Hedley to keep his wife (Sheila Hancock) pregnant. This financial arrangement is motivated, not by a yen for grandchildren, but by the hope that the poor cow's heart will give out.

The film is exceedingly well-acted by all concerned, but it's still Bette's show from start to finish. Her voice sweetly gurgling, her brows frenetically dancing, and her face wreathed in big, phony, simpering crocodile smiles, she goes beyond mere bitchiness; indeed, she scarcely seems like a human being at all (I mean that as a compliment). "Is she always like this?" Miss Taylor asks, and we find her perplexity quite understandable; such a perfection of viciousness does give one pause.

The missing eye is eventually explained: when Hedley was a little boy, he put it out with his big brother's air gun, and hasn't been able to look his mother full in the face ever since. However, we never do learn much of anything about her late and lamented spouse, the former head of this grotesque household. Some things are better left to the imagination.

Another Man's Poison   (G.B. 1952 B&W)

Another Man's Poison, one of those dreary English country house mysteries, is distinguished by the presence of Bette Davis in her scheming bitch mode (complete with riding crop). The plot—an orgy of motivationless behavior—indulges in meaningless melodrama for its own sake, piling complication on complication until the whole dramatic structure (such as it is) collapses under the excess weight. The players appear to be engaged in a competition to see who can deliver the most annoying performance. Co-star Emlyn Williams, in the role of a nosy neighbor, wins hands-down, though Bette certainly gives him a run for his money. I should mention that I can't abide cruelty to animals, whether it occurs on screen or off. Leading man Gary Merrill, out of sheer meanness, kills Bette's horse, so she does away with him. Then she goes into a swoon, and Williams, endeavoring to revive her, inadvertently gives her the same poison she just got done using on Merrill. The final fade-out finds her laughing hysterically as she realizes she's dying. Pretty sick stuff. There's a fine line between camp and just plain bad. I'm not sure where this movie falls.

Autumn Leaves* (U.S. 1956 B&W)

In the opening scene of *Autumn Leaves*, Joan Crawford is a busy little bee, frenziedly typing away in the tidy confines of her modest bungalow. Her closest chum, the elderly landlady (Ruth Donnelly) takes her to task for leading such an empty life. Joan half-jokingly protests that this is the curse of being too beautiful; men assume you're already spoken for. Ruth, on the contrary, claims that Joan is "too scared." And probably rightly so; it's a rough world out there, as we shall see.

A flashback informs us that, in her youth, Joan sacrificed her happiness to care for her ailing father. Now he's dead and she's just Millie, the middle-aged spinster typist. Then one night, acting on a wild impulse, she attends a piano recital and dines at a restaurant afterward. There she ends up sharing a booth with a gawky, boyish Cliff Robertson.

"You know something? You're lonely," Cliff idly observes.

"Lonely?!" she snaps, looking up from her menu, which she's been studying intently, as though to avoid just such conversational gambits as this one. "I think you're being rather presumptuous. My private life is personal."

Be that as it may, this unlikely pair make a date to go swimming the following afternoon. Chalk it up to Cliff's youthful charm. However, as we watch them dashing happily, hand in hand, into the surf, it occurs to us that maybe there's something funny about this nice young man. He seems to be an admirably attentive and devoted companion, but Joan has her doubts. "If you knew a girl your own age, you wouldn't want me," she tells him. She endeavors to break off the relationship, but Cliff is persistent, finally asking her to marry him. She wavers for a while, then gives her consent. "I hope you'll never be sorry," he tells her.

Hah! After the wedding, it turns out that he's a compulsive liar and thief. And nothing more than a humble tie salesman, whereas he led Joan to believe he was a full-fledged floorwalker. That ain't all: she discovers that he's been married before. That misalliance concluded catastrophically; he came home unexpectedly from work one day and stumbled on the ultimate in primal scenes: his blushing bride (Vera Miles) in bed with his own Dad (Lorne Greene)! Joan unwittingly causes a reenactment of this sordid incident: she forceably brings about a family reunion, but she and Cliff show up at a highly inopportune moment, finding Lorne and Vera fucking up a storm all over again! Joan is righteously indignant: "You're both so consumed with evil! So rotten! Your filthy souls are too evil for hell itself!" Actually, she saves this outburst for somewhat later on, when Ruth and all the rest of the neighbors are listening and Vera, the typical Fifties "other woman," is swathed in mink, no doubt paid for by Lorne, her loathsome, oily keeper. "You're more than a good wife," he coos to Joan, his voice oozing seductiveness. "You're like a friend and mother."

Which is precisely what poor Cliff needs, now that he's regressing into infantilism (he even sucks his thumb). His Oedipal traumas have turned him into a paranoid schizophrenic, and he even suspects Joan of plotting against him. There's a tight, mean little smirk on his face and a sinister glint in his eye; he looks like a psycho in a slasher movie. One particularly ugly squabble ends with him throwing Joan's typewriter at her. It lands on her hand, crushing it. (There are those who say that, in real life, Crawford was the one who ran round hurling typewriters at people. However, her offscreen relations with Robertson were entirely amicable: she used to always send him a cooler of Pepsi on his birthday.) Soon he's working her over on a regular basis; she's a mass of bruises and bandages. Why, she can't even go to the supermarket without putting on dark glasses to cover up the shiners he's given her!

This can't go on. Joan has no choice but to have him certified and committed. When the men in white suits are dragging him away, Cliff doesn't hesitate to let her know that he's peeved with her ("I'll get you! I'll cut your guts out!"). During his months in the boobyhatch, Joan frets and paces, worrying that his love for her was merely a symptom of his mental illness. "Am I a neurotic need?" she asks, pathetically.

Many a gay man has wondered something similar, at one time or another. *Autumn Leaves* may seem to be a grotesque caricature of a heterosexual romance, but it's really more a symbolic acting out of homosexual relations, particularly those which occur between young, volatile studs and older, more settled types. Crawford, who was never more masochistic than she is herein, tests the limits of a hellish Fifties world of pain, anxiety, and frustration. As one character gloomily puts it, "Being in love is never easy. And the more in love you are, the less easy and more lonesome it gets."

Baby Face* (U.S. 1933 B&W)

Baby Face is Barbara Stanwyck as a canny businesswoman who keeps her eye on the main chance. She starts out as a lowly tavern wench getting pawed by the likes of Nat Pendleton (with his shirt off and glistening with sweat), but she dares to dream of better things. The wise old man of the neighborhood tells her, "You don't realize your potentialities." She sees his point when her scummy dad tries to get her to "be nice" to a local politician. Dad gets killed when a still explodes in his face; as for the politician, he doesn't escape unscathed, either.

Barbara hops a freight to New York. On Wall Street she picks out a suitably phallic skyscraper and resolves to work there. "Have you had any experience?" inquires the horny young man in the personnel department. "Plenty," says Barbara, herding him into a deserted office. Voila! She's suddenly a filing clerk.

Co-star John Wayne is the one who nicknames her "Baby Face." He recommends her to his superior (Douglass Dumbrille), the head

BARBARA STANWYCK (1907–1990), strong-willed, no-nonsense star of countless films of the 30s, 40s, 50s and later. Publicity photo from her younger years (Warner Brothers/ Vitaphone Pictures).

of the mortgage department. The latter is not exactly oblivious to her charms. Indeed, he glances down the front of her blouse every chance he gets. She lures him into the ladies' john, where he's caught with his pants down and (pardon the pun) abruptly canned.

The cold-eyed executive who stumbles on this breach of decorum is Donald Cook. He's inclined to give Barbara her walking papers, but she prevails on his manly protectiveness. He gets her a place upstairs in accounting. Now she's a receptionist; his receptionist, as a matter of fact. Donald is engaged to a young woman of quality, but Barbara soon has him stopping by for a drink. (Dumbrille, looking very down at the heels, comes scratching at her door, literally begging for a quickie. She slams the door in his face, then tells Donald it was the paper boy.) Back at the office, she maneuvers Donald into a clinch just as his fiancée comes toddling over the threshold.

A brilliant match torpedoed, or so it would seem. But wait: the fiancée's father is the first vice-president of the company, and he tries to smooth things over. You can guess what happens when Barbara tells him how alone and defenseless she feels. Soon she's calling him "Fuzzie-Wuzzie." He sets her up as his kept woman, installing her in a plush apartment. Donald, crazed with jealousy, surprises the pair with a loaded gun. He shoots his would-be father-in-law dead, then blows his own brains out (in the bathroom, natch).

The scandal shakes the bank to its foundations. She's called to the very tippy-top floor, there to confer with the board of directors. Big deal, she thinks; they're just another bunch of men, as far as she's concerned. The newly installed president of the institution is a former polo player portrayed by George Brent. He suggests that Barbara might like to go to Paris and escape all of this unpleasant notoriety. Later, on a business trip, he encounters her there. In such a romantic setting, of course, he's a pushover, but their marriage threatens to topple the company. In other words, on her way to the summit, she devastates everything underneath. The moral is simple: it all goes to prove that men are at the mercy of their balls. But we knew that already, didn't we?

Beach Blanket Bingo* (U.S. 1965 C)

Beach Blanket Bingo has a running time of ninety-six minutes—rather long for a film of this type. I review it, not in order to sing the praises of Frankie Avalon, but of co-star John Ashley, even though he wears more clothes than the others and shows distressing signs of an incipient double chin. I like his bedroom eyes and bullet-proof pompadour, not to mention his gruff Southern accent. In the twist party scene, we can't help but notice his pertly pugnacious, hyperactive butt. And he's really no more diminutive than Frankie. Really.

The ever-effeminate Paul Lynde plays somebody called "Bullets," which certainly sounds suitably obscene, given the circumstances. "I didn't catch your name, boy," he says to Frankie, little black book at the ready. He hands the "boy" his business card. "Take one. They're free." "That's pretty tacky," Frankie replies, bitchily.

Lynde is cast as the press agent of an aspiring rock star played by Linda Evans. "Not too close, Sugar. He's a carrier," he warns her, when he notices that she's getting too friendly with Harvey Lembeck, a surf-Nazi motorcycle hoodlum. "I'll save the next dance for you," he says, with his trademark sarcasm, to Lembeck, who is careful to remind him, "I lead." (Honestly! These top men can be so *pushy*!) In the final pairing off, Linda Evans ends up with muscular Jody McCrea (whom she addresses as "Boney," yet another suggestively phallic nickname). Paul, overhearing Jody get sweetly romantic with Linda, comments as follows: "I knew he was stupid, but sickening, too?" The beach party genre is, in my considered opinion, offensively heterosexual. I enjoy subverting it; so did Paul Lynde.

Ben-Hur* (U.S. 1927 B&W with some color sequences)

The 1927 *Ben-Hur*, subtitled "A Tale of the Christ," hides its true nature behind sacred trappings, the better to wallow in kink. It is, I think, significant that Ben-Hur is played by Ramon Novarro (a homosexual murdered by stud hustlers in 1968). He is introduced to us after a brief prologue portraying the Christmas story (the Virgin Mary is Betty Bronson with an aureole surrounding her head). In his early scenes, this Hebrew prince wears naught but a hip-dusting mini-tunic—the sort of gam-displaying garment which, in later years, might have been worn by Betty Grable. His erstwhile friend, the villainous Mesala (Francis X. Bushman), comes clanking onscreen in the full-armor drag of a Roman soldier. His iron-clad butchness rings hollow, however: he seems to be playing Brunnhilde to Novarro's pin-up queen.

A freakish quirk of fate gets Ben-Hur arrested and sentenced to a life of servitude. In other words, he starts showing chest. Driven through the desert wastes, he collapses, half-mad with thirst. His captors torment him by tauntingly pouring water on the ground, then laugh at his abasement as he grovels in the mud and eagerly sucks up whatever moisture he can. Some guys can really dig such scenes of abject submission, but it turns out to be little more than a warm-up. Ben-Hur sweats more than he drinks: our hero becomes a galley slave, which means he wears almost nothing. Another, more muscular slave wears literally nothing: he's been shackled and bound in the background as an example to the others. This is one of the earliest instances of male nudity in a Hollywood film. (It's a rear-view shot, which means that this fellow must always remain an anonymous pioneer.) The scene furthermore includes a paroxysm of truly lurid homoerotic sadism: attacking pirates lash a seminude, hairy-chested hostage to the prow of their vessel; bound and spreadeagled, upside-down, quaking with fear, he's reduced to a living, breathing figurehead with which to ram the side of the Roman vessel.

In the ensuing battle, Ben-Hur's skimpy loincloth gets wet. When he turns his back to the camera, he might just as well be naked. The view is best appreciated by an august Roman tribune, who promptly decides to make Ben-Hur his "adopted son." Later there's a parade, with maidens scattering rose petals hither and yon. In the interest of fair play and equal representation, these bouncy babes wear nothing above the waist. The plot concludes with some incongruously joyous (and extrabiblical) events on the road to Golgotha. Tale of the Christ, indeed: as always, it is truly inspiring to behold what Hollywood can accomplish in the name of piety.

Beyond the Forest* (U.S. 1949 B&W)

Beyond the Forest stars Bette Davis as Rosa Moline, "a midnight girl in a nine o'clock town." That's how the ads described her when this febrile melodrama was first released. The script features one of her most notorious bits of dialogue: surveying her cozy living room, she grumbles, "What a dump!" This line has been immortalized, not only by Edward Albee, but by legions of impressionists and drag queens.

The film begins with a pious prologue that was obviously tacked on to placate the Legion of Decency (which nonetheless condemned the film as morally objectionable): "This is the story of evil. Evil is headstrong—is puffed up. For our soul's sake, it is salutary for us to view it in all its naked ugliness once in a while." Even before we've been properly introduced to her, a narrator describes Rosa "moving easily, freely, every man's admiring eye upon her." She's a girl to watch out for, all right. In the first reel, she knocks a reformed alcoholic off the wagon and casually shoots a cute little porcupine. She lets her poor, tired, selfless, hardworking husband (Joseph Cotten) scare up his own supper while she sits in the porch swing and files her nails. When she walks down the street, all the townsfolk turn and stare at her as if she had two heads. Somewhat improbably, she inspires and inflames the lust of a millionaire sportsman who's built himself a ritzy hunting lodge just outside of town. (He's played by David Brian, who, ironically enough, was a swain of Miss Joan Crawford at roughly the same time that this film was released.)

But mannerism, however entertaining, must ultimately make way for plot. Rosa guns down a luckless boob who tries to get in her way. The coroner's inquest rules it an accident, but she comes to a bad end, anyhow. She dies of complications from a self-induced abortion. (This is the sort of town in which a "good" woman is defined by her fecundity.) The best scenes come earlier: in Chicago, where she tracks down her big shot paramour and gets rebuffed. I felt like I was watching some crazed housewife who'd read too many Fifties romance comics and was trying to act out one of the stories on her own. She may be just a lurid, hopped-up Madame Bovary, but I, for one, could certainly relate to her wild, importunate hubris

—and so could any other homosexual male who's tried to turn his fantasies into reality. Her desperation seems weirdly appropriate, since, as played by the forty-year-old Miss Davis, she's all too obviously over the hill. Bette's portrayal has a bitchy, *Baby Jane*-ish intensity. Despite the assortment of good-looking men around, she saves all her *real* passion for the scene where she finds herself alone with a mink coat. (It belongs to co-star Ruth Roman. Rosa is positively verdant with envy.) Identifying with Rosa Moline is sort of like sympathizing with Imelda Marcos. But who says we've gotta be Politically Correct *all* the time?

Black Lizard* (Japan 1968 C)

Black Lizard is a mad soufflé stuffed with violence, sex, and Sixties gadgetry. The title character is an elegant drag queen (Akihiro Maruyama) who's got a drop-dead sense of style. She's Japan's master criminal; its master sleuth pursues her all over Osaka and Tokyo. They meet at a night club that's decorated with Aubrey Beardsley etchings. The mood is heavy with decadence and sexual ambiguity. "This was a world unknown to me, until a gaudy crime dragged me into it," complains the detective. (I think gaudy crimes are the best kind, don't you?) Later he says, "Black Lizard, you are an old-fashioned romanticist. In this age soiled by corruption and murder, you believe that crime should wear a gorgeous gown with a train fifteen feet long." That's right: they're in love. And sworn to destroy one another. How utterly surreal it all is! At one point an expensive sofa is brutally stabbed to death and buried at sea. Yukio Mishima makes a cameo appearance as a corpse. At first I thought the film was inspired by the Dr. Mabuse thrillers directed by Fritz Lang. I'm inclined to suspect, however, that the title villainess owes more to Gale Sondergaard and the "Spider Woman" character she originated in Forties B-films. The music score is mostly derived from baroque themes. Camp often requires a dash of genuine culture to set it off.

Blonde Venus* (U.S. 1932 B&W)

Blonde Venus begins with naked women frolicking in a sun-dappled pond. The setting is Germany's Black Forest. American students on a tramp through the woods discover and spy on these skinny-dippers. One of the guys is Herbert Marshall. One of the nude females is Marlene Dietrich. The girls are alerted to the presence of the guys when Sterling Holloway, overexcited as always, makes too much noise. One might almost suspect that he's trying to scare them away.

The scene shifts to New York. Marlene is now married to Herbert, but he is slowly dying of radium poisoning (he's a chemist) and needs to go back to Germany for a cure. Money, however, is a problem. Marlene considers returning to show business (she and all the other young ladies splashing in the pool were actresses), but Herbert won't hear of it. He'd literally rather die.

She pays him no heed and goes to an agent for an audition. The agent takes one look at her in the crowded waiting room and immediately invites her into his private office. He wants to see her legs. "Is that enough?" she asks, lifting her skirt demurely. "For the time being," he replies.

We begin to see why Herbert might have cause to oppose her career: from this point on, the film becomes an exercise in camp decadence. Marlene is now a night club chanteuse, billed as the Blonde Venus. She does a striptease in a gorilla suit. Then, wearing a blonde Afro wig and a costume made up of what seem to be giant zircons, she sings a remarkably suggestive number entitled "Hot Voodoo," while all around her prance nubile black women got up as native witch doctors.

Tasteless? You bet. And that's only the beginning. After the show, she begins an acquaintance with a well-to-do politician who can send her husband to Europe and never even notice the expense. He's played by none other than Cary Grant, who gives the role a fast-talking smoothness. He installs Marlene in a fancy apartment. He begs her for just one little kiss. She complies. Next thing you know, she's starting to wish that Herbert wouldn't come back from Germany. But he does, whereupon Marlene announces her intention to return to him.

39

"You still love him?" Cary asks, incredulously.

"He needs me."

"So do I, Helen."

"Not the way he does. You're strong, Nick. He's not."

So Herbert comes back early and trips to The Truth. He threatens to have her declared an unfit mother. (Oh, dear! Did I forget to mention that she and Herbert had a little boy?) She takes the kid and splits. The stylish shadows which bedeck the production grow more expressionistic as her money runs out. She's reduced to destitution, maybe even prostitution. Following hot on her heels is a detective played by Charlie Chan, or (excuse me) Sidney Toler. She lures him into a crowded, smoky tavern. "You don't look anything like these other women," says Sidney, referring to the strumpets loitering on the premises.

"Give me time," says Marlene, wearily. By now she's starting to think that maybe she *is* an unfit mother, so she tells Sidney to tell Herbert to come and get the kid. Herbert hands her a wad of bills and orders her to get lost. She passes the dough to a fellow vagrant and then, through the magic of montage, goes back to Europe, becomes a smash-hit singing sensation and is reunited with Cary. It's at this point she performs her big lesbo number, fondling the chorus girls while dressed in a white tuxedo with sequined lapels.

But even that isn't the end. Cary takes the fallen woman back to America, Herbert forgives her, and all ends happily. Some critics maintain that this film is a serious work of art, but I know it's something even better than that. There are plenty of clues: the large number of blacks in the cast, the persistent use of abrasive boogie-woogie music, and the constant leitmotif of return to Europe. It all adds up to one thing: a slap in the face to the Nazis, whose inevitable rise had made Marlene's flight to Hollywood advisable.

Bloody Pit of Horror* (Italy 1965 C)

Bloody Pit of Horror, perhaps the supreme jerk-off film of all time, begins with a hooded muscleman being led to his execution. He's dressed in red tights; the phallic bulge is obscenely prominent. (He isn't wearing a jock; we can see him bounce as he strides down the stairs to the dungeon.) He is put to death by a pair of guardsmen, also clad in tights, but with frilly skirted tunics concealing their crotches. With a wide, thick leather strap, they secure him within the iron maiden. Its spikes appear to be aimed at his groin. Slowly, slowly, they shut the door. A prolonged screech of agony follows. Through a window in the front, we watch the victim's head lifelessly slump to the side. The camera pans downward to show us the blood seeping and dribbling from the crack beneath the door.

We skip ahead three-hundred years. A bunch of bitchy models ("I'm not just a dumb blonde, you know!" "Who says you're a blonde?") arrive at the castle of Mickey Hargitay (in real life married to Jayne Mansfield, killed in a car wreck), the reincarnation of the stud we just saw killed. The girls are going to use this place as a backdrop for their latest assignment (they're posing for a series of horror novel dust jacket illustrations). The domicile is adorned with scads of kitschy bric-a-brac. Mickey resides in campy splendor with a pair of male servants who presumably see to all his physical needs. Mickey wears a silken kimono of hot salmon-pinkish hue. His retainers, meanwhile, are dressed in cute li'l sailor outfits: T-shirts with blue-and-white horizontal stripes and tight, white trousers. The costuming emphasizes the fact these two fellows have nice builds and full, firm, globular buttocks. Once again, bulges are noticeable between the legs. These footmen (or slaves, or suck buddies, or whatever they are) appear to be in a state of perpetual priapic excitement. We soon see why. Mickey has taken it upon himself to "punish" heterosexual fornicators. Clad in a very butch assortment of leather belts and bracelets, with gold chains and sporting a kinky mask, his award-winning chest exposed and his cock clearly evident in his highly revealing tights, he's the personification of cruel, virile, masculine potency.

The psychosexual mechanism at work here is basically quite simple. Mickey's titillating attire is geared to bring out the latent homosexuality of even the most macho male viewer. As quickly as it comes to light, however, this lurking femininity is ruthlessly repressed, through the symbolic means of endlessly repetitive murder scenes in which Mickey slays women identified as being sexually active. (Effeminate men are similarly dealt with: the models are accompanied by a faggy photographer named Dermot, who gets shot through the neck with an arrow.)

Hargitay is essentially playing a psychotic inversion of himself:

the script announces that the killer was once an actor in Hercules pictures. (In actual fact, Mickey's best-known film was *The Loves of Hercules*.) He gruesomely mutilates seductive females. Whatever else the film might be, it accurately portrays the narcissistic egotism so rampant among compulsive bodybuilders. Mickey admires his own rippling muscles at every opportunity. "Mankind is made up of inferior creatures, spiritually and physically deformed, who would have corrupted the harmony of my perfect body," he comments while oiling his bulging pectorals (a task which, incidentally, he carries out with a teasingly slow, lascivious, masturbatory flair). Such dialogue is surpassingly difficult to concentrate upon, since our eyes are constantly straying to the lower half of his torso, while our fevered brains speculate as to whether he's semi-erect or simply hung like an Arabian thoroughbred stallion.

The scenes of voluptuous girls getting broken on the rack and bathed in boiling pitch are really just heterosadean window dressing. The heart and soul of the film is the moment when the boringly conventional, conservative "good guy" awakens in bed with a darkly handsome young man. The latter fellow's a corpse, of course, but that circumstance, I suppose, is merely intended to give this lewdly exploitative film a bit of additional decadence. As a work of Gothic horror, the movie is luridly, laughably, woefully inept. Hargitay's heavily stylized performance, however, is brilliantly erotic. It's hard to believe they could make 'em this nasty in 1965.

The Boys in the Band* (U.S. 1970 C)

Nowadays *The Boys in the Band* is practically an historical document. What was it like to be a queen in the late Sixties and early Seventies? This movie tells us, by showing the campy, bitchy behavior of a bunch of queens at a birthday party.

Anti-gay religious nuts should watch this picture at least once a month; it would keep them firm in their resolve. Indeed, it's the mother lode of fag stereotypes. (Anita Bryant quotes dialogue from it in one of her many books.) In this movie, homosexuals tend to be rather unhappy creatures. However, I hasten to add that there's really no reason the ones at this party couldn't be very happy indeed, if only they had sense enough and guts enough to hurl their insulting, bullying host off the balcony.

Does *The Boys in the Band* qualify as a camp film? I think it does. In fact, it virtually summarizes the content of this book that you are reading. There are references to Maria Montez and Vera Hruba Ralston. (This movie should jolly well vindicate me with the younger generation of gay men, who refuse to believe that there once was a time when male homosexuals talked and cared and knew about such bizarre people.) There are references to *The Wizard of Oz* ("He's about as straight as the yellow brick road.") and to *Sunset Boulevard* ("I'm *not* ready for my close-up, Mr. DeMille, nor will I be for the next two weeks."). At one point, a guest is even seen perusing *The Films of Joan Crawford*.

But what's *really* camp is the way in which straight men are portrayed. Doesn't matter if they're parking lot attendants or delivery boys; they are all gorgeous hunks. Furthermore, by their sneers and querulous looks, we can tell that they all despise homosexuals almost as much as the director of this movie does.

Breakfast at Tiffany's* (U.S. 1961 C)

I once had a friend who absolutely adored Audrey Hepburn. When *Breakfast at Tiffany's* came to town, he was so excited, his legs were scarcely able to carry him to the theatre; he kept falling down along the way. What's really interesting is the fact that he was a mere twelve years old—a good little Catholic boy—and not yet in touch with his true sexual nature. The fascinated fondness which he felt for *Breakfast at Tiffany's* was, of course, a dead giveaway. Under the circumstances, and at such a tender age as his, no further manifestation of gayness was possible, or, for that matter, necessary.

The fact that *Breakfast at Tiffany's* was so symbolic in (and of) his life is appropriate, since the film itself deals with gayness so symbolically. Words such as "gamine" and "pixie" would seem to have been invented for the sole purpose of describing Audrey Hepburn. Holly Golightly, the character she portrays, is officially defined in the film as a "glamour girl." Unofficially, Holly is a transvestized stand-in for her creator, Truman Capote. She's the new boy in town, the pretty boy, the little prince who reigns supreme at the bar on Saturday night. Androgynous, flitting from one transitory love affair to another, decked out in Givenchy coats and dresses, and twiddling a cigarette holder approximately the length of a TV antenna, she's what a typical young urban male homosexual either wants to be, sees himself as being, or (less typically) is.

The film has virtually no plot at all. A dumb stud (George Peppard) moves into the apartment just upstairs from hers. He fancies himself a writer, but he's actually the kept boy of a rich old queen (Patricia Neal, cast against gender, same as Hepburn). Holly and the stud fall in love, teach each other self-respect, and, next thing you know, he's selling stories to *The New Yorker*.

It is, in short, a film without substance—so wispy, it threatens to float off the screen. If one fails to see through its heterosexual disguises, the film is merely bad, as cop-outs and compromises generally are. Whenever "Moon River" wells up on the soundtrack, however, my eyes inevitably well up with tears. For the sake of my friend, however, and not at all because of the movie.

The Bride and the Beast   (U.S. 1958 B&W)

Although *The Bride and the Beast* is directed by Adrian Weiss, the actual auteur of the production is clearly its screenwriter—Edward D. Wood, the transvestite sex fetishist responsible for such memorable movies as *Glen or Glenda?* and *The Sinister Urge*. His trademark cross-dressing motif is readily apparent in the latter pair of films. *The Bride and the Beast*, however, goes considerably beyond this theme. Instead of blurring mere gender lines, it blurs the lines between entire species.

Lance Fuller and Charlotte Austin are newlyweds honeymooning at Lance's country estate. He's a big game hunter and keeps a live gorilla penned up in the basement. When he shows Charlotte this unusual pet, it's love at first sight. The gorilla reciprocates her affection, caressing her wrist and fondling her angora sweater (Wood had a thing about angora). Lance brings Charlotte up to the bedroom; he's eager to get to know her better. Unsurprisingly, this occasions some mighty breast-beating on the part of the gorilla. Late that night, he breaks out of his cage and goes upstairs for sloppy seconds. He rips Charlotte's frilly nightgown right off, whereupon she collapses, naked, at his feet. Lance, meanwhile, goes for his gun (no, not *that* one) and, as any jealous husband might do, shoots the intruder dead.

Lest you think this film more unseemly than it is, I should probably point out that the gorilla is merely a man dressed in a monkey costume. His lust is, after all, only human. And, speaking of human lust, Lance Fuller is aptly named, indeed. In the wedding night scene, it seems we can actually sense his lance growing fuller. His passion is enhanced when, under deep hypnosis, Charlotte reveals that she's the reincarnation of a gorilla. His bride is a beast, which, at any rate, serves to explain her fondness for angora sweaters. Soft, fur-like material such as this is precisely the sort of thing with which she prefers her flesh to be covered. Lance makes the mistake of bringing her with him on an expedition to Africa. Of course, she meets up with another gorilla and gets swept off her feet again— quite literally. This time there's no hope of winning her back; that sultry jungle fever is in her blood; she simply can't help but go ape. Lance is left with no one to solace him (or service him) save "Taro" (Johnny Roth), his young, well-muscled, stripped-to-the-waist valet and general factotum. Somehow I get the impression that Big Bwana's gonna make out just fine.

Bullwhip * (U.S. 1958 C)

The combination of Rhonda Fleming and Guy Madison in a movie entitled *Bullwhip* sounds, if nothing else, commendably formidable. And you may rest assured that our lord and lady of the lash comport themselves impressively. Miss Rhonda is cast as a buffalo huntress who is "half Injun," as they say in films of this type. In order to satisfy the requirements of her eccentric father's last will and testament, she's obliged to marry, so she sets about finding herself a conveniently disposable husband. A corrupt judge sets her up with Guy, cast as a condemned—or, to be more precise—railroaded

GUY MADISON (1922–   ), left, handsome American leading actor of post-war films. Publicity photo.

prisoner sentenced to be hung at sunrise. The wedding, as one might expect, is rather brusque. When asked if he takes this woman, etc., Guy says, "Yeah. Sure, judge," instead of the customary, "I do."

The action begins to get kinky when Guy escapes death and catches up with Rhonda's wagon train, which he promptly takes over, exercising what he feels to be his husbandly right. Rhonda bullwhips him right across his pretty face. That doesn't faze him: they play tug of war with the whip, he wins, and she tumbles off her horse, into the mud. Guy takes custody of the whip from here on in. "You won't be needing this anymore," he smirks.

The question at this point becomes—Will he fuck her? Rhonda, needless to say, doesn't want him to. "You don't know what you're missing," he says, unbuttoning and removing his shirt to reveal a mouth-wateringly hairy chest. He does have a point, doesn't he? He's also got a tough, gritty voice, flinty eyes, and a nose so long and tapered that our imaginations can run amok. Quite a hunk, as they say. Rhonda wears lovely gowns in this picture, and Guy strips his clothes off on a fairly regular basis. What more could the discerning viewer ask for?

Can't Stop the Music* (U.S. 1980 C)

In 1980 there was every reason to believe that Can't Stop the Music, the disco extravaganza starring the Village People, was going to be a huge success. Variety's advance review went so far as to suggest that a sequel should be made entitled Can't Stop the Money. Unfortunately, when Can't Stop the Music was released, it sank without a trace. Its failure effectively ended the disco boom.

There were several plausible explanations for this, not the least of them being the fact that mainstream audiences probably just weren't ready for a movie that was built around an openly gay singing group. (Bear in mind that Saturday Night Fever, the only seriously profitable disco flick, concerned itself with working class heterosexuals.) AIDS has since imbued the production with an even more disreputable aura. Watching the onscreen festivities is rather like reading about the party in Poe's "Masque of the Red Death" as written up in a Sunday society column. We get the same sense of eerie poignance that we'd feel if viewing a pre-World War II documentary celebrating the culture and diversity of Polish Jewry. Some scenes are inadvertently macabre; the prettiest song in the film is entitled, with stunning prescience, "I Love You to Death."

Yes, I'll admit this is a bad, stupid, corny sort of movie, but it's also mega-sexy and ultra-gay. However, the word "homosexual" is never uttered. "Gay" isn't used, either. Nothing overt takes place. It's more a matter of subliminal suggestion. "Oh, boy! One hot night coming up!" enthuses aspiring songwriter Steve Guttenberg as he's stripping off his shirt. Meanwhile, Felipe Rose (the seminude Native American member of the group) bends over a bicycle, revealing a perfect expanse of bronzed thigh.

The film comes out of its closet during the fairly frequent musical interludes. Co-star June Havoc tells Guttenberg, "It's your music that's bringing all of these talented boys together. They ought to get down on their knees!" Careful attention to the lyrics would seem to indicate that they get on their knees rather often. Moments after June's outburst, they're singing, "So let's all / try tonight / to feel love / when we come inside each other." ("Hey, let's go down!" exclaims someone eager to join in the fun.) By Nineties standards, this sounds unmistakably like a paean to unsafe sex.

The highlight of the film is the big "Y.M.C.A." number. ("When you're short on your dough, you can stay there / and I'm sure you will find many ways to have a good time!") In the shower room shots, if you look quick, you can actually see cock. "This is *the* sound of the Eighties!" Guttenberg assures a record promoter (Paul Sand). Whereupon the Village People launch themselves into a rousing rendition of an anthem called "Liberation": "We won't let those small minds stand in our way. / If there's a price, then we are willing to pay!" (Had they but known.) Later they sing a song about milk shakes (draw your own conclusions), during which lead singer Ray Simpson seems to be impaling his butt on a spiked heel. The grand finale is staged in San Francisco and consists of a gala performance of the title song: "You can't stop the music! / Nobody can stop the music!"

But somebody certainly did. Despite its many detractors, this movie presently qualifies as a fond remembrance of the days when the music—and the sex—were still going strong.

Cobra Woman   (U.S. 1944 C)

Cobra Woman gets underway with outbursts of choral croon-
ing, as clouds of incense rise before the sinister, sinuous statue of
the Cobra God. This film, a delirious extravaganza, is probably the
quintessential Maria Montez vehicle. She plays twin sisters: one
good, one evil. Which is destined to rule as high priestess of Cobra
Island? The good Maria, kidnapped by Lon Chaney, Jr. on the eve
of her marriage to Jon Hall, is only of interest when attempting to
impersonate the bad Maria, who is much the more entertaining of
the two. The bad Maria wears a golden sunburst headdress, a flam-
ing-red robe, and, beneath it, a tight, slinky, sequin-studded snake
dress, in which she performs a kootch dance during the course of
which she points out those of her people whom she has selected as
victims for human sacrifice (they are promptly borne away, shrieking). We are told that she has turned the happy natives of her tropic
isle into a race of "religious fanatics." At her word, they willingly
hurl themselves into the mouth of an active volcano. ("The cobra
ritual appeals to their emotions," explains the Queen Mother, portrayed by Mary Nash.) "I'm de law here!" announces the bad Maria,
squaring her shoulders manfully. This should give you some idea of
what we're dealing with here: no less than four times in the course
of the film, she concludes a speech with the words, "I haf spoken!"
   The director is Robert Siodmak, a noir specialist who tricks things
out with the occasional weird, Teutonic, unexpected camera angle.
He seems to be trying to draw a comparison between Cobra Island
and Nazi Germany, but any pretension toward "meaning" gets pretty
much buried beneath all the glitz, the corn, and the kitsch. Comic
relief (redundant, under the circumstances) is provided by Sabu, who
seems to be engaged in a competition with Miss Montez to see
who can give the worst performance. For a while, he actually looks
as though he might be a contender, but Maria, with a truly ludicrous climactic fainting fit, pins his ears back rather decisively. The
screenplay enhances his primitive charm by having him say "I are,"
instead of "I am." He and Jon Hall are constantly rescuing one
another from peril. At one point Sabu is captured by the bad Maria's
henchmen. "We have ways of punishing little boys who don't tell
the truth," intones the chief torturer, as a half dozen studly young

Maria Montez (1919–1951), star of several 1940s adventure camp classics, often with exotic locales. Publicity photo from the 1943 South Seas adventure, *White Savage* (Universal).

guardsmen threateningly hover in the background. Caramba! The last we see of Sabu is his ass: the final shot of the film finds him bending over while a chimpanzee, armed with needle and thread, mends a gaping hole in the seat of the poor lad's trousers. Penetrating drama, indeed.

College Confidential (U.S. 1960 B&W)

College Confidential begins with a scene of traditional family values. Mom is Pamela Mason, Dad is Elisha Cook, and the spawn of this hellish union is none other than Mamie Van Doren. We witness a domestic quarrel. Mamie has arrived home at three in the morning on a school night. In fact, we see her rudely ejected from a hot rod after a heavy petting session on Lover's Lane. When Elisha attempts to gently remonstrate with her, she deflects his wrath by getting him all hot and bothered about a sex survey which she's participating in for sociology class.

In the scene which follows, Elisha accuses Steve Allen, Mamie's Soc professor, of "practicing sex, instead of surveying it." Steve is the poor, embattled liberal, victim of a dirty-minded misunderstanding which could easily blossom into a right-wing crusade. If it hasn't already: Steve is confronted by the head of his department (Herbert Marshall, no doubt appalled to find himself slumming like this), who has received an anonymous letter accusing the poor sap of being a corrupter of youth. Steve's fiancée demands that he be more circumspect: "I want you to abandon this dangerous project, which people are interpreting in the worst possible way! You can accuse me of being melodramatic, but you must make a choice! The project . . . or *me*!"

Meanwhile, down by the old swimming hole, the students discuss the developing controversy. "Am I missing out by not taking part in this extracurricular survey?" wonders a young lady in a two-piece bathing suit. Jayne Meadows, an inquiring reporter equipped with binoculars, climbs a tree, the better to eavesdrop on the conversation. Steve helps her down again, the better to explain that all he really wants is to help the kids avoid letting sex distract them from their homework. On a visit to his bachelor pad, Jayne provides comic relief by trying out his gym equipment. Steve gets all flustered when he shows her his bedroom. This, I take it, is supposed to establish his innocence.

On Friday night he has the kids over to show them his home movies. He fixes them banana-and-ketchup sandwiches, which may have Freudian significance, but I think it's just meant to show how endearingly goofy he is. Unfortunately, someone slips a stag reel in amongst the films Steve had planned to run. When the lights come up, an interesting array of comments are heard. "This is too much, even for *me*!" blurts the class tramp (Ziva Rodann).

Later we learn that the porn flick (which we never actually get to see, of course) was absurdly softcore. In fact, it's not even that: the participants were wearing flesh-colored body stockings. You'd think that a group of reasonably alert college students might notice a little detail like this; we can only conclude that we're dealing with some sadly unsophisticated youngsters here. Suffice it to say that Steve is hauled into court, where he's asked to justify his teaching methods.

But how can he get a fair trial in a town full of prudes? When the word "virginity" comes up in the course of the testimony, we hear a stunned intake of breath from everyone in the courtroom, including visiting columnist Walter Winchell, who claims, "This is a shock! Enough to make Dr. Kinsey blush!" The real horror comes later, when Steve makes his impassioned plea for academic freedom; a sorrier collection of pious platitudes has seldom been heard. Then the local druggist (Mickey Shaughnessy) has a nervous breakdown (an embarrassing histrionic display that almost makes the rest of the acting in this movie look good) and confesses that he planted the porn, wrote the anonymous letter, etc., etc., in order to draw Winchell, Earl Wilson, Sheilah Graham, and all the other journalist guest stars into town. He hoped, you see, that they would notice his pretty daughter and make her a movie star.

So what does it all mean, exactly? Well, as Steve so aptly puts it in his courtroom summation, it means "the triumph of stupidity over reason." Well may you wonder why a male homosexual would want to sit through this aggressively heterosexual film. But think again, and ask yourself: has any film ever made heterosexuality look worse?

Colossus and the Amazon Queen*
(Italy 1964 Released in color. Available in video generally in b&w)

Colossus and the Amazon Queen, a gladiator picture starring
Rod Taylor and Ed Fury, is listed as being a 1964 release. This
presents us with an intriguing puzzle. In 1963 Rod Taylor was
the principal star of *The Birds* and also played a major role in *The
V.I.P.'s* with Liz and Dick. No wonder he looks so befuddled in this
movie. He's probably thinking, "What am I doing here? I thought
my career was going rather well. A year ago I was being directed
by Hitchcock. How did I wind up providing comic relief for Ed
Fury?" Still, it's nonetheless interesting to see him in a beefcake role.
He's boyish and nimble, with nice legs and thighs. However, as far
as I'm concerned, the star of the show is Gianna Maria Canale as
the glamorous queen of the title, much given to midday tippling. She
somehow manages to be the least offensive member of the cast.

The best sword-and-sandal epics are the ones that take themselves very seriously and end up being inadvertently hilarious. This
one intends to be funny (the music score keeps nudging us to let us
know) and is therefore a disaster. Furthermore, the film is a manifestation of Sixties sexism at its most absurd extreme. The legendary
Amazons are portrayed as being a bunch of silly, temperamental
women clumsily clunking around in heavy armor. They're always
in a snit about something. Plus they fall down a lot, usually because
they're either drunk or pregnant.

Their men are mainly kidnapped studs who, once they're in cap-
tivity, abruptly turn into screaming queens, complete with earrings
and full drag regalia. Rod Taylor, for instance, becomes a beautician. On the river bank and in the all-male marketplace, we overhear a series of typical manly exchanges:

"Say! Did you hear that in Greece they have soapflakes that don't
give you those ugly chapped hands?"

"You don't say! Well, it's high time, if you ask me. I'm just ruining my complexion with these cheap detergents."

"I just can't understand! I never seem to get my wash as dazzling
as yours."

"Tell me, Orestes, what's new with you?"

"Oh, my dear, don't even ask me! I'm slaving day and night!"

And so forth. An Amazon warrior comes swaggering home after a hard day of military maneuvers. "Soup's on?" she curtly inquires of her husband, who's wearing a dress.

"Why, you've just arrived!" he exclaims. "And you want to eat already?"

"Well, I'm in training, butch, and I don't want any back talk from you!"

I will admit such sexual role reversals can be amusing. Furthermore, in the course of their initiation into fagdom, the guys are forced to sit through a ballet performance involving a trio of copiously oiled musclemen dancing on tippy-toe, their hips swaying and swishing, dressed in nothing but helmets and skimpy loincloths with tassels attached at the crotch. I was scarcely able to believe my eyes. Which brings us to another mystery: where, besides Greenwich Village and San Francisco, could this movie be shown in 1964?

Conquest* (U.S. 1937 B&W)

The opening scene of Conquest plays like a Nazi propaganda film about subhuman Slavic savagery and debauchery. A horde of Cossacks ride their horses right into the parlor of a Polish castle. They burn the tapestries, smash the candelabra, shoot the manservants, rape the maidservants, and generally reduce the decor to rubble. Then Greta Garbo appears at the head of the staircase. When those uncouth Russkies catch sight of the Divine Garbo, they all freeze in their tracks, instantly overcome with awe. Fortunately, before they've had a chance to regain their bravado, they are routed by the Polish lancers. Garbo turns to her elderly husband (struck in the face with a whip by a departing blackguard) and entreats him as follows: "It didn't happen! It was a nightmare!"

"A nightmare we shared with our furniture," he replies, gesturing to indicate their vandalized surroundings. Never mind all the dead servants; life is cheaper than furniture. Garbo's brother rides in with the lancers and tells her of his hero, the Emperor Napoleon: "When he walks among the wounded, they seem comforted, proud, and die happy." Napoleon is Charles Boyer, who, of course, takes a fancy to Garbo. Elder statesmen beg her to put love of country ahead of virtue: "You are a woman. Napoleon is, after all, only a man." She gives herself to the Emperor, who, in exchange for her honor, frees the Poles from their oppressors. Thoroughly disgusted, her husband sets out for Rome to seek an annulment of their marriage. Greta, however, is soon past caring: she and Napoleon have found true love.

From this point on, the film becomes a collection of tenderly passionate interludes before and after battles that we don't get to see. The camp qualities remain constant throughout. They are particularly noticeable when Napoleon announces his intention to escape from Elba and take the road which will lead him to Waterloo (every clause of this fateful declaration is punctuated with thunderclaps and lightning bolts). Yes, this is a tiresome movie, but it casts a romantic spell (of sorts). I have yet to meet a homosexual effeminate enough to read bodice-ripper romance paperbacks. Many of us, however, find the cinematic equivalent quite irresistible.

Cry-Baby* (U.S. 1990 C)

Cry-Baby, a John Waters version of a typical Fifties rock-'n'-roll extravaganza, is as stringently stylized as an M-G-M production number. As always, Waters has a great eye for guys. Like so many of the great Hollywood directors of yesteryear, he's got a talent for taking an essentially heterosexual narrative and then homo-eroticizing it ruthlessly and relentlessly. Cry-Baby has basically the same plot as Grease. It's a boy-meets-girl story, but this time the boys have all the best camera angles.

The cast is a camp phantasmagoria: Johnny Depp, Traci Lords, Patty Hearst, David Nelson, Troy Donahue, Joey Heatherton, Joe Dallesandro, Mink Stole, Ricki Lake, Willem Dafoe, Susan Tyrrell, and Polly Bergen. Nelson and Hearst are the standouts. We even get to hear Patty say "Fuck." Donahue and Stole look like they could have been contenders, too, but they barely have a minute's worth of screen time. Stole, in fact, is confined to an iron lung and is only seen in a mirror. Dafoe is memorable as a prison guard who struck me as being a closet case. As the heroine's high society grandma (who runs a charm school), Bergen gives a spirited, energetic, admirably silly performance. Depp, in the title role, clearly didn't do his own crying. Seldom have I seen such gelatinous-looking tears. This movie is badly in need of Divine. Her presence is sorely missed. Susan Tyrrell plays the Divine part, but she is hardly an adequate substitute, though she does get to throw a dart at a picture of Mamie Eisenhower.

The Damned* (Italy 1969 C)

The Damned, Luchino Visconti's film about corrosive ambition among the evil rich of Hitler's Germany, is decadent in all sorts of picturesque ways, but never once did it give me the feeling that I was seeing the Third Reich as it really was. From a camp standpoint, I suppose that this is all for the best. On the other hand, you can't really blame me for getting impatient. This is a film in which the stray hint and the ominous detail reign supreme. The constant obliqueness eventually becomes both tiresome and frustrating.

The centerpiece of the picture (now a minor gay cult film), of course, is the "Night of the Long Knives" sequence, which amounts to being a big homosexual orgy cut short by Nazis with machine guns. Oddly enough, though the rest of the film is in English, this particular scene is played in German, without subtitles. The sex is low-key; it looks more like a boozy excess of macho high-spiritedness.

One of the movie's principal villains is played by Helmut Berger, a frequent performer in Visconti's films. Early on, he gets himself up in drag and does a Dietrich impression. Don't be misled, however: he's cast as a heterosexual child molester, reminiscent of the title character in Fritz Lang's M. He rapes two little girls and murders a third. He finally ends up raping his own mother (for reasons unclear to me). She is portrayed by Ingrid Thulin as the definitive Fascist bitch. Why, she's even muscular! She wears a lot of weird Nazi evening gowns—the kind with bare shoulders and straps in the back. The incident of incestuous rape, however, turns her into a dope-addicted zombie. She's married to a Macbeth-like cold-blooded killer. He's played by Dirk Bogarde, who comes across as too weak and wimpish for the part. The cast also includes

Charlotte Rampling, a notable cult figure of the Seventies. Her role, however, is small. Before very many scenes have elapsed, she gets deported to a concentration camp.

Damon and Pythias   (Italy 1962 C)

Even as just a bare outline, the legend of Damon and Pythias is loaded with homoerotic potential. That's why the notion of filming it as a beefcake epic verges on blatant pornography.

Bisexual porno, I hasten to add. Our title characters are, of course, provided with pulchritudinous female companionship. Pythias (Don Burnett) is a native of Athens who travels to Syracuse, a fascist dictatorship ruled by Dionysius the Tyrant. There he gets mugged by Damon, a charming rogue portrayed by Guy Williams (best known as the star of TV's *Lost in Space*). This would seem to get their relationship off to an inauspicious start, but the two nonetheless become surprisingly intimate friends. Early on, Damon retires to a bedchamber with his main squeeze (Liana Orfei). He invites Pythias to join them. "Come on in. Make yourself comfortable."

"Uh . . . May I?" asks Pythias, shy and hesitant.

"Please," replies Damon, who ends up reclining in the middle, between the other two. "Brothers and sisters, eh?" he murmurs contentedly, referring to the fraternal ideals which characterize Athenian philosophy.

Damon is soon getting drunk over Pythias, and also getting into barroom brawls over the guy. Ms. Orfei wants him to just settle down and fuck her, but by that time the Greek (and, I fancy, Greek love) has gotten into his blood. In a jealous snit, he betrays Pythias to the bad guys (the henchmen of Dionysius) and then, overcome with remorse, risks his own life to rescue him. "It's something I never felt before," he explains, when asked about this new and tempestuous friendship.

After several nicely staged action interludes, the famous story kicks into gear: Dionysius captures the subversive Pythias and condemns him to death, but the doomed prisoner has a pregnant wife back in Athens, so Damon offers himself to serve as a hostage while Pythias goes home to see her through her confinement. He returns just as Damon is about to be executed in his stead. Moved by the drama of it all, the Tyrant pardons them both. Despite his macho appearance, Williams delivers a strikingly fey performance. And Liana Orfei has a much stronger presence than is usual for women in films of this type. This Italian production has a Hollywood director: Curtis Bernhardt, whose credentials mark him as being peculiarly well-suited to gay cult material. With a pair of Bette Davis films to his credit *(A Stolen Life* and *Payment on Demand)*, he was obviously the right man for the job.

Dead Ringer* (U.S. 1964 B&W)

Were it not for its campy cast, *Dead Ringer* would be nothing more than a dreary, overlong B-picture. Indigent good twin shoots wealthy bad twin and then attempts to supplant her. The perfect crime? Hardly. The good twin gradually awakens to the fact that the bad twin was guilty of murder, also.

The film is full of such cheap, obvious ironies as this. The proceedings, however, are partially redeemed by the presence of Bette Davis, popeyed and fish-faced in her dual role as the twins. Her performance is more entertaining than convincing. ("Pooah *fah*-thuh!" the bad twin histrionically declaims, when informed that dipsomaniacal Dad was dragged away to the boobyhatch in a straightjacket.) Appropriately, smoking is a factor in this saga of homicidal sisters: one smokes; the other doesn't. The grim goings-on are lightened by some flavorsome supporting turns. Estelle Winwood looks practically mummified as a dour religious zealot. Jean Hagen is contrastingly plump and perky as a loudmouth arriviste. Interestingly, these two actually have a scene together.

Like many other movies, this one asserts the moral superiority of dogs. The family pooch loves the good twin, hates the bad twin, and thereby almost blows the good twin's cover. He also hates the bad twin's evil gigolo boyfriend (Peter Lawford), who conspired to help her poison her husband. So naturally, when Lawford starts roughing up the good twin, the dog attacks him and kills him. Someday I would dearly love to see this plot enacted with a house cat taking the place of the dog.

Desperate Living* (U.S. 1977 C)

"I have never found the antics of deviates to be one bit amusing," Mink Stole solemnly declares in *Desperate Living*. Fortunately, I cannot say the same. This John Waters opus stars Stole as a recently released mental patient who isn't quite ready to face the outside world. When some children accidentally knock a baseball through her window, she accuses them of trying to assassinate her. When the phone rings and it proves to be a wrong number, she hysterically castigates the luckless caller ("How can you ever repay the thirty seconds you have stolen from my life?!"). And, when her husband attempts to give her a badly needed sedative, she orders the overweight housekeeper (Jean Hill) to sit on his face, thereby suffocating him.

The two women flee to Mortville, a kind of hobo jungle that serves as a haven for fugitives. They find this sanctuary with the help of a depraved policeman, who will only give them directions if they'll fork over their underpants. Once there, they room at a shack belonging to a lesbian couple: Mole (Susan Lowe) is a wart-faced wrestler who's been residing in Mortville ever since putting an opponent's eye out and stomping on it; her lover, Muffy (Liz Renay), is merely in for snuffing a babysitter (who got a mite confused and put the baby in the fridge). Mortville is ruled by the tyrannical Queen Carlotta (Edith Massey), who compels her subjects to eat cockroaches and wear unbecoming clothes (the hefty Miss Hill looks especially ludicrous, clad in a chartreuse tutu). The populace ultimately rises in revolt; the queen becomes the main course at a cannibal victory banquet.

This grim fairy tale has an appropriately medieval aura. The film is borderline porno and the action is mainly lesbian. It should be noted, however, that Queen Carlotta's palace guardsmen regularly strip off their clothes in order to service her. As is often the case with early Waters, the grunge becomes a bit much, after a while. That's why the film is ideal for video—you can take it in small doses. Acting honors go to Ms. Stole, who starts at full power and keeps right on going. It's also fun to see Massey play a villainess, for a change.

Dishonored* (U.S. 1931 B&W)

Dishonored starts out with Beethoven on the soundtrack, so we know right away we're in for something Germanic and heavy. Marlene Dietrich is cast as a prostitute whose love of country (Austria, in this case) leads her to become a spy. World War I probably didn't really look like it does in this movie, but it should have. The rancid romanticism is ubiquitous. A traitor (Warner Oland), fingered by Dietrich, casually munches a grape before blowing his brains out. Dietrich herself thinks nothing of cradling a cat in one arm while brandishing a gun with her other hand. She takes the cat with her everywhere, even behind enemy lines, into occupied Poland. There she develops a kinky love/hate relationship with a Russian colonel (Victor McLaglen, rather oddly cast). First he's going to have her shot at sunrise, then she's going to have him shot at sunrise, etc. She ends up getting shot at sunrise for helping him to escape.

The film is like an illustrated catalog of unhealthy, destructive soldier-male attitudes toward women and sex. At the casino, McLaglen is seated by the roulette wheel. The man standing behind him rests his hand on McLaglen's shoulder, till McLaglen tells him to desist. Meanwhile the sexually ambiguous Dietrich is taking her leave of a girlfriend at the bar. Affectionately, she grasps the woman's hand in parting. The director, Josef von Sternberg, does not bear down heavily on this moment; nevertheless, a comparison is indubitably being drawn.

Doctor of Doom* (Mexico 1960 B&W)

The *Doctor of Doom* is a crazed surgeon who likes to transplant the brains of pretty girls. Trouble is, they die on him; he thinks it's because of their low IQs. So he kidnaps a lady chemist, but she also expires on the operating table, probably because she forgot to bring her lucky rabbit's foot that day.

The doctor decides he needs a victim with more stamina. Turns out the chemist had a sister who's a wrestler (Lorena Velazquez). Down at the gym, Lorena is being introduced to Rubi, a new contender.

"Know something? I've watched you," says Rubi to Lorena, "and your eyes have such a sad look. Tell me—is anything wrong?"

"No," Lorena replies evasively, then changes her mind. "Well . . . all right. My poor sister! It's just something I can't forget. See, they murdered her three nights ago!"

"I'm so sorry! Forgive me, but I really—"

"No, I don't want you to feel bad about it."

"But if there's anything I can do to help—"

"Thank you. You're a real swell girl. Are you staying nearby here, Rubi?"

"At the Splendid Hotel. Why?"

"My new apartment is large, and you must be lonely. I thought maybe you'd like to come and live there."

"I'd be delighted to!"

So that's how lady wrestlers get together. The Doctor of Doom, however, is going to disrupt their tender idyll. Lorena, of course, can vanquish him without even mussing her bouffant hairdo; all she has to do is throw acid in his face. But he's not finished yet: he kidnaps one of her rival wrestlers and gives the poor woman the brain of a male ape (as if she wasn't butch enough already). This results in a somewhat more spirited wrestling match than usual.

Believe it or not, some of the humor in this movie is intentional. Like, for instance, when a male bodybuilder comes swaggering into the ladies' gym and tries to make off with some of their weights. All the girls pile on top of him. As if they needed an excuse to pile on top of each other.

Doll Face* (U.S. 1945 B&W)

Doll Face is Vivian Blaine in a B-grade musical programmer. She auditions for a distinguished impresario (Reed Hadley) who turns her down because she's a stripper currently headlining at the Gayety Theater. He tells her she needs to acquire culture, which is easier said than done, since she hasn't been to school since she was expelled from the sixth grade. Carmen Miranda, her friend and co-star at the Gayety, tells her it's all for the best, since, without Doll Face, the "whole show go floozy and we all lose our jobs." Then Doll Face writes a best-selling autobiography which establishes her as a woman of cultivation. Hadley signs her up and builds a lavish production around her and her pals. Carmen, who plays someone named Chita Chula, sings a song called "Chico Chico." Perry Como sings "Hubba Hubba Hubba." The lyrics for the latter have a certain post-Hiroshima topicality: "I got it from the guy who was in the know—it was mighty smoky over Tokyo." I'm not sure whether camp's the word for this sort of stuff. Some things go beyond being bad taste.

Dragstrip Girl* (U.S. 1957 B&W)

Fay Spain has the title role in *Dragstrip Girl*. We can tell by the grease stains on her pert little bottom: this is a gal who knows her way around a crankshaft. "A speed demon for a daughter!" her prim and proper mother despairs. Fay just shrugs: "It's a speedy age we live in."

She is romanced by Steve Terrell, who takes her out for a spin in his hot rod. "Lean on it!" she enthuses. Against his better judgment, he does, and very nearly runs over a Fifties housewife pushing a baby carriage. Fay shrugs again: "She shoulda used the crosswalk."

Steve's rival for her affections is John Ashley. He's the local rich kid, and he really looks the part: all that shop talk about rear ends makes it hard to ignore that his is rather plump and puffy. He does a fair Elvis impersonation, however. (Accompanying him is Frank Gorshin, in drag.) In the big fistfight scene, Steve knocks him unconscious. There's a moment of glorious kinkiness here: while John reclines so adorably supine, someone garnishes his face with whipped cream and a maraschino cherry.

But let's not dwell too long on symbolism. At one point Gorshin wolfs down a slice of pizza with a scoop of chocolate ice cream on top, and I'd rather not attempt to decode that. Even my dirty mind draws the line somewhere.

JOHN ASHLEY (1934–   ), star of 1950s camp classics such as *Beach Blanket Bingo*, *High School Caesar*, and *Dragstrip Girls*. Publicity photo.

Drum* (U.S. 1976 C)

Drum, a sequel to the notorious *Mandingo*, is distinguished by its particularly warped sense of humor. Coarse, lurid, and even downright crude, this film is still basically a comedy of manners—sort of like a concentration camp version of *Upstairs, Downstairs*.

The movie mainly transpires at Falconhurst, a slave-breeding plantation owned and operated by an amusingly uncouth oaf (Warren Oates). His pert and pretty daughter (Rainbeaux Smith) may look like Alice in Wonderland, but she deports herself with all the modesty of a nanny goat. The girl is constantly groping the resident studs and endeavoring to unbutton their trousers. Obviously, the dear child requires the guidance of, if not a mother, then some other shining example of Southern womanhood. Toward this end, a charming governess (Fiona Lewis) is imported from New Orleans. However, she turns out to be a designing woman, who successfully plots with her fellow servants to finagle Master Warren into bedding and wedding her. As Oates so elegantly puts it, "Fornicatin' is what Falconhurst's all about."

The Afro-American hero of the piece is Ken Norton, who fulfills an identical function in *Mandingo*. Practically everybody wants to get in his pants. The one who wants him most, unfortunately, is a demented old queen (John Colicos), whose shenanigans precipitate a slave uprising which brutally interrupts the bedroom farce of the preceding reels. Conflagration and holocaust descend upon the entire cast, including nominally innocent bystanders such as the pretty young man (Alain Patrick) whose bad luck it is to be the kept boy of Colicos. As for the villain himself, he is castrated by Norton, who (it is implied) crushes the bad guy's balls with his bare hands. Obviously, this film is a degenerate classic of homophobic cinema. However, its wretched excessiveness precludes our taking it seriously.

Duel of the Titans   (Italy 1962 C)

Romulus and Remus, fabled twins of ancient myth, begin their story as infants floating down a river on a makeshift raft, from whence they are rescued by a merciful she-wolf. Ere long this unlikely step-mother is slain by a shepherd, who confiscates her human wards. These grow up to be Steve Reeves and Gordon Scott, the crown princes of peplum; this movie, *Duel of the Titans*, is their only co-starring collaboration.

We first encounter Steve and Gordon at a sacrificial ceremony honoring Pan. A goat is slain; gory strips of its skin are seized by half-naked youths who use them to flagellate the orgiastic onlook-ers. Steve steps in to prevent Virna Lisi from tasting the lash of a lustful whip-wielder. "My name's Romulus. What's yours?" he blurts, as if they were at a Shriners convention.

He carries her off when he learns she's a Sabine princess. She pretends to be haughty, but she digs those biceps. Steve and Virna get caught in the rain, poor things, and have to take their clothes off. While wringing out his wet shirt, Steve fills her in on the back-ground he shares with Gordon: "Once we were just shepherds . . . and so peaceful, we'd kiss the hand that whipped us." I've heard of guys who were into that.

Steve's words are quickly put to the test. He's apprehended, stripped, and then spread-eagled on a wheel which is spun while the whips bite his flesh from many and various angles. Meanwhile his true mother looks on in tears; she's a vestal virgin who consigned her kids to the shifting currents of the river, rather than admit she'd been knocked up (and by a deity, no less).

At her word, Steve and Gordon set out to found "an Eternal City" (i.e., Rome). It's a long trek, and Gordon turns surly. "What's tormenting you?" Virna asks him. He's probably peeved about the fact he has second billing, and also because the script doesn't give him much to do. Furthermore, what he does do doesn't work out very well. When Gordon defies the gods by climbing "the holy mountain that vomits fire," the screen is riven in two by an earth-quake and half the cast gets swallowed up.

This is a very sensual film, laved in Brucknerian music and luridly voluptuous color. At times, the screen seems almost to pulsate.

And, in the end, we get the satisfaction of watching Steve beat the living shit out of Gordon. (Take that, you imitative upstart!) Actually, it's Steve who takes a beating, but then he and Gordon get to roll around on the ground together. The fight—and the movie—end with Gordon clumsily impaling himself on his brother's sword. Earlier, he'd petulantly snarled at Steve, "I'll never share anything with you!"

Eyes of Texas* (U.S. 1948 B&W)

Eyes of Texas is an amazingly decadent Roy Rogers western. The plot pits Roy against a seemingly sweet old lady named Hattie (Nana Bryant) who bakes cakes and lives in a pretty little house with a white picket fence. Types like her are the ones you have to keep an eye on; hence the title. Down in the basement she's got a secret kennel filled with dogs that she's starved into a state of bloodthirsty savagery. She's scheming to take over an orphanage for homeless boys and boot them all out into the street. Anyone who stands in her way gets mysteriously devoured by "wolves." She hires roughnecks to horsewhip Roy. (Students of homoerotic sadism in the cinema should note that his shirt gets ripped in this scene.) A gat clutched tightly in her hand, she advises him, "You should never trust a woman."

Conveniently enough, she's got a weak (though certainly not soft) heart, so, at the end, she just drops dead and nobody has to kill her. Seems to me that she was in the wrong line of work for someone with a heart condition. This 1948 release is a vivid manifestation of postwar malaise. I mean, we know things must be getting pretty noir when Grandma's pet pooch is the Hound of the Baskervilles.

Fellini Satyricon* (Italy 1970 C)

One might naturally wonder what a Federico Fellini film is doing in a book on gay camp. In point of fact, however, this movie has plenty to offer us. The plot centers on a pair of handsome young men (one blonde, one brunette) vying for the favors of a barely pubescent boy. (The straightest of my straight friends once confided to me that he found himself sexually responding to this provocative child. Chicken conquers all, apparently.)

Set in the ancient world (on a series of heavily stylized, theatrical sets), the film has the look of a peplum, except that the guys are mostly either gay or bisexual. Our heroes, separated from their boylove by unhappy circumstance, chance to encounter an African slave girl and settle down for a threesome . . . which doesn't work out; they forget about her and concentrate on each other, while she giggles at them good-naturedly. Later they try to satisfy a nympho who has to be kept tied up all the time. They kidnap an albino hermaphrodite, who dies of thirst in the desert. The labyrinth of the Minotaur is explored, but he turns out to be—not a monster—just another musclebound queen. They come to a town which only grants entrance to those who can fuck the female reclining at the gate. "He's a dead fish," she contemptuously says of the blonde, who can't get it up for her.

A wrestling match concludes with the victor kissing the vanquished. Later the two men are wed to each other at sea, but the marriage doesn't last; the "bride" is beheaded before they get back to land. Anyway, some wedding. The movie ends with a funeral. The mourners devour the corpse.

Female Trouble* (U.S. 1974 C)

Female Trouble is a heartwarming celebration of traditional family values. The opening scenes transpire during the Christmas season. There's surely nothing more traditional than Christmas: a typical American family gathered at the hearthside, singing carols and happily opening their Christmas presents. But what's this? The daughter of the household is disappointed with her gift. She'd been hoping for cha-cha heels, but her parents have selected a more conservative style of shoe.

"Nice girls don't wear cha-cha heels," Father explains, while Daughter overturns the Christmas tree on Mom and angrily stomps on the unopened gifts. Since she's played by Divine in his portly prime, the packages are irreparably flattened. After reducing the room to a shambles, our heroine delivers a touching yuletide benediction: "I hate you! Fuck you! Fuck you both, you awful people! You're not my parents! I hate you, I hate this house, and I HATE CHRISTMAS!"

Seriously, folks, this is a vintage John Waters movie, which means that it's a subversion of everything Dan Quayle holds dear. Fleeing her formerly happy home, Divine attempts to hitchhike out of town. She is promptly picked up by a pervert, who rapes her and then performs cunnilingus on her. This masculine role is also interpreted by Divine, wearing thoroughly befouled underpants.

Knocked up, our heroine delivers her own baby, without assistance, while reclining on the davenport of a cheap hotel room. The character's name, by the way, is Dawn Davenport. (She's tough: she severs the baby's umbilical cord with her teeth!) Now that she's got a kid to support, her life becomes a downward spiral. First she's a waitress, then a go-go dancer, then a hooker, and then she rolls drunks for a living.

Right next door to Dawn's hideout are the lodgings of a leather-clad dominatrix played by Edith Massey. She resides with her nephew, a hair stylist who, she's grieved to learn, is straight. "Oh, honey, I'd be so happy if you'd turn nellie!" she tells him. "I'd be so proud if you was a fag and had a nice beautician boyfriend. . . . The world of heterosexuals is a sick and boring life!" Boyd McDonald couldn't have said it better.

She is, of course, heartsick when her nephew weds Dawn, who, I might add, wears a see-through bridal gown that's definitively tacky. And, true to Edith's predictions, married life proves to be lackluster. Dawn's husband reads magazines while he screws her. Afterward, he invites her daughter, Taffy (Mink Stole), to sit beside him on the bed. "I'd sooner jump in a river of snot," she pertly tells him. Next he asks her to suck his cock, which gets him this reply: "I wouldn't suck your lousy dick if I was suffocating and there was oxygen in your balls!" Later the child pays a call on her bio-logical father. But he pukes on her, so she stabs him to death. Then she atones by becoming a Hare Krishna. Dawn, utterly appalled, strangles her, then dies in the electric chair.

The last half hour drags a bit. Even so, this is definitely the tape I'd like to run for Jesse Helms, if he ever honored my typical American home with his august presence. I'd love to watch his face as he heard Edith Massey say, "I just use common sense. I mean, if they're smart, they're queer, and, if they're stupid, they're straight." Sure beats *It's a Wonderful Life*, doesn't it?

The 5,000 Fingers of Dr. T. * (U.S. 1953 C)

During the McCarthy era, Hollywood showed its loyalty by churn-ing out several anti-Communist parables. Of these, the most bizarre, the most stylized, the most homoerotic was surely *The 5,000 Fin-gers of Dr. T.* The star is Tommy Rettig, whom my generation will always remember as "Jeff" from the *Lassie* television series. Like any healthy, normal, red-blooded, clean-cut American chicken, Tommy hates having to take piano lessons. Unfortunately, his widowed mother (Mary Healy) insists upon them. Piano playing equals classical music equals foreign tyranny, or so Tommy imagines when he has a nightmare about his instructor (Hans Conried). In the dream, Conried is keeping him prisoner in an elaborate gulag sur-rounded by an electrified barbed-wire fence.

Conried's ardent desire is to capture five hundred little boys (the 5,000 fingers of the title) and have them perform in unison at a supercolossal concert. Toward this end, he's brainwashed American mothers (who, we surmise, use their feminine wiles to bring hus-bands into the fold, as well). Deep in the dungeons languish male proponents of other musical instruments, clad in tight pants and no shirts. Miss Healy is on the premises, also. He keeps her in a deep hypnotic trance. While under his sway, she wears sexy Jean Louis gowns. (Once free, her shoulders are demurely covered.) Just when Dr. Conried seems to be on the brink of triumph, Tommy whips up an A-bomb and blows everything to smithereens.

Conried is clearly a Commie, but he's just as obviously a queen.

For one thing, he's constantly dancing with men (usually Peter Lind Hayes; Miss Healy functions as a beard). In preparation for the huge recital, his quintet of valets attire him in swishy finery: "undulating undies," "lavender spats," a "purple nylon girdle," a "peekaboo blouse," a "pink brocaded bodice," an "organdy snood," a "chiffon Mother Hubbard," and, to top it all off, "leather vests."

Do you need further evidence? Well, we're told that he hates dogs and baseball. For a mirror reversal of this film, see the review of *Storm Center* elsewhere in this book.

---

*Flamingo Road** (U.S. 1949 B&W)

Flamingo Road has Joan Crawford playing a regular dame for a change. She's a kootch dancer in a carnival (yeah, you read that right). She stays behind when the show pulls up stakes. The local deputy sheriff (Zachary Scott) takes a shine to her. She thinks that he thinks she's cheap, but he turns out to be a perfect gentleman. Which doesn't mean he doesn't want to fuck her. The whole town thinks they're doing it, including Zach's boss, the corrupt sheriff (Sydney Greenstreet), who's grooming him for a high-tone political career. Sydney takes an instant dislike to Joan. She thinks that he thinks she's cheap, and she's right. He wants her out of town, so he gets her fired from the waitress job that Zach lined up for her. And he nudges Zach into a loveless marriage to a society girl. (Honestly, Zachary Scott can be such a weakling at times!)

You can hardly blame Joan for giving Greenstreet a good slap. So then he gets her arrested and sent to a work farm on a trumped-up prostitution charge. Once she gets out, she quickly hooks up with a powerbroker played by David Brian. He marries her and sets her up in a mansion on Flamingo Road. From here on in, she's a fancy lady.

This film could have used a more imaginative screenwriter. I kept wanting to hear that there was a more-than-political reason for Greenstreet's obsession with Zach. Greenstreet, mumbling unintelligibly (as is his wont), is easily the picture's campiest component. But it's Crawford, surveying him bleakly, who gets off the nastiest line of dialogue: "You just wouldn't believe how much trouble it is to dispose of a dead elephant."

362-52

From left to right: SIDNEY GREENSTREET (1879–1954), ZACHARY SCOTT (1914–1965) and DAVID BRIAN (1914–   ) in the 1949 film *Flamingo Road* (Warner Brothers). Also starring Joan Crawford. Greenstreet steals the show as a corrupt Southern sheriff, with Joan a close second.

Flash Gordon* (U.S. 1980 C)

Flash Gordon, a relentlessly smirky, decadent, and homoerotic remake of the seminal sci-fi serial, is a very expensive, very ugly film. It's extremely gay, mainly due to the costuming, or, in some cases, the lack of costuming. Flash is now a celebrity football quarterback (Sam J. Jones), his face on the cover of People magazine. He is spirited away to the planet of Ming the Merciless (Max von Sydow), who wants to destroy the earth. Flash is put to death in a bubble-shaped gas chamber, his muscular body completely unclad, except for a black-leather jockstrap. But he's brought back to life, and successfully unites the various local oppressed minorities into a victorious army of rebellion. The pivotal moment is when he and the handsome Prince Barin (Timothy Dalton) swear a bond of undying loyalty and devotion. What turns the tide of battle, however, are the Hawkmen: a race of burly, seminude winged warriors who look like oversexed angels. Ming is impaled on the rapier-like point of a missile nose cone. Earth is saved.

This celebration of kink came out in 1980, a decisive year in American politics. The film combines the dregs of Seventies disco culture with the chauvinistic cruelty of nascent Reaganism.

Flesh* (U.S. 1968 C)

The title is appropriate. Flesh depicts a day in the life of a male prostitute, portrayed by Joe Dallesandro, who is naked more often than not. We see a few of his johns. With one exception, they are better looking than he is.

This is an Andy Warhol production, directed by Paul Morrissey. Not only are the people unattractive, but so are their voices. I heard so many abrasive New York accents, I began to wish that the movie was silent.

The cast includes transvestites. Candy Darling is impressive, Jackie Curtis less so. (Chatting about film stars of the Forties, she mispronounces the names of Eugene Pallette and Jane Frazee. What kind of a queen would do that?)

Flying Down to Rio* (U.S. 1933 B&W)

Flying Down to Rio is generally remembered as being the first of the Ginger Rogers and Fred Astaire musicals. The topbilled stars of the film, however, are the glamorously gorgeous Dolores Del Rio and the dazzlingly blonde Gene Raymond. (This is all right with me, since I like them better, anyway.) In the opening scenes, we may be forgiven for supposing that the star is Franklin Pangborn, the Thirties character actor whose specialty was fussy, fretful faggot types. He's cast as an employee of the Hotel Hibiscus whose job it is to keep the boys in the band from getting too familiar with the guests.

In their first number, Rogers and Astaire dance on seven wedge-shaped pianos that are fitted together, like pieces of a pie, to form a circle. This tendency toward extravagance culminates in a climactic production number which has chorus girls securely fastened to the wings of airplanes and gesticulating wildly (which is all they *can* do, under the circumstances). What makes this concept campy is the supposition that such antics could possibly be appreciated by an audience on the ground.

Frankenstein's Daughter* (U.S. 1958 B&W)

John Ashley, heartbreakingly gorgeous, his pants tight, his eyes huge and soulful, is top-billed in Frankenstein's Daughter, though he's clearly unequipped to play either Frankenstein or his daughter. Remaining on the sidelines for much of the movie's length, he portrays a young man who has much to complain about. For one thing, he's engaged to a girl named Trudy. Worse yet, she periodically turns into a monster and consequently causes him public embarrassment. I mean, we're talking front-page headlines here.

Even without Ashley's smoldering presence, this movie would still have had a sexually subversive subtext: after all, its monsters are female. (There are two of them, as it happens.) Midway through the proceedings, there's a pool party, but John keeps his clothes on: he's stuck in the kitchen making shish kebab, while, out on the patio, Page Cavanaugh and his Trio are performing a song called "Special Date." I like the way John casts an uneasy glance over his shoulder, just after catching his initial glimpse of the monster's shadow. (It's the other monster, this time; by this point in the narrative, Trudy has reverted to Fifties adolescent normalcy.) Moments later, his other shoulder is being patted very paternally by the presiding police inspector. The next scene is the last one in the film; we're back at the pool and John is finally dressed in bathing briefs. In closing, I should mention that this film bears no relation to the even more flamboyantly titled *Jesse James Meets Frankenstein's Daughter*.

The Gang's All Here   (U.S. 1943 C)

The Gang's All Here, a phenomenally florid Carmen Miranda musical, gets underway with a number so bizarre and phantasmagorical, we doubt the evidence of our own senses. We're on the New York waterfront. We can actually see the water (more about that later). A ship from Brazil has just docked. We watch its cargo of fruit being unloaded (more about that, too). Carmen appears. She sings about the excitement of finding herself "on gay Broadway." (In her numbers this time out, she seems determined to mention the word "gay" as often as possible.) The camera pulls back to reveal that we're in a night club. The ship, the water, the fruit are all mere components of a mammoth stage set. Show girls are seated at the row of tables nearest the stage. They croon right along with the other chorines. The overall effect is extremely disorienting. Where does the show begin and reality leave off? Co-star Edward Everett Horton gets so mixed up, he starts dancing with Eugene Pallette.

If I were to pick a single image that is emblematic of camp, it would probably be Carmen Miranda adorned with a towering headdress of fruit. She wears her tallest one ever when she sings "The Lady in the Tutti Frutti Hat": indeed, the number concludes with the world's most gigantic bunch of bananas sprouting from the top of Carmen's head as she stands at the end of a runway formed by two rows of monumentally huge strawberries. Bananas are the key motif, transforming a seemingly innocuous floor show into a garishly surreal masturbation fantasy. Chorus girls wave giant bananas up and down and back and forth to form archways and tunnels and hypnotically undulating waves. (Freud would've had a field day.) They also play a xylophone made of wooden bananas. We wonder what to expect for an encore. A song about penis envy?

Carmen also wears a turquoise turban garnished with gold and purple butterflies. She's the star of the show, but Alice Faye gets top billing. Alice is lit rather unflatteringly; in both of her big numbers, we can plainly see the mole on her upper lip. (She and director Busby Berkeley were apparently feuding when this picture was made.) Her romantic interest is James Ellison, very actor-ish in the role of a soldier. Horton keeps wanting to throw him a stag party, or, at the very least, a "bachelor dinner," but Ellison isn't interested.

This movie seems to have been made by people who could never believe that there's such a thing as "too much." We find ourselves wondering where and how it will all end. The final, climactic number features a horde of ugly dwarf children dancing a polka and wearing electric pink polka dots, which somehow turn into neon hula hoops carried by chorus girls. To top it all off, we get to hear Eugene Pallette sing. (Or do I mean croak?) What's that you say? You're asking about the plot? This movie, despite all its hidden meanings, wouldn't know the meaning of the word.

Gentlemen Prefer Blondes* (U.S. 1953 C)

Gentlemen Prefer Blondes presents us with a pair of Fifties glamour icons, both in the same show. This movie dates from 1953, a year when Americans were hot on the trail of subversion. The Rosenbergs were executed. Even comic books were suspect. HUAC had already investigated Hollywood. So what are we to make of it when the two reigning temptresses of the screen—Jane Russell and Marilyn Monroe—make their entrances dressed as weird aquatic anomalies, lobster-red and covered with sequins?

Not that these girls would ever dream of abolishing capitalism. Quite the contrary. Monroe, the more mercenary of the two, seeks marriage with a millionaire's son. He's played by Tommy Noonan, who is meek and mild-mannered as always and gives every appearance of being as adorably addled as she is. His eyes have a hurt puppy-dog look which I find quite irresistible. (The test of a true invert: when Tommy and Marilyn share a two-shot, I find myself ogling him instead of her.)

Our heroines set sail for France with the U.S. Olympic team. These boys mean business: they wear red-white-and-blue neckties. They also wear flesh-colored swimming trunks. This is most disconcerting, though it certainly enhances the film's choreography. When Jane performs a number in the gym, a dozen of these semi-nude athletes arrange themselves before her, six on each side. Then they turn 'round, bend over, and commence to do some very deep knee-bends, so that she proceeds along a pathway lined with wildly pumping male posteriors.

Also on board is Charles Coburn, surely the dirtiest—and the oldest—dirty old man that ever was. This should give you some idea: his character is nicknamed "Piggy." In real life, he donated a goodly share of his earnings to the radical right. In this movie he inadvertently kisses the hand of George "Foghorn" Winslow. It was surely his only excursion into pedophilia.

The girls end up in Paris, favorite destination of so many Fifties musicals. This is where Marilyn sings "Diamonds Are a Girl's Best Friend." She touches her breasts when she gets to the part about "These rocks don't lose their shape." In such a hypocritical era, it must have been difficult to know what was harmless fun and what was unacceptable. A chorus line of practically naked men flexing their butts? Tits equated with jewelry? The Fifties weren't innocent—just schizo.

The Giant of Marathon* (Italy 1960 C)

A haze of homoeroticism suffuses and permeates *The Giant of Marathon*. Male wrestlers grapple behind the opening titles, sinewy muscles straining in a contest of strength and will. Athletic competitions of this kind can get rather heated, as they say; the grimaces of the contenders as they collapse in each other's arms, one man irrevocably submitting to the other, speak of another, more pleasant form of friction.

The top man in the tussle is none other than Steve Reeves. The script, of course, takes care to place his man-to-man antics within a safely heterosexual context, which, I might add, is a trifle more elaborate than usual. There are scenes of war and scenes of amour; director Jacques Tourneur articulates both with consummate skill, and with a major assist from cinematographer Mario Bava. The mise en scène is bedecked and adorned with statuary, lush color (the blue of the midnight skies is especially rich), and stunning wide-screen panoramas. The scene in which Reeves pursues Mylène Demongeot's chariot through a picturesque wood has a charming, fairy-tale quality such as I've never seen before in a peplum. (It's likely that Bava directed this scene.) The dastardly villain (Sergio Fantoni) misleads and deceives poor Steve into suspecting Mylène of harboring Fascist sympathies. He rejects her and retires to his country estate, where he works off his sexual frustration by arduously plowing the soil into deep, straight furrows. (That's my kind of farmer, by God! If he can't have access to the orifice he wants, he'll fuck the very earth itself, instead!) We see a new side of Steve Reeves in this opus. His clean-shaven face radiates a fresh, open, healthy allure. Furthermore, he makes a convincing case for himself as an actor.

But he's also a juicy slab of meat who doesn't want to disappoint his slavering fans. In the final reel he garbs himself in a pair of white bathing tights which bear a startling resemblance to a diaper. This attire leaves his tushie looking singularly vulnerable, particularly when he announces his intention to defend Athens against those pesky Persians and their sneak attacks from the rear. His comrades and cohorts are clad just as he is, and, in the underwater fighting, their trunks have a tendency to cling, thus defining their buttocks to an almost indecent degree. Which is why, for the true connoisseur, this final battle scene can be climactic in more ways than one.

The Giants of Thessaly* (Italy 1960 C)

The Giants of Thessaly is directed by Riccardo Freda, a former art critic. The esthetic nature of his background is readily apparent, particularly in an early scene depicting a storm at sea. Such attractive, alluring, well-muscled sailorboys! And they fall down so much! And their clothes get so clingingly *wet*!

Not that they wear much. I guess I hadn't realized that Jason and his Argonauts put out to sea in such skimpy attire: tight bathing briefs with flaps of studded leather hanging in front. The highly refined—even rarified—lewdness of Freda's distinctive vision transforms their mythic exploit into an epic poem of crashing waves, surging seafoam, straining muscles, and undraped thighs. Never have I seen an episode of such extended and elaborate eroticism, even in this intensely physical genre. At one point a brawny youth is swept overboard. Jason (Roland Carey) hastens to the rescue and, by the might of his arm and the strength of his sinew, pulls the poor lad back to safety. This sequence includes what is perhaps the most beautiful shot of a male armpit in the history of the cinema. Even if only on the basis of this shot alone, Freda merits a place in the pantheon of the truly great directors.

Whoever designed the costuming (or, to put it more plainly, swimwear) must have been a genius of obscenity. The graceful fold of fabric at the seat makes us think we're seeing butt cracks even when we're not. In the battle scenes, it's perfectly easy to tell one side from the other: the good guys are always the ones who don't have anything on above the waist. Even when they do "dress up," they favor shirts and vests with cutaway pieces that leave their tits exposed. On the isle of the evil enchantress, the Argonauts are temporarily transformed into sheep. Unsurprisingly, they find this experience excruciatingly uncomfortable. These boys just aren't accustomed to being all bundled up in wool.

The enchantress, by the way, is named Gaea (draw your own conclusions). She sails across a pool of bubbling mineral water in a cute little putt-putt. Sounds very glamorous, of course, but she proves to be an illusion—a cackling harridan in beauteous disguise. This is the least heterosexual peplum ever made. In this movie, even the music score is homoerotic: an all-male chorus chanting to a pulsating, pile-driving beat. At the climax, Jason is at last reunited with his faithful, long-suffering wife (Ziva Rodann). However, perversely enough, the scene's entire emotional emphasis is placed on the fond farewell that he bids his mortally wounded buddy, Orpheus. The film has its myths all mixed up, but never mind. It ends with a shot of the Golden Fleece placed atop a statue of Zeus, the exalted father of the gods. He suddenly looks like a drag queen sporting a long blonde wig. Lest we forget, even Zeus had his Ganymede. Art critics know this, and so do we.

Gilda* (U.S. 1946 B&W)

In her title role as *Gilda*, Rita Hayworth has one of the all-time great entrances. A man comes into her boudoir and says, "Gilda! Are you decent?" All we can see of her is what seems to be an unkempt mass of hair. Then she tosses her head back, revealing her face, and says, "Me?".

Glenn Ford also gets a somewhat unorthodox entrance. The camera comes up from underground, and there he is, on his knees, shooting craps. We're somewhere in Argentina, and a thief attempts to relieve him of his winnings. George Macready, a local bon vivant, comes to his rescue. "You must lead a gay life," says Glenn, sizing up George's natty attire. He lights George's cigarette. The byplay here is sophisticated, but fairly obvious. George owns and operates a casino. He invites Glenn to come over and try his luck.

Glenn takes him up on the offer, and even asks him for a job. Says George: "This I must be sure of—that there is no woman anywhere. Gambling and women do not mix." Glenn couldn't agree with him more.

Things just keep getting cozier and cozier. George and Glenn drink a toast. "To us," says George. "To the three of us," he adds, indicating his lethal walking stick, with its concealed rapier blade. Glenn, I might add, is holding this cane at a very suggestive angle as they drink.

Then Hayworth comes along and upsets the apple cart. She used to be Glenn's girlfriend. Now she's married to George. Glenn doesn't know who to be jealous of first. It's his task to keep her in line, which is not at all easy, since (a) she's a tramp and (b) she enjoys pissing him off. She at least knows who to be jealous of. You see, she's well aware that all he cares about is protecting George's feelings.

"I hate you so much that I would destroy myself to take you down with me," she says to Glenn. He parries the blow by asserting, "There are more women in the world than anything else . . . except insects." Co-star Joseph Calleia is moved to comment on this acrimonious relationship: "You two kids love each other pretty terribly, don't you?"

Indeed. Glenn marries Gilda when it looks as though George has been killed in an airplane mishap. His sole motivation, however, is to keep her faithful to her late husband's memory. "You wouldn't think one woman could marry two insane men in one lifetime, now would you?" she asks rhetorically. George comes back, of course, but he gets stabbed to death with that very symbolic walking stick. This story has a heterosexual surface gloss, but I deem it significant that the wise old man of the movie (Steven Geray) is a men's room attendant.

Girls in Prison* (U.S. 1956 B&W)

Girls in Prison was probably the first film of its genre to acknowledge the existence of lesbians in stir. Joan Taylor is the new kid in the cell block. Sweet and comparatively innocent, she's disturbed to find herself sharing a cell with a hard-bitten floozy (Adele Jergens) and a dyke (Helen Gilbert) whose voice is artificially sweetened with the scent of magnolia blossoms.

"Ah declayuh!" says Gilbert to Jergens, while caressing Joan's coiffure. "Doesn't she have the loveliest skin? And that hair!"

Joan cringes in horror, while Adele reassures her as follows: "Don't let that phony Southern talk get you, kid. It comes straight from Duluth, Minnesota!"

"Keep away from me! Don't touch me!" Joan later snarls at Helen, when she tries to lead her by the hand to the chow line.

"Just trying to be friendly," says Helen.

"I don't want any friends!"

"This can be a pretty terrible place without friends."

How true. A couple scenes down the line, there's a rock-'n'-roll dance party. No boys allowed, natch. Joan sits on the sidelines, pouring her heart out to the handsome and ever-so-sympathetic chaplain (Richard Denning). "These women!" Joan shudders. "You know what I'm afraid of most? That I'll become like them. It's contagious!" Cut to women dancing with each other.

"It's funny how scum like us thinks alike," Adele sighs ruefully to Helen, whom she now refers to as "a woman scorned." The two of them end up sharing the shelter of a bunk with Joan when the jail is struck by an earthquake (very fortuitous; the trio make their escape in the chaos which ensues). Not much of a movie, but at least it's a juicy character part for Adele. Gutsy and glamorous, gritty and gravel-voiced, she was the consummate B-movie gun moll of the Fifties. This is surely the only one of her films in which she shows no liking for men.

Glen or Glenda?* (U.S. 1953 B&W)

Glen or Glenda?, a drag queen drama written and directed by the noted transvestite, Edward D. Wood, is, by definition, a deeply personal artistic achievement. More so, at any rate, than Wood's other masterworks, which include *Bride of the Monster* and *Plan 9 from Outer Space*. The film gets underway with Bela Lugosi ranting and raving incoherently at the camera. Via a horizontally split screen, he glowers omnisciently down upon the passing parade of the cityscape that takes up the screen's lower half. "Pipple!" he grumbles. "All goink somewhere! All with their own thoughts, their own ideas. All with their own person-alities!" Shock cuts back to Bela and his enigmatic pronouncements periodically interrupt the proceedings that follow, undermining the film's already feeble narrative pulse.

Scene Two confronts us with the tacky suicide of a dowdy crossdresser, clad in a prim, buttoned-up frock which he wants to be buried in. It's his/her last wish: "Let my body rest in death forever in the things I cannot wear in life." This apparently has a poignant effect on police inspector Lyle Talbot, who seems like a typical

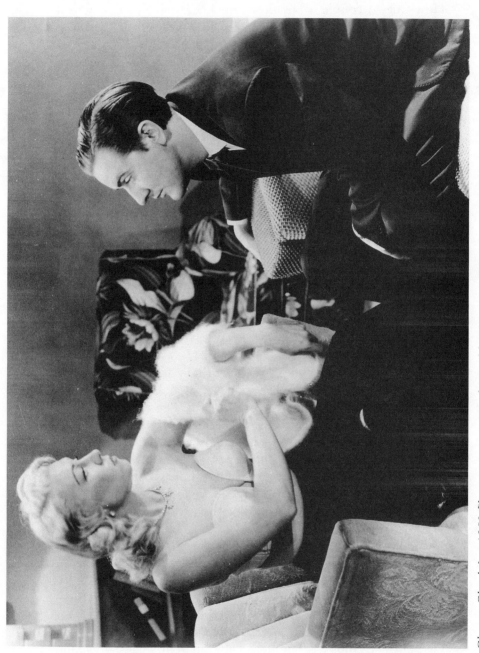

Glen or Glenda?, a 1953 film on transvestism directed by the inimitable Edward G. Wood Jr. Perhaps the campiest film in this book! Must be seen to be believed!

tough cop, but who secretly is a softie at heart. He seeks out a psychiatrist to explain the "problem" of transvestites. The doctor (Timothy Farrell) relates a case history which takes up most of the movie. This, of course, is the story of Glen (or Glenda).

Wood casts himself in these pivotal title roles (using the pseudonym of "Daniel Davis"). Although it may not be saying much, he's far more proficient as an actor than as a writer or director. In his capacity as scenarist, he permits himself numerous unfair advantages. For one thing, he's essentially playing himself. For another thing, the dialogue he gives himself is nowhere near as bad (which is to say, not as florid) as the lines he assigns to the other performers. This leads me to suspect he was actually aware of how truly lousy his writing could get. If that was indeed the case, then he must have known he was being unkind to leading lady Dolores Fuller, who portrays the college girl who becomes Glen's fiancée. She's definitely not an actress, but even the most accomplished diva couldn't hope to breathe life into clinkers like, "Our fourth term in Psychology explains a lot of the facts, but I'm afraid the end of study is only the beginning of reality." That may be taken as a typical example of Wood's clunky, pompous, meandering prose. Here's her final statement on her would-be husband's sartorial quirk: "Glen," she says, after a bout of meditation so painfully intense, it resembles electrocution (no, folks, she's not undergoing shock therapy; she's merely mulling things over), "I don't fully understand this, but maybe together we can work it out." Then she takes off her fluffy angora sweater and lets him try it on.

Glen's fixation dates back to his childhood. He borrowed his sister's dress to wear as a costume to a Halloween party. It won first prize. "Then one day it wasn't Halloween any longer," but Glen was still dressing up. Now he's all grown up and prowling the streets, disguised in a blonde wig, falsies, earrings, a tight-fitting skirt, and a white pullover sweater.

This crazy movie, with its ramshackle, improbably complex structure, gets more and more nutty as it goes along. The centerpiece is a lengthy phantasmagoria of delirium induced by Glen's indecision as to whether he ought to confide in Dolores. She's trapped beneath a phallic-looking fallen tree which, significantly, Glen is unable to lift (or erect) till he takes off his frilly "Glenda" duds. This is followed by a couple of utterly extraneous bits which seem to have been specifically inserted for the straight male audience. First there's a sado-lesbo-porno bondage scene with women tying each other up to the accompaniment of what sounds like Slovenian polka band music. Next we witness a heterosexual rape, and the music switches to a honky-tonk arrangement of ballet music from *Aida*. The mind reels. Words fail me. But nowhere near as often as they failed Edward D. Wood.

Goliath and the Barbarians* (Italy 1960 C)

"Whooo is heee?" breathes Chelo Alonso, when she catches her first glimpse of Steve Reeves in *Goliath and the Barbarians*. Then she goes into a swoon so he can carry her off in his brawny arms. She might not have been so romantically inclined if he'd been wearing the fright mask with which he terrifies her father's troops. But fortunately, in this scene, he's bare-headed. In the following scene he's also bare-chested, so *he's* the one who gets carried off—by Arturo Dominici, who's got some really sadistic tortures lined up. Arturo almost has an orgasm when Steve's hands are tied to a pair of horses which are driven in opposite directions. But Steve isn't vanquished; he merely looks a mite uncomfortable, that's all. As soon as he gets away, he has another love scene with Chelo. I think he's attracted to her because she's the only woman in the movie whose tits are bigger than his are. Watching Reeves and Alonso try to kiss is downright comical.

Chelo's a good barbarian; Steve polishes off the bad ones and rides off into the sunset with her. Was it intermarriage that brought the Roman empire so low? The battle scenes in this movie tend to go on too long; just bear in mind that Rome didn't fall in a day.

Gladiators of Rome* (Italy 1962 Released in color. Available in video generally only in b&w)

Gladiators of Rome, a meandering beefcake opus, compensates for its lack of narrative drive by offering a somewhat more explicit

STEVE REEVES (1926–) in *Goliath and the Barbarians* (AIP Italy). Holder of the body-building titles Mr. Universe and Mr. World, Reeves starred in numerous 1950s–60s muscleman films of the sword and sandal genre.

homoeroticism than is normally found in films of this sort. The star—and center attraction—is Gordon Scott, whose bulging biceps and curvaceous pectorals are enhanced by his genuinely pleasant, friendly-looking face. (His eyes, however, are darkly dangerous; they are, I think, his best feature.) His screen time is mainly devoted to killing people and balancing massive phallic objects atop his mighty shoulders. There's also a scene in which he's bound and spread-eagled and threatened with white-hot pokers.

These supposedly heterosexual films seldom provide a focus with which the gay male viewer can truly empathize. Usually the best we can do is try to imagine ourselves in the place of someone like Sylva Koscina, Scilla Gabel, Isabelle Corey, Chelo Alonso, Gianna Maria Canale, or, in this case, Wandisa Guida. *Gladiators of Rome*, however, actually does include a sympathetic homosexual character, who functions as the principal comic relief. This jester type is first seen giving Gordon a remarkably thorough massage. Back, neck, arms, belly; nothing escapes this fellow's cunning, teasing, ultimately captivating fingers. I noticed his hand lingering inordinately long on Gordon's right nipple. Both actors appear to be enjoying themselves immensely, though Gordon, playing coy, does ask, in tones of mock impatience, "Now what's all this attention for?" As if he didn't know.

After risking his own neck to help Gordon rendezvous with the leading lady, this gay sidekick complains, "They'll be kissing each other and I'll probably get beaten up. There's no justice!" We certainly don't have any trouble empathizing at that point, nor when he expresses admiration for Gordon's glorious physique: "One careless touch from one of your great paws and I'd be broken right in half," he swoons, exultantly. Gordon, cast as a slave named Marcus, is hardly the only attractive hero on hand. "Valerian is a handsome man," the sidekick enthuses. "If I were a girl, I'd fall in love with him myself!"

In short, this guy is practically an Italian version of Franklin Pangborn. He even gets to die cradled in Gordon's naked, brawny arms. So this otherwise tedious epic does at least have one thing going for it. As for the gladiatorial action, much of it entails breastplates, unfortunately, but it does lead to a memorable line of dialogue: "You, Aeneas, are interested in creating gladiators, and I, in breeding bulls." In the context of this movie, I'm not at all sure that there's a difference.

Hairspray* (U.S. 1988 C)

Hairspray, a camp musical, marked the entry of writer-director John Waters into the mainstream. Which is to say that the only really gross thing in the film is the sound of a pimple being popped. Early Sixties nostalgia is the keynote here. Indeed, the action transpires in 1963 (which, coincidentally enough, was the year I wrote my first film review). Integration's the topic under discussion, and the movie functions as a timely reminder that racial confrontations were what got the political side of the Sixties rolling. In fact, the film is almost like a parody of the preachy propaganda movies that people like Stanley Kramer were actually cranking out back in those days. *Hairspray* immediately establishes which ideological side it's on: practically the first thing we see is someone carelessly and contemptuously discarding a Pat Boone record.

The star of the show is undeniably Ricki Lake as the "pleasantly plump" Baltimore teen who campaigns to integrate an afterschool dance program broadcast daily on local TV. She's superb, but I must confess a generational prejudice in favor of performers my own age: people who experienced the decade firsthand. I'm thinking particularly of the late Divine, cast as the heroine's mother, who, when told to turn on her TV at once (Ricki's making her video debut), instantly assumes it's an urgent national news bulletin and dolefully inquires, "Did poor Debbie Reynolds have a nervous breakdown?!" Learning so abruptly that her daughter's a celebrity, she promptly has an ecstatic conniption of eyeball-rolling pride ("She could be one of the June Taylor Dancers!").

The host of the big dance show that's so central to the plot is a Dick Clark type, a perfect example of the kind of groomed-for-TV smoothie I've always found irresistible. He's portrayed by a snub-nosed hunk named Shawn Thompson and I must admit that, by the end of the film, I couldn't keep my eyes off him. The character he's playing is called "Corny Collins." At this point, I could say something very crude and alliterative about what I'd like to do to him, but instead I'll tastefully refrain. In the interest of journalistic fairness, I should probably also mention that, the first time I saw this film, the gay male couple in the row ahead of me seemed quite taken with Michael St. Gerard, the sloe-eyed actor cast as Ricki's "common-law boyfriend."

An utterly delightful entertainment, all told. Credit must also be given to Vincent Peranio for his gorgeously tacky sets. I was especially impressed with Divine's hideous combination rec room/dining room, paneled in knotty pine.

Heat* (U.S. 1972 C)

Heat is doubly qualified for inclusion in this book: it's a camp re-working of Sunset Boulevard, which is itself a recognized camp masterpiece. Joe Dallesandro gets top billing in his customary role as a dumb stud. We're given plenty of chances to ogle his beautiful, unclad body. (Dallesandro got his start posing for beefcake photos at the studios of the Athletic Model Guild.) I feel obliged to mention, however, that, in this, his ponytailed hippie phase, he looks distinctly unsavory and more than a little bit unhealthy. Furthermore, as heroes go, he's hopelessly inarticulate; his most frequent comment is "Oh, yeah?"

Histrionic honors, such as they are, go to Sylvia Miles in the Gloria Swanson part. Miles is cast as a fading TV actress eking out a living on the talk show and game show circuit. It's 1972 and expectations are scaled down accordingly. Everyone's a "star," but nobody's got any glamour. In Sunset Boulevard, Swanson complained that the movies became too small to contain her. The people in Heat are insects; even a television screen looks big to them.

Just like William Holden in Sunset Boulevard, the Dallesandro character is named Joe and is shacking up with a has-been leading lady. All around the edges are intimations of polymorphous perversity. The Sylvia Miles character has a daughter, for example, who claims to be a lesbian, but has a baby and, midway through the action, goes down on a guy. Despite all the raunch, however, we get the feeling these people are almost too enervated for sex; they'd rather be out sunbathing.

The film is a product of the Andy Warhol "factory," which means that there's plenty of ad-libbed dialogue, ludicrous non-acting, inept camerawork, and obfuscating artistic pretentiousness. In Sunset Boulevard Gloria Swanson laments that the era of great screen faces like hers is past. *Heat*, however, is a film more concerned with crotches than with faces. And Gloria's right: at least at the movies, faces are more interesting.

Hercules* (Italy 1960 C)

Steve Reeves delineates the title role in *Hercules*, strutting his stuff in the sort of classical setting to which he's accustomed. The plot has all the young men of ancient Greece yearning to emulate this semi-sacred hero. His athletic prowess inspires a national physical fitness campaign. "He's conquered the hearts of our sons," remarks one venerable worthy. (Though this line is sufficiently provocative when properly transcribed, I misunderstood it at first, and thought that the man had said, "His cock is the talk of our sons.")

"I wanted you to notice me," pants Ulysses breathlessly, after pole-vaulting up a steep hillside to land sprawling at Hercules' feet. The doughty redhead becomes the demigod's protégé, but soon is frightened off when Herc hurls a discus so far that it vanishes from sight.

Reeves would have had to throw me at least that far, before I'd begin to lose interest. Although I suppose it dates me to admit it, I must confess that my very first wet dream was about this darkly, brutally handsome actor. By now, of course, I'm well aware that there is no direct and logical correlation between bulging biceps and a big dick, but in those days, apparently, my pubescent subconscious was not too sure about that. Even today, Reeves is still a looker and well worth dreaming about.

Hercules Against the Moon Men* (Italy 1964 C)

As the title makes abundantly clear, *Hercules Against the Moon Men* is a hybrid: part sword-and-sandal epic, part sci-fi/horror. When genres collide on such a scale, the results are often unstable and unpredictable. In this particular instance, we are faced with what seems to be a work of inadvertently Fascist art. Like most Hercules pictures, it comes from the country that gave the world Mussolini.

For members of the warrior caste, the world is a threatening place. In this film, the very earth itself is incontinent. Every breach and fissure brings forth tongues of flame, rivers of lava. The Fascist mentality is sore afraid of all things hot and flowing. Soldier males perpetually seek some mountain fastness, high and dry, where the integrity of a man's bodily boundaries may be safely maintained. The moon men are literally monolithic: animated pillars of impermeable rock. These goose-stepping creatures dwell in the "Mountain of Death," surrounded by desolate, arid wasteland. In this arena, men of stone confront a man of steel: Hercules, who, in this movie, is actually played by someone named Alan Steel.

The light holds no warmth here (moonlight never does). Set in the face of a cliff is a sliding panel, and, when this portal of doom opens, admitting a host of humans for sacrifice to the Moon Goddess, these victims are bathed in the unfriendly glare of a searchlight, which serves as a handy metaphor representing the totalitarian gaze. Later, through an eye-shaped cleft in the rock, we peer out at the full moon, which is positioned to seem like the iris of the aperture. Big Sister is watching!

The villainess, however, turns out to be an earthling: an evil queen wearing tightly clinging, glistening gowns straight out of the Forties. She looks like a typical glamour girl of the Nazi era. (The heroine is her half-sister: a blonde dressed in white. She is, quite literally, a "white sister.") The palace of the queen is patrolled by a pair of guardsmen who rigidly hold their spears at precisely the angle of an erect penis. At the (you should pardon the expression) climax of the movie, this nasty woman, this emblem of damp, sticky femininity is squooshed to death by the stomping men of stone. Then they, in turn, are buried beneath an avalanche . . . which, when you stop and think, may signify, not defeat, but a joyous commingling. The film concludes with a coda which has the logic of a dream: shots of serenely flowing streams that lead to a peaceful sea. The messy orgasm has brought us to a state of afterglow, and all things dirty have apparently been washed away. Till next time.

Hercules and the Captive Women* (Italy 1963 C)

Reg Park stars as the title muscleman in *Hercules and the Captive Women*. He's an endearingly squat and chunky version of the standard beefcake model/bodybuilder type. There is, however, something about his languid smile and lazy, carefree manner which suggests that perhaps he's not quite as macho as one might suppose. Not very bright, either, but that's okay by me.

The plot concerns his visit to Atlantis, the lost continent. The citizens of Atlantis worship the planet Uranus, a fact which, predictably enough, leads to hilariously filthy-sounding dialogue whenever they discuss their religion with Hercules. He may look like a "top man," but appearances can sometimes be deceiving; it would seem that his charms as a passive partner are widely celebrated. "Today is dedicated to your anus!" he's told, upon his arrival in Atlantis. "The queen is in the temple for the sacred ceremony." Her name is Antinea and she's played by Fay Spain. Furthermore, she's got a political purpose for plumbing the depths of the demigod's sex habits. The high priest informs him, "Antinea has found the mystic secrets of your anus and will use them to make herself omnipotent." (Perhaps she's intending blackmail?) The priest also claims that he and all the other men of Atlantis have become "the heirs to all the powers of your anus," but the promised gang-bang never occurs. In the end, Atlantis sinks into the sea. Fortunately, Hercules gets his ass out of there, thus fulfilling a prophecy voiced earlier: "Your anus has abandoned us!"

I regret to note that the movie takes a dim view of women in positions of authority. The kings and governors of the Grecian city-state are portrayed as being a bunch of henpecked husbands whose wives have forbidden them to participate in valorous deeds and heroic quests. Queen Antinea is so crazed with power, she cannot abide the concept of having a royal successor; therefore she orders that her own daughter be put to death. This is contrasted with the affectionate relationship which is shared by Hercules and his attractive adolescent son. Maybe a little bit *too* affectionate: Hercules, so exceedingly fond of this handsome youth, is reluctant to ever leave home! And the King of Thebes, his patron, shows remarkable understanding and sensitivity with regard to this peculiar domestic predicament; "If I had a beautiful wife and son, I would think the same way," he comments. As a loving father, Hercules is maybe even somewhat possessive: at one point the "beautiful son" tells the queen's daughter, "If my father finds me here with a girl, he'll never let me out of the house."

Perhaps the producers should consider making a sequel, all about the horrors of being "grounded" by an incestuous parent. At any rate, the title of the film is misleading: there is only one captive woman on hand, whereas the movie features at least a legion of captive (and captivating) men.

Hercules Unchained* (Italy 1960 C)

Ah, the joys and attractions of indolence! Steve Reeves spends much of *Hercules Unchained* asleep, on the verge of sleep, or feigning sleep. Trouble is, everyone is trying to violate his wife (Sylva Koscina). So naturally he heads for the tall timber with a pubescent lad, to whom he confides: "My boy, I've discovered something very important. Up to now, I've been making one big mistake. You should sleep in the daytime and stay awake at night. Otherwise, you'll lose the best part of your life." Hear, hear!

Can this be the Hercules we all know and love? He's been drinking the Waters of Forgetfulness and has fallen under the spell of Queen Omphale (Sylvia Lopez), who dwells with her bevy of handmaidens in a cavern behind a waterfall. These ladies-in-waiting weave garlands of flowers to place on his forgetful brow. But amnesia inevitably recedes; memory returns, and, with it, responsibility. An iconic image: Omphale hugging his hairy leg, in an effort to restrain him. She's got a mausoleum of mummies, in which she preserves the remains of her former studs. In this hidden chamber, a little pedestal already has Hercules' name on it.

The mise en scène is saturated with sex and sensuality. Lurid lighting and bright, vibrant colors complete the effect. This is a movie entirely of its time: an era when the realms of myth and literature were plundered to provide schlock cinema for adolescent boys.

*Hero of Rome** (Italy 1963 Released in color. Available in video generally only in b&w)

Hero of Rome, a sword-and-sandal spectacle that seems to be all about the connection between bloodlust and hairy thighs, is an admirably orgasmic vehicle for Gordon Scott, the patron saint of homoerotic slaughter. Never a slouch when it comes to killing men with his bare hands, Gordon outdoes himself here. He's an animal! He's a mad dog! His eyes positively blaze with homicidal fury! At one point, he uses the edge of his heavy shield to snap 'n' crush the necks of two attractive "bad guys" simultaneously. He growls with regard to an enemy, "This very night, I'll kill him in his tent. In his very *bed*, if necessary!" Then he grins with carnal anticipation. The script makes a point of placing all this violence in a clearly sexual context: the principal villain is Tarquinius, one of history's most famous rapists. He's portrayed as the very incarnation of hetero-sexual horniness. It's no wonder that Gordon spends the entire picture longing to disembowel him.

Cinematically speaking, the film is a cut above Gordon's usual. It's even got an impressive music score. Gordon's in great shape and he wants the whole world to know it. He's got a perfectly fabulous crotch shot as he uses one of his legs to knock down a tree which he wants to employ as a bridge spanning a vertiginous chasm. Then he gives us a good look at his underarm hair as he clambers across. He's cast as Rome's "most glorious hero: Caius Mucius, called Scaeveia (that is 'Left Handed')." Early on, he deliberately roasts his right hand in a brazier. Thus disabled, he must adjust to his handicap. There are, after all, an assortment of exciting things one can do with a strong left hand. "One hand is as good as another. You must exercise it and keep on exercising it!" urges Gordon's handsome male sidekick, who adds, with a touch of hopefulness, "If you like, I'll help you." The script never bothers to tell us whether Gordon ever regains the use of his injured member. Then again, with such willing and eager buddies, he probably never really needs to use either hand.

High School Caesar* (U.S. 1960 B&W)

High School Caesar is John Ashley as "Mat Stevens," a rich kid who wants to be king of the campus. Ashley, a strutting pretty boy type, practically invites the audience to take inventory of his many physical assets: shirt very casually unbuttoned at the neck, exposing a fairly generous expanse of brawny chest hair; brunette pompadour glistening with the high-gloss sheen of "greasy kid stuff"; dangerous eyes that don't miss a trick; a perfectly chiseled profile with a perky little upturned nose. In short, a babyface . . . with a smirky, jokey tentativeness that serves to indicate a basic insecurity underlying all that swaggering bravado. "High School Caesar!" proclaims the title song. "You're gonna get it in the end!" And a nice, neat, snugly packed, tight little rear end it is.

As emperors go, this guy seems more inspired by *Little Caesar* than by *Julius Caesar*. His tyrannical rule is based on rackets: selling protection and purloined exams. Like so many supposedly macho gangsters, he's got a punk hanger-on who sees to his every need and desire. This one's called Cricket: a fidgety, girlish kind of guy. Mat wears his collar up and is constantly smoothing back that glowing mass of jet-black hair. Cricket's hair is more closely cropped and he's partial to shapeless, baggy sweaters.

"Hey, Mat?" whines Cricket. "Ya really think I'll get to be student body treasurer?"

"Yeah, I think so, Cricket," Mat replies. "You'll be even *more* important to me then." His hand gently settles on the kid's shoulder, then gracefully glides up to playfully caress the nape of his neck. It's enough to make you wonder whose body is being treasured.

These two are subverting our country's democratic system by fixing the senior high election. At the victory dance Mat finally takes time out from fondling Cricket to dance a little with the surly brunette vamp (or fag hag?) who's constantly dogging his tracks. I mean, that's really the American way, isn't it? Boys for private fun; girls for public display.

But Mat has an even more guilty secret: in the privacy of his own home, he listens to Muzak! "Home" is a palatial Southern mansion with crystal goblets to drink from and servants to wait on him hand and foot. His parents are off in Europe somewhere and he's got the whole joint to himself. But Mat's still not happy. Alone in his room, he throws himself facedown on the bed and sobs into his pillow. On the bedside table beside him is a radio decorated with a pair of bronzed baby shoes. I guess that all this tough-guy he-man really wants is someone to mother him. Any volunteers?

The imagery is unmistakably homoerotic as Mat, the dark, burly conqueror, hovers and kneels, trembling and diffident, over the corpse of a blonde male victim, sprawled picturesquely, face up, in a ditch. (In this sort of movie, victims are always blonde.) Then Mat kidnaps and tries to molest the heroine (also a blonde). Cricket flies off in a jealous fury and runs squealing to the local teen hangout. After Cricket has spilled the beans to the other boys and girls, they all gang up on Mat, who says, "Not you too, Cricket?" as if to remind us that this movie is, after all, derived from Shakespeare. Nothing can beat a firm background in the classics, right? However, the most classical thing about this film is John Ashley's body, which looks commendably firm both back and front.

Hot Rod Gang   (U.S. 1958 B&W)

John Ashley gets to camp it up in *Hot Rod Gang*. He's an aspiring rock star and drag racer who, unfortunately, is forced to live in a mansion with a pair of rich maiden aunts. So he's obliged to "lay it on thick," you might say. He goes about dressed in a suit and horn-rimmed glasses. One scene has the family lawyer introducing him to a prospective fiancée. "Has she been scrutinized?" Ashley inquires. "Most thoroughly," the girl's father assures him.

"Ree-ahlly?" John enthuses, when informed that the girl sings madrigals. He gets so excited, Aunt Anastasia has to fetch him a tranquilizer. John avers that he himself has been practicing to solo in a performance of the Mendelssohn Violin Concerto. Later, however, he's down at the clubhouse, lip-synching ditties like "Hit-and-Run Lover." The kids get so worked up, they just about tear his false beard off. Why the whiskers? The script says he wants to disguise himself as "one of those Greenwich Village characters." Maybe the term implied something different, back in the Fifties.

High School Confidential!* (U.S. 1958 B&W)

Russ Tamblyn has always been, well, kind of cocky. Cute, too. His shell-like ears are surely among the most adorable in Hollywood history. His brooding facial features and pert-yet-full, well-defined butt are additional points in his favor, doing their part to make him look all the hotter. In *High School Confidential!*, a 1958 teen-spleen extravaganza, he flashes a sublimely insolent sneer. His first morning of classes starts out with him proclaiming, "Before this crummy day is over, every crummy stud in this whole crummy school is going to know who Tony Baker is." He's Russ Tamblyn, of course. And he's got what it takes to get a stud's attention.

A devil abroad, he's even more attractive when he gets home. He's the product of a broken one, alas. He resides with his aunt, a platinum blonde bombshell played by Mamie Van Doren. Finding her clad in a flouncy dressing gown in the middle of the afternoon, he inquires, "You gettin' up or going to bed?" "You looking for excitement?" she replies, biting into an apple and casting him a meaningful leer. He's not impressed. (He only has eyes for Jan Sterling, cast as a frosty, uptight schoolmarm with a hairstyle that makes her look like a boy.) Toward the end of the movie, Mamie comes striding into Russ's bedroom. "I don't remember inviting you in here," he chides, removing his shirt to reveal his remarkably hairless chest. "I won't look," she promises, having already gotten an eyeful. "I found some marijuana cigarettes when I cleaned your room today," she remarks with studied casualness, and then attempts to blackmail him into giving her sex. Little does she know that he is, in fact, a narc. Fifties rebels almost always cop out in the end. By actually *being* a cop, Tamblyn does them one better.

Russ Tamblyn (1934–   ), dancer, actor, and teenage heartthrob of the 50s. Publicity photo.

Hush . . . Hush, Sweet Charlotte* (U.S. 1964 B&W)

The historical significance of Hush . . . Hush, Sweet Charlotte resides in the fact that it brought graphic gore into the mainstream. There had, of course, been other gory films before this one, but they didn't have stars and weren't nominated for Oscars. (Contrary to popular perception, Psycho contains no gore.) Before we even get to the opening titles, Hush . . . Hush, Sweet Charlotte shows us Bruce Dern's hand being severed with a meat cleaver, blood splashing on a plaster Cupid, and Dern waving the gruesome stump of his arm at the camera.

The idea was to reassemble the personnel of What Ever Happened to Baby Jane? for a Southern Gothic rehash. This time Joan Crawford was slated to have top billing, but she took sick and was replaced by Olivia de Haviland. Olivia looks great, but reads her lines as if she's on Valium. On the other hand, Agnes Moorehead overacts dreadfully (she's the one, by the way, who got nominated). Leading lady Bette Davis gives a performance which she obviously hopes is as bravura as her Baby Jane tour de force. Hers is the title role: a wealthy recluse, generally believed to have been the one who hacked up Bruce. Olivia is seeking to drive her insane and then take charge of the family finances. Agnes is the slovenly housekeeper, with crypto-lesbian inflections. The best acting is done by Victor Buono, oddly moving in a cameo role as Bette's father. (In reality, he was certainly more than young enough to be her son.) Routine Grand Guignol at best, the film is not a camp classic. In the mid-Sixties, however, it was hugely popular with gay audiences and therefore rates at least a mention here.

I Could Go on Singing* (G.B. 1963 C)

I Could Go on Singing was Judy Garland's last film. The title is somewhat ironic, since she really couldn't go on for very much longer. We can tell by just looking at her: she's in pretty rough shape. Cast as a famous singer named Jenny Bowman, who's come to London for an engagement at the Palladium, she is, for all practical purposes, playing herself. The way she parades her neuroses and vulnerabilities for our delectation becomes not only tedious, but also embarrassing, even excruciating.

Her leading man is Dirk Bogarde, who looks slick and was reportedly thrilled to be working with her. All the more drain on his acting abilities, therefore, since he's called upon to delineate her cold, distant, stand-offish ex-lover, a distinguished Harley Street specialist who has custody of their illegitimate son. He takes her to see the lad perform in a production of *H.M.S. Pinafore*. Which means we get to see lots of English public schoolboys dressed up as girls. (Unsurprisingly, it's the ones dressed as sailors who look gay.) The kid doesn't know she's his mother. So then, of course, we get the scene where he comes in on his parents squabbling and unexpectedly overhears the facts of the matter. Oh, it's all so poignant, you could just about puke.

Poor Judy. Even Edith Head fails her, this time out: the clothes are dumpy and she ends up looking like one of the Munchkins from *The Wizard of Oz*. The script seems to be making unflattering commentary on her life and career, like when Bogarde complains, "She takes more love than anyone can possibly give," and when he calls her "a self-centered, grasping, egocentric little bitch." The dialogue becomes so stunningly self-revelatory, it ultimately begins dropping hints about the film's intended audience—as when Judy, drunk, announces, "I've had enough to float Fire Island."

I, Mobster* (U.S. 1958 B&W)

Steve Cochran is smooth and slick in the title role of *I, Mobster*. And why shouldn't he be? The part fits him like a glove. Or should I say holster? He's all gat in this film—cocked and ready for action, with slicked-back hair, bedroom eyes, and a smirky, defiant sneer that I find sweeter than any smile. "I grew up fast," he tells the audience. And that's not the half of it: Steve was about forty when this picture was produced, but he's got all the mannerisms of a punk kid down cold. In blue jeans and a tight-fitting black T-shirt, he almost looks as young as he acts. There are furtive sexual undertones as he delivers packets of heroin in a shiny black leather jacket. His gullible Italian Mama (Celia Lovsky) is plenty proud of him. "A very responsible job," she crows. "Delivering medicine all over the city."

Yvette Vickers offers Steve sexual favors in exchange for dope. He ain't interested. Indeed, he ignores her, concentrating instead on chewing his bubble gum. She's so insulted, she blows the whistle on him; he lands a stretch in the slammer. It's over with in a blink. "I did the whole trick standing on my ear," he says. We read the implicit homosex between the lines. No need to spell it out. Which is more dangerous? His big, black, loaded gun? Or his black Irish mug with the leprechaun eyes flashing and darting, and those bushy, coal-black eyebrows dancing a veritable jig just above them? The gun kills quickly; the face, on the other hand, promises slow, sweet torment. In one scene, he comes home from pulling a hit and finds a strange boy awaiting him in his bedroom. Steve stashes the gun in a drawer. "You used that, didn't you?" asks the kid, globular buttocks glowing in a pair of tight, white britches. The notorious Lili St. Cyr performs her patented striptease, disrobing and bathing for the edification of a full night club audience. Except for a single reaction shot in which his eyes almost shine with horniness, Steve seems more interested in the cigarette that he's smoking. Face it: the guy's got an oral fixation.

The arrival of a bevy of chorus girls interrupts a gangster confab. One of the hoods spills a drink down a girl's four hundred dollar gown. Straight men have no respect for a woman's clothing. "Thought this was a business meeting," Cochran mutters disgustedly. "C'mon, Frankie. Let's blow." He says he's holding out for a girl just like the one who married Dad. I've heard that one before. He plays his most passionate scene with his back to the camera, beating the shit out of a tousle-haired junkie in a pool hall. (It's the boy from the bedroom scene mentioned above . . . except that he's all grown up now.) Lovsky hits the nail on the head when she says to Cochran, "It is a great pity there is so little feeling in you . . . so little love."

In some respects, this is a rather anomalous Cochran vehicle. Steve was always a whiz at sexual chemistry; here he gets by without it till the film is more than halfway through. But there comes a time . . . He's wearing a glossy dressing gown (gold, I think, though the film is in black-and-white), exposing a generous expanse of his hairy, hunky chest. And leading lady Lita Milan comes strutting in, wearing a clinging, form-fitting cocktail dress, with sequins. She looks like a moll and he tells her so. And she says she doesn't care, she just wants to be near him. Cut to waves crashing majestically on the beach. I'm a sucker for romance any day of the week. And for hairy chests.

I'm No Angel* (U.S. 1933 B&W)

The opening reel of *I'm No Angel* finds Mae West performing her patented swagger, grind, and bump in a freak show. There are, I suppose, more appropriate places, but, offhand, I can't think of any. She makes an impressive entrance: a runway is quickly assembled; a flourish of trumpets sounds; and there she is, performing moves that might astonish a chiropractor. Actually, she doesn't really move around that much. It's what's left to the imagination that counts. "Penny for your thoughts," she leers to the crowd (exclusively male, of course), before launching into her rendition of "They Call Me Sister Honky-Tonk." Afterward, she's got the brass to say she's tired out from dancing. She saves her energy for rooking the suckers; watching her at it is like seeing an artist at work. Mae West isn't an actress; she's an event.

As always, she shows an affinity for minorities. Her lawyer in the film is named Pinkowitz. "P like in pansy," she begins, when asked to spell it out. The second reel finds her performing in a circus. This, of course, means another grand entrance: the trumpets are back, and she comes in riding an elephant. The highlight of her act is when she shares a cage with the King of Beasts. She tells the lion to open wide; then she bends over and takes a close look at his molars. It's certainly a new way of giving head.

This is the film in which she utters the immortal line, "Beulah, peel me a grape!" She also wears a dress bedecked with sequined spiderwebs. Cary Grant is the fly who comes into her parlor while she's thus attired. When he shakes her hand, she doesn't let go. Later she advises him to "come up and see me." "When I'm good, I'm very good," she tells him, "but when I'm bad, I'm better."

The film has its climax in a court of law. "You must answer

questions directly," the judge warns her. That's a stiff requirement, since indirection is her customary route. She elects to question the witnesses herself. "How'madoin'?" she asks the all-male jury, as she saunters past. She wins the case and Cary, too. "What are you thinking about?" he asks her at the close of the film. "Same thing you are," she slurs in reply. In movies, sex is better evoked than spelled out. And, in this particular movie, the detours are elegant.

The Importance of Being Earnest* (G.B. 1952 C)

It is, I think, a ringing indictment of Victorian society that Oscar Wilde was obliged to support himself by writing heterosexual fluff like *The Importance of Being Earnest*. The title is a play on words, since one of the two heroines (Joan Greenwood; the other is Dorothy Tutin) is absolutely and unshakably determined that her husband, should she marry, must bear the name of Ernest. Unfortunately, the man she loves, and who also loves her, is known as Jack, a name to which she is unalterably opposed, perhaps because it suggests something unseemly and indelicate.

The dialogue is brimming with witty epigrams. For camp value, however, we must look to the performances, all of them hilariously replete with arch affectation. Michael Denison and Sir Michael Redgrave, cast as the suitors of Tutin and Greenwood, are, according to plot context, portraying heterosexuals. Their manner and bearing, however, suggest that they'd be happier in each other's arms, and probably more comfortable in feminine attire. As for the two aforementioned ingenues, they trill and coo like birds of peculiarly neutral gender. Dame Edith Evans is cast as Lady Bracknell, who is rightly called a "gorgon" in the text. Close-ups of her petrifying countenance are brazenly employed for shock effect. Co-star Margaret Rutherford is appropriately fluttery as the governess, Miss Prism. Perhaps Wilde was correct in portraying names as being all-important. It occurs to me that characters with names such as these virtually demand to be played with a degree of ostentatious artificiality.

In This Our Life* (U.S. 1942 B&W)

In This Our Life is sublimely silly Southern-fried melodrama. Permit me to introduce you to the Timberlake family. Mama (Billie Burke) is a snuffling hypochondriac. Daddy (Frank Craven) is an ineffectual milquetoast. (The names these two are saddled with, by the way, are Lavinia and Asa.) Uncle (Charles Coburn) is a cranky old right-wing hypocrite (an instance of typecasting, if ever there was one), who harbors an incestuous passion for one of his nieces. She's Bette Davis playing a demented Southern belle, and we can tell she's poison the minute we lay eyes on her. We can tell by her flouncy hairdo and her cheap, flashy tastes, the devil-driven look in her huge, haunted eyes, and the petulant way she's always pursing her lips.

On the eve of her wedding (to an idealistic lawyer portrayed by George Brent), Bette runs off with a doctor (Dennis Morgan) who's married to her sister (Olivia de Havilland). "Ah adoah you, Pe-tuh," she huskily murmurs to Morgan. These two don't live happily ever after. Before very long, Davis has driven Dennis to drink and suicide. Somewhat chastened, she goes back home; her family shows an admirable willingness to forgive and forget. By this time, George has commenced to court Olivia. Bette, back to her old bad habits, sets out to come between them. Driving home from a thwarted rendezvous (George didn't show), her car collides with a couple of pedestrians: a mother and child out for a stroll. Bette doesn't hang around to find out how badly they're hurt; that would spoil her track record. Instead she proceeds to pin this hit-and-run accident on a struggling black law student (Ernest Anderson). The cops catch on, thanks to George and Olivia. A frenzied chase concludes with Davis dying when her automobile goes hurtling off an embankment.

Olivia does well by her role, but so what? All *she* has to do is play a normal person. Davis, on the other hand, has a histrionic field day in a part that doesn't permit her a single sympathetic or unselfish moment. At one point, when George and Olivia make a detour because of a forest fire, we catch ourselves assuming that Bette's to blame for this calamity also. During this scene, the back projection is about as convincing as a magic lantern slide. The entire plot unfolds in a milieu of picturesquely phony studio settings. The script is flavorsomely rich in high-camp silliness. "Parks are for the very rich or the very poor," asserts Olivia. "Say! You've got intelligence!" George responds in tones of wonderment. Fifty years ago, men could still get away with being surprised about such things.

Jail Bait* (U.S. 1954 B&W)

Jail Bait is directed by the adorably incompetent Edward D. Wood *(Glen or Glenda?)* and features several members of his usual, equally untalented stock company, including Lyle Talbot, Dolores Fuller, and Timothy Farrell. Although he never really showed a knack for selecting actors, Wood has a good eye for hunks: in a prominent supporting part, *Jail Bait* stars Steve Reeves, who, five years or so down the line, would be playing the title role in *Hercules*. Though cast as a police detective, Reeves is nevertheless given a chance to display those massive pecs of his: he strides onscreen while putting a shirt on. Tragically enough, bad camera placement sabotages this potentially spectacular moment, but the hilariously perfunctory dialogue (straining to explain why he's undressed while on duty) does provide at least some small gesture of compensation—

TALBOT: Why don't you do your shaving at home?

REEVES: Never home long enough to do it.

TALBOT: You've got a point there.

Timothy Farrell also goes about bare-breasted. From a strictly conventional standpoint, his physique is not impressive. His flabby midriff and droopy tits eloquently indicate that he spends far less time at the gym than Steve does. His chest, however, is much, much hairier than Steve's, and, frankly, that's what I like. Steve's the one, however, who shows a provocative preference for men—

TALBOT: Dr. Gregor's a great man, both in his personal life and his business life.

REEVES: Sounds like a man I'd like to meet.

No one so much as attempts to give a decent performance. Steve is stolid oak. On the other hand, Dolores Fuller (Mrs. Wood, in real life) is all insouciant ineptitude and abrasive nasalness. "I hope

I'm happy to know you," she simpers, upon being introduced to Steve. She's come to the station house to bail out her brother. "He was carrying a gun," Talbot grimly points out.

"There are much worse crimes," shrugs Dolores.

"Carrying a gun can be a dangerous business," Talbot persists.

"So can building a skyscraper," Dolores parries.

This movie has a penchant for guns. "Messy things, these shootings," someone remarks after the first murder. The script keeps getting funnier and funnier. "This afternoon we had a long telephone conversation earlier in the day," says Dr. Gregor (Herbert Rawlinson). Dolores gives him a look of blank befuddlement which, under the circumstances, is entirely appropriate. The doctor is given to making deep, portentous statements such as, "Plastic surgery at times seems to me to be very, very complicated."

"Where have I failed?" he asks, later on.

"You haven't failed, Dad," Dolores assures him, fondly patting his bald pate.

"Words, my daughter, just words," sighs the doctor.

So might the scriptwriter. The hard, flat visuals, caught in the camera's icy stare, lend the film a certain distinctiveness, while helping its more laughable components to stand out all the more. There's also a surprise ending, but you can see it coming from miles away. In a camp classic like *Jail Bait*, plot doesn't matter much.

Jezebel* (U.S. 1938 B&W)

Jezebel is a survey of quaint customs in antebellum New Orleans. George Brent gets killed in a duel. Henry Fonda finds out—the hard way—that yellow fever is carried by mosquitoes. This is a great movie for queens, since the whole plot hinges on what color dress Bette Davis wears to a ball. The rest of the girls are in white, but she shows up in red. They treat her as if she was wearing one of those T-shirts that say "SHIT HAPPENS." Grim stuff, but entertaining and indubitably well-made. Davis won an Oscar for her role. This gay cult film presents a fairly brazen display of her classic mannerisms.

Johnny Guitar* (U.S. 1954 C)

Even in a book on camp, this Gothic, operatic, multifaceted western comes off as sounding somewhat bizarre. Joan Crawford stars as Vienna, a saloonkeeper who stands to profit enormously when the railroad crosses her property. She is opposed by Emma Small (Mercedes McCambridge), a frustrated spinster who's the richest woman in town. Emma loathes progress and, more especially, is pathologically jealous of Joan and her cronies: the Dancing Kid (Scott Brady) and his gang of could-be criminals. As Joan puts it, "She's in love with the Kid. He makes her feel like a woman, and that frightens her."

Several critics have pointed out that Emma's fanatical determination to rid the range of riffraff is actually an elaborate parody of early Fifties witch-hunts intended to purge the country of Communists. Director Nicholas Ray is careful to make the correlation perfectly clear, as in the scene which finds Emma and the black-clad lynch mob she leads (they've just come straight from her brother's funeral) interrogating a frightened prisoner. Their lying lips promise clemency, if only he'll name the right names.

The passage of time has increased the film's relevance. McCambridge may not look much like Joe McCarthy, but she bears a passing resemblance to Anita Bryant, and the plot has more than its share of homoerotic resonances. Crawford is a mannish sexual aggressor. She dresses in male attire: tight black jeans and a close-fitting black shirt. A tie and a gun belt complete the ensemble. She plays housemother to Brady and his all-male band, who share a cozy cabin in a hidden valley. Like the seven dwarfs, they're miners, and she's their Snow White (in fact, Joan wears a virgin white gown in a scene which has her pleading innocence and embracing martyrdom). The youngest member of Brady's bunch is a boy called "Turkey," though "Chicken" would do just as well. With her darkly intense, glowering face and quick, darting, birdlike gestures, Emma herself has a bold-as-brass, latent lesbian look about her. She seems unwholesomely fascinated by the Crawford character. At the climax the two women stalk one another with big, phallic pistols. "I'm coming up, Vienna!" Mercedes shrills. "I'm waiting!" is the heroine's cool reply.

JOAN CRAWFORD (1906–1977), American leading lady of numerous films from 1925 to 1970 and one of gaydom's camp icons. Shown here in a publicity release photo from *Johnny Guitar* (Republic Productions Inc.).

Admittedly, the neuroses portrayed in this Freudian horse opera are primarily of a heterosexual nature. *Johnny Guitar* is unique among westerns because, for a change, it's the male protagonists who function as passive and peripheral sex objects. Crawford almost crudely eyes co-star Sterling Hayden, who is the title character principally because we'd otherwise forget his name. She blatantly enjoys pitting her men against each other and likes to listen to them bickering over her favors; she provokes and stage-manages their every verbal volley. Contrariwise, when Brady embraces Emma in a brief and teasing dance, one can almost smell the musk of feverish, frustrated desire arising from the folds of McCambridge's oppressive woolen skirt. Emma's id desires the Dancing Kid, but her superego thinks he's just terrible and wants to blow his brains out with a great big gun. He ultimately robs her bank; that's just the kind of rape she's been yearning for. With the forces of law and order behind her, she embarks on a homicide binge. It's an orgy she's long awaited: she sheds her psychic restraints as readily as the veil she discards when she joins the posse. When they burn Vienna's tavern, she prances around the blaze like a witch out of *Macbeth*. And when Brady attempts to intervene in the final shootout, she plugs him squarely between the eyes. This transcends mere murder. Like a stern schoolmarm, she is chastising him for missing the whole point of the movie, for presuming to poke his masculine nose in a spat between two ladies, when, in fact, it was really Vienna that she wanted all along.

Sometimes life emulates melodrama: the set of this film was the scene of a bitter feud between Crawford and McCambridge. Tensions ran high: Nicholas Ray was quoted as saying that he threw up on his way to work every morning. He also claimed that, the night after McCambridge received an ovation from the crew, a drunken Crawford broke into her room and vandalized her wardrobe. With so many well-known boozers both behind and in front of the camera (McCambridge, a recovering alcoholic, now lectures on the subject), it's a wonder they ever got this film in the can, let alone that it turned out so brilliantly.

Jubilee Trail* (U.S. 1954 C)

Jubilee Trail shoots its brightest shaft in the very first scene: a colorful production number built around Vera Hruba Ralston, the leading lady. She's the resident chanteuse at a posh New Orleans eatery, surrounded by chorus girls, all of them noticeably prettier than she is. Vera struts, sashays, and even strips (very slightly), serenely and sublimely confident in the strength of her own sex appeal as she winks and squints and gapes and often wrinkles (with adorable insouciance) her moderately large nose. The audience joins in on the third verse. We wonder how they come to know the words. But this is a Republic picture, which means we're not supposed to think very hard about anything.

Her song over, Vera exchanges her glitzy blue sequined stage costume for a cream-colored gown with scarlet trim and matching picture hat. She settles herself in the restaurant proper and orders a bowl of stew. In short order, she has befriended the innocent newlywed bride (Joan Leslie) ensconced at a neighboring table. Miss Leslie asks her her name. "Florinda," she replies, in a husky, foreign-accented voice—the voice of a down-to-earth Dietrich without pretension, mystique, or, for that matter, talent. (I've named my favorite cat Florinda, in honor of this moment.)

In the following scene, she wears a dress of green and turquoise stripes. Her picture hat is black and adorned with artificial roses. Since she's hiding from the cops, this outfit is rather inadvisable attire. Miss Leslie conceals her in a cupboard while her husband (John Russell) fends off the law. After the danger is past, Mr. Russell addresses Vera as follows:

"I've known a lot of women like you, Florinda."

"I'm sure you have, Mr. Hale, but this time it isn't going to cost you anything."

The script variously designates Vera a "strumpet," a "harlot," a "Jezebel," and a "copper-penny doxy." But all we really know about her is that she's loud, in speech, demeanor, and appearance. By mule train, she and the prissy newlyweds are soon traversing the Jubilee Trail to California. After numerous adventures (and the demise of Mr. Russell), the two women wind up managing a saloon in old Los Angeles. Toward the close of the picture, Vera has a prayerful scene, bathed in moonlight at the end of a long corridor, while an organ and strings can be heard in the background. It's her big dramatic moment—the dramatic highlight of her career, in fact. Ironically, the film itself was an expensive failure, which helped put both her and her studio out of business. I once celebrated New Year's Eve by watching this movie with a friend of mine who claims that he's straight. "She sure wears a lot of interesting hats in this movie," he commented. I would tend to question the sexuality of any man who spends time contemplating Vera Hruba Ralston's hats.

Jungle Woman   (U.S. 1944 B&W)

No book on camp can be truly complete without some mention of Acquanetta, the Native American starlet (billed as "the Venezuelan Volcano") who was employed by Universal in the Forties. She is principally remembered for a pair of horror pictures in which she plays a girl who intermittently turns into an ape. Even in her more comely form, she's dangerous. She hates women and has super-

ACQUANETTA (1920–   ), 1940s star of such camp adventures as *Arabian Nights, Jungle Woman*. Publicity photo.

human strength. The first of the films was *Captive Wild Woman*, but its sequel, *Jungle Woman*, is much more ludicrous. For one thing, in *Jungle Woman* Acquanetta has dialogue (earlier, she'd had the wisdom to maintain an ominous silence). This film also includes a funny/spooky scene in which our shapeshifting heroine overturns a canoe in which a sappy pair of heteros sit mawkishly admiring the starlit sky. Furthermore, she tries to frame kindly old J. Carrol Naish on a sex harassment charge. Yes, when it comes to monkey business, you just can't trust those ape women.

---

*La Cage aux Folles** (France 1978 C)

The star of this homosexual farce is Ugo Tognazzi, who portrays the proprietor of a night club that features a transvestite revue. Michel Serrault is cast as his lover, a neurotic queen who dresses and behaves like an aging Hollywood actress. This couple employ a "maid": a handsome black who thinks he can break into show business by traipsing around the house clad in little more than a skimpy pair of hot pants. It's a highly unconventional ménage, over which Tognazzi presides with incongruously dignified composure.

The plot has complications. Ugo's son (the offspring of a youthful indiscretion) has grown up to become something of a prig. He's engaged to marry a girl whose father is a professional prude in charge of a national campaign for moral rearmament. Of course, the parents of the bride (who reside in rooms of brown austerity) are eager to meet the family of the groom. Tognazzi, after inviting them to come over for dinner, perceives that some sort of housecleaning is in order. He radically alters the decor of his home: frilly flamboyance gives way to a pious, severe medieval style. The "maid" is obliged to clean up his act and attire himself in the duds of a proper butler.

But how is Serrault to be made presentable? He must modify his mincing walk and dainty table manners. Ugo drives the poor fellow to the brink of nervous collapse by nagging him to walk like John Wayne. Such a charade is doomed from the outset. Serrault has a different trick up his sleeve. With the aid of a matronly wig, a dowdy housedress, and a faltering falsetto voice, he is introduced to the guests in the guise of Tognazzi's wife. This deception also proves unsuccessful, not that it really matters. Through a chain of disastrous happenstances, even the bluenosed father of the bride is obliged to go about in drag before the awful evening is over (he bears an astonishing resemblance to the late Elsa Maxwell). The humor in this classic camp film is often "politically incorrect." Still, in its very unfashionableness, the movie qualifies as an interesting curio.

The film was sufficiently successful to inspire a pair of sequels. *La Cage aux Folles II* * (1981) is a spy spoof involving the gay couple in a web of foreign intrigue. I found it to be at least as amusing as its predecessor. In *La Cage aux Folles III* * (1985), the femme half of the duo comes into a vast inheritance, the only condition being that he must get himself married to a woman. This premise sounds funny on paper. On the screen, unfortunately, it falls flat.

Ladies of the Chorus * (U.S. 1948 B&W)

For the casual film fan, *Ladies of the Chorus* is merely of interest in its capacity as an early Marilyn Monroe vehicle. For the cognoscenti, however, the film has deeper dimensions and more complicated facets. The meaty role of Marilyn's mother is delineated by Adele Jergens, who, even as early as 1948, was a seasoned B-movie veteran. Adele is cast as an aging burlesque queen. Marilyn is following in her mom's professional footsteps. Furthermore, both are employed in the very same chorus line. Talk about family values!

Adele doesn't permit Marilyn to go out on dates with married sugar daddies. Marilyn complains that Adele is treating her like a child. Why should the other girls have all the fun? But, when one of them dares to call Jergens a "hag," Monroe unsheathes her claws and rushes to Mom's defense. Cat fight time, and Monroe acquits herself admirably. Afterward there's the added thrill of watching her straighten Jergens' wig before they go "on."

Marilyn eventually meets a nice boy who sends her flowers and takes her to dinner at the Waldorf. There's a very unsettling scene when he comes backstage to meet Mother. She's in costume (skimpy) and the first thing he sees are her gams. Next he sees her take off

ADELE JERGENS (1922–　), American star of the 1940s–50s, shown here in a publicity photo by Ned Scott from *Down to Earth* (Columbia Pictures).

her glamorous blonde wig, revealing the gray-streaked hair under-neath. Later, when he asks her for Marilyn's hand in marriage, she's dressed far more sedately, but then she launches into a flash-back sequence which finds her clad in a Jazz Baby fringe skirt. Just how old was Adele when this picture was shot? Twenty-six, as a matter of fact. Casting her as the parent of Monroe (then a mature 22) must have led to a certain degree of tension on the set. At any rate, this is a good little programmer with plenty of loaded issues on its mind: not only questions of age, but also social class and couture. The sensitive viewer will savor the superabundance of camp ironies.

Laura* (U.S. 1944 B&W)

In *Laura*, Dana Andrews is cast as a police detective investigating the murder of the glamorous title character (Gene Tierney). Grad-ually, he becomes obsessed with her. Before too long, he's hitting the sauce and hanging out at her empty apartment (it's the scene of the crime). Although repelled by the coterie of bizarre hangers-on with which she once surrounded herself, he inexorably finds himself falling in love with secondhand memories and hearsay evi-dence regarding this mysterious female whom he can never hope to possess. Or can he? Midway through the movie, Laura turns out to be very much alive. This complicates the case, not to mention the state of Dana's emotions.

One of Laura's more outlandish associates is Waldo Lydecker (Clifton Webb), a waspish wit, conceited and bitchy. The film begins with Andrews interrogating this suspect, who is interrupted while bathing. As he arises from the tub, we watch a near-sublim-inal smirk dart across Dana's face. One gets the impression that Waldo must be rather modestly endowed. The script makes clear, however, that he has ways by which to compensate for any per-sonal shortcoming.

Under the hothouse conditions prevailing, even the ostensibly "normal" characters end up seeming strange and feverishly exotic. For instance, Laura's servant (Dorothy Adams) comes across as being a repressed lesbian, a fervid religious fanatic, and a ferocious cop-hater, all at one and the same time. Besides which, she's supposed to be sympathetic.

The movie's campiest component is probably the relationship between co-stars Vincent Price and Judith Anderson. She's a rich old lady, he's the gigolo type, and so they share a sick symbiosis. We are given to understand that these two ne'er-do-wells will be wed, not so much out of love as because they have mutually arrived at the conclusion that they deserve nothing better than each other. This is typical film noir reasoning, carrying self-awareness to grotesquely fatalistic lengths.

We are also led to assume that Andrews and Tierney will ultimately get together. However, I harbor doubts regarding the future of such a match. Price is Laura's former fiancé. Anderson is her aunt. Blood is thicker than water. I can foresee some highly uncomfortable family gatherings.

Law of Desire* (Spain 1987 C)

Pedro Almodóvar's *Law of Desire*, a gay sex melodrama, is delightfully lurid in its campy outlandishness. The show starts right out with a handsome young man stripping off his clothes, reclining on a bed, and jacking off. This turns out to be a scene from a film-within-the-film, the director of which (thirtyish, blonde, good-looking Eusebio Poncela) is *Law of Desire*'s hero. He's at the apex of a queer love triangle involving a pair of darkly attractive young men in their twenties. He's in love with one and pursued by the other. Furthermore, the one who's crazy about him turns out to be literally crazy: he pushes the other boy off a cliff (hard by a more than usually phallic lighthouse). Poncela, blinded by tears of grief, drives his car into a tree and gets amnesia. Thus he's unable to defend himself when the police, armed with circumstantial evidence, accuse him of the murder. His memory returns when he's visited by his transsexual sister (Carmen Maura), who tells him all about how she was sexually molested by their father back in the days when she was a boy.

You got all that? This is a movie loaded with hot men and gay sex. It's the only movie I've ever seen in which the killer, holed up in a building surrounded by cops, bargains with them for one more hour of freedom and then gets into bed and has sex with a man.

The Little Foxes* (U.S. 1941 B&W)

The Little Foxes is the one where Bette Davis sees her husband having a heart attack and simply sits there, refusing to fetch him his medicine. She coldbloodedly watches him croak because his death will serve to maximize her profits from the cotton mill that her awful brothers are planning to build. The film is a fairly caustic comment on "success" and what's required to achieve it. In 1941 it must have seemed a rather momentous event in the history of the motion picture Production Code; in those days, getting away with murder was strictly against the rules. In the context of the narrative, Bette is "punished" in the sense that her only child abandons her, but this doesn't really amount to much, since it's perfectly clear that the character whom Davis is delineating doesn't give a fig about anyone other than herself.

The script is by Lillian Hellman, based, of course, on her famous play. Significantly, the action is set in the year 1900. It's the start of a crass, ugly century and a look at the class who made it that way. Despite the horse-and-buggy ambience, we are able to plainly sense the times to come. Hubbard is the name of the sleazy clan to which the title refers. The Hunts, the Luces, the Buckleys, the Nixons, etc., are waiting in the wings. Like several other Davis films, this is primarily a gay cult film with camp very much secondary.

The Lost City* (U.S. 1935 B&W)

The Lost City, a twelve-chapter saga of apocalyptic doom, somehow does not elicit an appropriately solemn response from the viewer. Earth is faced with destruction, catastrophic disasters take untold lives, and here I sit, contemplating the young inventor who thinks he can save the world. Do I wish him success? Frankly, no;

I'm too busy thinking about what a hunk he is. He's played by Kane Richmond, and there's something about his long, white neck—thick and sturdy, firm yet limber, and smooth as polished marble—which brings out fantasies better not expressed by me in print.

The plot carries him and his sidekick (Eddie Fetherstone) to darkest Africa, where they tumble through a trapdoor, then slide down a slick-surfaced chute while all tangled up in each other's arms and legs. (Beats the Tunnel of Love, in my book.) They end up in the private office of the evil mastermind, who introduces himself as follows: "As you may know, the Legurians were master scientists. I am the last of that race, carrying on the electromagnetic traditions of my people."

Ethnicity is so special, don't you agree?

This electromagnetic bad guy is a maniacal slavemaster played by William Boyd (a barnstorming actor not to be confused with the cowboy star of the same name). He's in the business of turning the local natives into horrible, giant, cross-eyed, frizzy-haired black zombies. (I should note that their rippling muscles have been copiously oiled to a glistening sheen.) He's assisted in his nefarious task by a seminude fairy boy (Jerry Frank) who watches the enlarging process with rapt fascination, grinning with orgasmic enthusiasm. (It's fair to say that he's probably excited about the enlargement of one body part in particular.)

Frank is clad in a truly obscene garment: a glitterboy swimsuit (with sequins and suspenders) which serves to accentuate both his buttocks and his crotch-bulge. A cardboard bolt of lightning is emblazoned on his otherwise naked chest; another one garnishes his groin. He's got a really butch way of walking, but his tough guy demeanor is superficial at best. ("Quick! Untie me!" he snivels during a bondage scene.) In a fight scene, he's hit on the head with a monkey wrench and topples over, thrusting his glitter-clad butt into the camera lens as though offering it to be fucked.

Richmond, the hero, may not be quite the scientific genius he's cracked up to be. For one thing, he has a habit of saying "lavatory," instead of "laboratory." Perhaps he's a urologist (certainly an appropriate field of interest, given the circumstances and the surroundings). But the only really smart thing he does is to wear a shirt with torn sleeves, thus giving us provocative glimpses of his shapely biceps.

Kane also has the distinction of appearing (with Mr. Fetherstone) in the kinkiest bondage scene that this serial has to offer. During its course, he rolls over onto his belly and offers the cords that bind his wrists to be nibbled on by Fetherstone, who also is all tied up at the time. The wrists are coyly positioned over his ass; Eddie's busy mouth and teeth have a lot of munching to do. "You making any headway there?" Kane inquires nervously, not entirely certain of his sidekick's intentions.

The second kinkiest bondage scene has Kane at the mercy of Gabby Hayes (the only significant "name" in the cast). With indelible ink, Gabby painstakingly prints the word "DESIRE" upon the milk-white canvas of Richmond's naked, remarkably hairless chest. This mad flourish of homoerotic decadence is a surrealistic gesture almost worthy of Cocteau. (Our hero's principal "desire" at this point is presumably a simple wish to get untied.)

By no means, however, would I want to imply that this show has an all-male cast. Quite the contrary: mention must be made of Margot D'use as Queen Rama, a low-camp exotic who wants to rule all of Africa. To realize her ambition, she must first subdue an obsessed scientist who alone knows the secret of turning black men white. (In case you haven't already guessed, this serial is morbidly racist.) Claudia Dell is the irritatingly fidget-prone heroine. ("He's so croo-ell!" she complains of the mad mastermind portrayed by Mr. Boyd.) As emblems of sexual tension, however, both these ladies are ludicrously, pathetically beside the point.

There is, if not a bona fide climax, at least a grand finale of sorts. Mr. Richmond, he of the broad and voluptuous neck (". . . a throat which . . . has the smooth and supple muscularity of the male organ in its early stage of tumescence."—Tennessee Williams), is Back in Bondage Again, strapped securely in a chair by Mr. Frank, the fairysuited flunky, who, of course, cops a free feel in the process, and who then proceeds to tease and torment our unhappily ensorcelled hero with a lethal laser beam. While wielding this phallic instrument of torture, Frank is potency personified; the lightning bolt which adorns his crotch seems literal, not symbolic. His eyes dance with sadistic glee; his toothy grin sparkles. He's caught up in an erotic transport of ecstasy, and, if it had gone on much longer, he would surely have needed to change his bathing briefs. But then . . . some idiot turns off the power. We are left to contemplate, not the sticky, musky residue of a spent and drying passion, but the lavish profusion of homoerotic notations which have lewdly and lubriciously led up to this point. Too profuse, I think, and too blatant to qualify as coincidental.

Lost Horizon* (U.S. 1937 B&W)

Lost Horizon, a Frank Capra inspirational tract, is deservedly famous for its depiction of Shangri-La, a hidden haven of peace in a world of turmoil and conflict. In my childhood, I appreciated this film simply as a romantic story that would carry me a million miles away from the workaday world to a distant, exotic past. (To my young eyes, the turmoil looked as appealing as the peace, since both were of Thirties vintage.) Now, however, I tend to be more captivated by the operatic, strictly esthetic qualities of the production. Which is not to say that this is a particularly well-made film. On the contrary: the narrative, derived from James Hilton's novel, is so clunky and arbitrary, we wonder how the movie ever managed to get made.

The protagonists, along with the audience, arrive at Shangri-La by way of an elaborate pilgrimage through an assortment of pulp magazine adventure clichés. The hero is Ronald Colman, who, as always, is almost nauseatingly noble and stalwart. In the opening scene, he and his annoying kid brother (John Howard) are introduced in a war-torn Chinese setting, where we find them shepherding a group of orphans to safety. Need I add that all of these children are white? And that, when first seen, Colman and Howard are literally carrying a couple of them in their arms? Colman's entourage includes a rouged, consumptive prostitute (Isabel Jewell), a plucky fugitive from justice (Thomas Mitchell), and Edward Everett Horton as a prototypical nervous Nellie. Horton's offensive fag routine is somewhat counterbalanced by the presence of H. B. Warner, who brings a more patrician, dignified queenliness to his role as Shangri-La's obsequious majordomo, to the extent that we practically burst out laughing when Colman incredulously asks him, "You have no disputes over women?" and we instinctively know that Margo is lying when she claims that he's madly and possessively in love with her.

The real star of the show (and its campiest element) is Shangri-La itself: a utopia of flat-topped Art Deco architecture, with gardens and fountains and happy, carefree natives. Since the people stay youthful indefinitely and hardly anyone ages and dies, we wonder about the population problem. The principality is located in "the Valley of the Blue Moon" and H. B. Warner tells us that the locals are "moderately chaste." Perhaps that's another way of saying that they only have sex once in a blue moon. At any rate, the place is a magical realm where tame deer graze, off-screen choirs are in constant ululation, flocks of pigeons dart and swoop, and the cherry blossoms are always in bloom. At times it's like something out of a Disney picture, as, for example, in the scene where Jane Wyatt goes skinnydipping in a mountain stream; an intruder approaches, whereupon a friendly squirrel warns her with chirrups that she seems to literally comprehend. But, however warm the climate, there is something distinctively chilly about the interiors. They are bathed in a white light that is soft, diffuse, and hazy. The art director, Stephen Goosson, was awarded an Oscar for his efforts. Translucency is the name of his game. If this film were a poem, it would probably be called "Ode to a Glass Brick."

The Loves of Hercules* (Italy 1960 C)

The Loves of Hercules gets underway like many another sword-and-sandal fantasy, with bodybuilders in skimpy fairy suits looking and acting excessively chummy. However, it abruptly turns into a whole other kind of movie upon the arrival of camp icon Jayne Mansfield, whose top-heavy charms are here enhanced by the fact that she's surrounded by a retinue of half-naked men. Attired in an assortment of cross-your-heart bodices that look like they were designed by Frederick's of Hollywood, she is cast in two roles, both of them queenly (of course). It's hard to say which is more humorous: her royal predicaments or the manner in which she responds to them. Attacked by a maddened bull, she lies sprawled in an attitude of ostentatious defenselessness. But naturally she's also given ample chance to act imperious. For instance, at one point she declaims, "Are you forgetting I am the Queen? You will pay for this treachery!" Then she gets to smack a cute little gong. "You are a woman," points out the evil Prime Minister (rather needlessly), "and the burden of government is too heavy for you alone." "Yes, I know I need help," replies Jayne, acknowledging that she's probably got enough to haul around already.

Hercules is portrayed by Mickey Hargitay, her real-life consort (at the time). A Mayfair accent has been dubbed into his grimacing Hungarian mouth ("The gods have smiled on me at lahst!"). The dubbing is unfortunate for Jayne's fans, too. We miss all her characteristic kewpie-doll squealing and moaning. Mickey gets to decapitate a three-headed Hydra which, when it takes a victim between a pair of its patently mechanical jaws, resembles nothing so much as a hydraulic ride in an amusement park. Yes, this ex-Mr. Universe is definitely a man to be reckoned with. The script even hints that he might also be formidably physical in the sack. Take, for example, the scene in which Magda, a Gypsy hag, urges Hippolyta, the wicked queen of the Amazons, to sorcerously shape-shift herself into a carrot-topped semblance of Jayne—

MAGDA: If you want him to be in love with you, you must take the face of that woman.

HIPPOLYTA: I must disguise myself?

MAGDA: There's nothing else to be done, I assure you.

HIPPOLYTA (regally): That's the most insulting price any woman could pay for love!

MAGDA: That may be true, Hippolyta, but Hercules is *worth it*!

As a matter of fact, I rather doubt that this was so vehemently the case, despite the clinically impressive shot of his firm and sturdy posterior as we watch him go clambering over a collapsing drawbridge. That sort of thing is mere trivial ornamentation. In the case of a film like *The Loves of Hercules*, the truly dyed-in-the-wool gay man will only have eyes for Jayne.

---

*Lust in the Dust** (U.S. 1985 C)

In the opening frames of *Lust in the Dust*, the title of the movie, spelled out in red, raw, rough-hewn lettering, emerges from out of a desert landscape. This, together with the blaring, surging back-

DIVINE (1945–1988), American transvestite star of such camp classics as *Female Trouble*, *Hairspray* and *Pink Flamingos*. In this photo a frightened Divine attempts to hide from marauding outlaws in the 1984 production of *Lust in the Dust* (directed by Paul Bartel, Fox Run pictures). "Of course, the last thing my parents wanted was a son who wears a cocktail dress that glitters, but they've come around to that."—Divine.

ground music, denotes a definitely retro sensibility. The film, director Paul Bartel's ludicrously passionate parody of Fifties westerns, owes most of its rollicking resonances to overheated Republic pictures such as *Johnny Guitar* and *Jubilee Trail*.

Tab Hunter, tight-lipped and flint-eyed, seems to be doing an impression of Clint Eastwood in a spaghetti western. But the centerpiece of the picture is Divine's delightfully overdrawn delineation of a dance hall girl. Her florid emotionalism makes for hilarious incongruity in all of her scenes with Tab. Equally amusing is the disparity between her physical appearance and the horniness which she almost always inspires in the men who cross her path. Here is where comparisons with Republic are especially instructive, for, at such moments as these, Divine bids fair to be the new Vera Hruba Ralston. In a sense, the plot sets up Tab as being Divine's opposite number: every female in the film has a bad case of the hots for him. However, he doesn't seem unduly responsive to their advances.

Need I point out that this is a very gay movie? Director Bartel has made a specialty of kinky, provocative films such as this. His credits include such titles as *Eating Raoul* (1982) and *Private Parts* (1972)—neither of which, however, is as erotic as it sounds.

Madam Satan* (U.S. 1930 B&W)

In *Madam Satan* Kay Johnson is cast as a high society wife who discovers a powder puff in her husband's roadster. She asks the lisping chauffeur how it got there, but he is unable to offer a satisfactory explanation. For distraction from her marital woes, she sits down at the organ and performs an aria from Flotow's *Martha*. By the time she's done, her hubby (Reginald Denny) has returned from his revels. She discovers him taking a shower with a male companion. (Don't worry; they both have their clothes on.) The two men retire to bed (twin beds; I said not to worry). Kay, meanwhile, asks advice from the upstairs maid, who replies by launching into a soprano aria.

In point of fact, Kay's fears are justified: there really is an "other woman." She's Lillian Roth and, at one point, she delivers a speech that could serve as inspiration to gay men everywhere: "What do

I give him? I laugh when he does. I drink when he does. I give him a pal with lips to kiss and shoulders to hug. I give him a dream made out of perfume and soft lights. I jazz all the dullness out of his soul for him." Set it to music and I'll sing it myself.

The grand finale is a camp pièce de résistance: a wild costume party aboard a doomed dirigible. Kay wins Reggie back by showing up as "Madam Satan," complete with a horned headdress and a black-and-platinum gown that's a swirl of beguiling concealments. Her entrance provokes a production number (of course), which concludes with all the guys getting down on their knees at the she-devil's feet. "Who wants to go to hell with Madam Satan?" she scoffingly asks them. (Something tells me this movie wouldn't go over too well with the fundamentalist set.) She and Denny wind up in the chart room, where they sip flaming cups of cafe diable. But then a bolt of lightning strikes the zeppelin, causing it to break free of its moorings. This is, after all, a Cecil B. DeMille movie, which means that picturesque debauchery must be punished with spectacular disaster in the final reel. No matter: the guests simply parachute to safety. You'll be interested to hear that Miss Roth lands in an all-male steam bath.

The Magic Christian* (G.B. 1969 C)

The Magic Christian is an absurdist comedy about greed and corruption. This in itself is unremarkable. What's extraordinary is the fact that the tale is presented in such unmistakably homoerotic terms. Peter Sellers portrays a billionaire businessman clearly intrigued by a penniless drifter (Ringo Starr) whom he encounters one day in the park. The sequence of shots leading up to this meeting is intended to contrast the wealth of one man with the poverty of the other. At the same time, however, the essential loneliness of both men is firmly established.

Sellers adopts the scruffy young fellow as his legal son and heir. When the papers are signed, we hear wedding bells chime and the two men embrace like long-lost lovers. Together they embark on a research project of sorts; they're studying the effect of money on human integrity. For starters, Laurence Harvey is bribed to do a striptease while performing Hamlet. By modern standards, we don't see much, but we certainly see enough to get the idea. Raucous honky-tonk music interrupts the "To be or not to be" speech, the camera watching closely as the zipper slowly descends.

So much for British arts and letters. The next target is British sportsmanship: Sellers calls in field artillery and flamethrowers in order to down (and simultaneously cook) a pheasant. He arranges to have a leopard smuggled into a dog show and passes off the resultant carnage as an antiwar statement. He goes to a fancy French restaurant and plays with the food—grossly, rather in the style of John Belushi in *Animal House*. Then he traipses back to the kitchen for a passionate waltz with the chef. "That's the last we shall see of *him* tonight," someone says.

Next to be subverted is a boxing match. At stake is the heavy-weight championship of the world. The two contestants, both in the pay of Peter, abruptly abandon their aggressiveness and commit a homosexual act in the very first round. "The crowd seems to be sickened by the sight of no blood," remarks a ringside commentator.

From land we move to water: the annual Oxford-Cambridge boat race is thrown. And then comes the maiden voyage of "The Magic Christian," a luxurious cruise ship sailing from London to New York. The passenger list is impressive: John and Yoko, Jackie and Ari, etc. Of course, Peter and Ringo are on board. The fun begins with a floor show in the dining lounge: a pair of Mr. Universe types, one black, one white, both with loincloths voluptuously bulging, perform a graceful adagio act hard by the table of a racist imperial major (Terence Alexander) who positively cringes with distaste.

There's something definitely queer about this ship. The steward is Christopher Lee, his fangs flashing. The ship's doctor is a simpering fag (Leonard Frey) who prescribes marijuana to his patients. In the bar, Roman Polanski is approached by a transvestite (Yul Brynner) who serenades him with a rendition of "Mad About the Boy." A visit to the engine room reveals that the ship is powered by a battalion of female galley slaves wearing nothing above the waist. Lording it over them is a dominatrix (Raquel Welch, obviously in training for her title role in *Myra Breckinridge*) dressed in a costume of ornately studded leather. "During my reign as Priestess of the Whip, I have never seen such unmitigated sloth!"

complains Raquel, in a moment that defines camp. Pandemonium (and, if you look quick, an orgy of homosexual lovemaking) promptly erupts all over the vessel.

In the final sequence of the film, Peter and Ringo simply dump a load of money into a vat of raw sewage and let people dive for it. The moral would seem to be that every heterosexual has his price. Seldom have I seen the straight world so explicitly equated with avarice and bloodlust. Would that such comparisons were still fashionable! I take at least a small measure of comfort in the knowledge that someday the pendulum must inevitably swing back to where it was in 1969.

The Maltese Falcon* (U.S. 1941 B&W)

The Maltese Falcon stars Humphrey Bogart in what may be his single most celebrated role. However, Sam Spade, the detective he portrays, strikes me as being a singularly unappealing sort: tough, cynical, incapable of genuine feeling, contemptuous of people in general and of homosexuals in particular. His habitat is the usual noirish urban underworld, where alliances are transient at best and no one can ever be really relied upon. He dislikes being touched, especially by members of his own sex.

Can the negative stereotyping of homosexuals be camp? Perhaps, if it's sufficiently dated and indirect. Not that there's anything subtle about the lisping, mincing, gardenia-scented, downright hysterical faggot delineated herein by Peter Lorre (complete with pinky ring). He's not been on the screen so much as a full minute before he comes suggestively close to fellating the handle of his walking stick! Elisha Cook, looking remarkably young and unwholesomely sexy, portrays the paid bodyguard and kept boy of unscrupulous mastermind Sydney Greenstreet (who claims that this unsavory fellow is "like a son of my own"). Elisha is dismissed by Bogie as belonging to the category of "cheap gunmen" who have "their heaters bulging in their clothes." I'll wager that Mae West could have done a thing or two with that line. Despite Elisha's many commendable qualities, his sugar daddy nonetheless betrays and abandons him. Under the circumstances, it should come as no surprise that the only human relationship which the picture takes seriously is the one between Bogart and leading lady Mary Astor. And he even sends *her* up the river!

Dennis Kelly, author of *Chicken*, has made cogent comments of his own about this film. He writes, "One can't take too seriously the villain roles, since they're such ingeniously understated caricatures. For many straights, Peter Lorre's performance is like running a fingernail down a blackboard. Bogart's attitude is that he can't take either Cook or Lorre seriously, a typical camp attitude of straights toward gays. There's a certain dry, almost British sense of humor one must have to appreciate the camp in *The Maltese Falcon*—the wry humor, say, of Peter Lorre's gestures with the pistol to his lips."

Nonetheless, bad guys are still bad guys. Audiences in 1941 weren't ready for gays in any other capacity.

Mandingo * (U.S. 1975 C)

In 1954 Richard Fleischer directed James Mason in the famous Walt Disney movie, *20,000 Leagues Under the Sea*. Twenty years later, he directed him in *Mandingo*, which is about as far a cry from a Disney picture as you can get. *Mandingo* is Southern Gothic at its most depraved. The setting is a somewhat shabby plantation in antebellum days. It would appear that young Master Hammond (Perry King) is in love with two of his slaves, played by Brenda Sykes and Ken Norton. To satisfy convention, however, he weds a white woman (Susan George). On their honeymoon, he's chagrined to discover that she is not exactly a model of purity (at a tender age, she permitted her pervert brother to deflower her). Her marriage a flop, she takes to the bottle and, when Ms. Sykes conceives, causes her to miscarry by pushing her down the stairs. Then she perversely sets about ruining the other object of her husband's affections: by threatening to accuse him of rape, she successfully forces herself on Norton—not once, but several times. When Perry finds out, he poisons her, then scalds the unfortunate Norton to death in a huge vat of boiling water.

Not a pretty picture, but at least it isn't boring. Maurice Jarre's

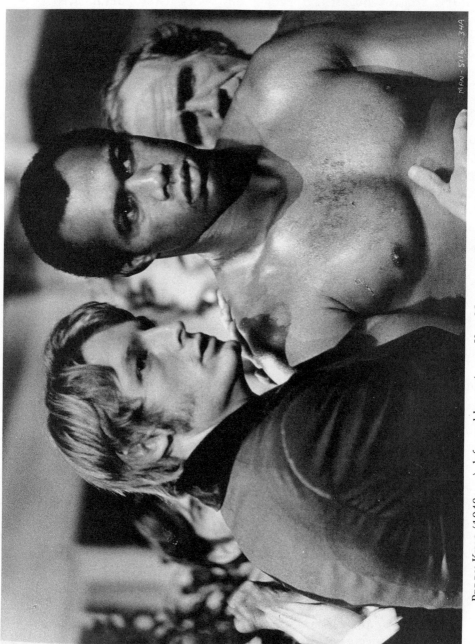

PERRY KING (1948–), left, and boxer/actor KEN NORTON (1945–) in a scene from *Mandingo* (Dino de Laurentiis Corp.).

inappropriately pastoral music score tends to suggest that these sordid goings-on are all merely quaintly bucolic. Perry King has a scene of full frontal nudity, which probably would not have qualified as camp, if he hadn't gotten down on his knees and started saying his "Now I lay me down to sleep . . .". James Mason, cast as Perry's pa, gets to be rather campy also: in one scene he superstitiously attempts to cure his rheumatism by sleeping all curled up with a cute little black boy. As for the conspicuously muscular Mr. Norton, suffice it to say that his name in the film is Mede, which is short for Ganymede.

[Drum, *a successor film with similar themes, is reviewed elsewhere in this book.*]

The Mark of Zorro* (U.S. 1940 B&W)

The Mark of Zorro qualifies as tragicomic camp. I mean, here we have a certified gay-but-closeted actor (Tyrone Power) cast as a dashing masked hero who, to divert suspicion, poses as an effeminate fop. The ironies are endless.

When first we encounter Tyrone, he's attending a Spanish military academy, where he acquires the sobriquet of "The California Cockerel" (for his swordsmanship, I hasten to explain). Later, back in his homeland, and having seen how the local peons are abused, he quickly decides on his course of action, establishing a clearly defined identity for himself: "I love the shimmer of satin and silk, the matching of one delicate shade against the other," he sighs to co-star Gale Sondergaard. "Then there's the choosing of scents and lotions . . ."

The bad guys are nearby, absorbing this pretty speech. Basil Rathbone rolls his eyes in disgust. "There's one little peacock that won't give us any trouble," crows J. Edward Bromberg.

The village padre is Eugene Pallette (with his croaking voice it's difficult to imagine him preaching a sermon). He also takes an interest in the exotic young newcomer. "I feel good muscle here," he exults, squeezing Tyrone's biceps. (I noticed good muscles popping out all over him. California caballeros tend to wear awfully tight breeches.) The priest becomes Power's confederate, as Zorro

TYRONE POWER (1913–1958), shown here in a 1930s publicity photo, was in few camp films (*Mark of Zorro* is a rare exception). Married three times, his affairs with men have been detailed in recent biographies.

embarks on a career as the Robin Hood of old Los Angeles, taking from the rich, giving to the poor, and scratching Z's on every available surface. But I, of course, am more entertained by his frivolous "official" self, squinting through a monocle and performing parlor tricks with fans and handkerchiefs. Rathbone at one point compares him to a fruit.

Sondergaard was married to one of the Hollywood Ten and, like her husband, was blacklisted. Here she plays a vain and silly aristocrat. Rathbone, an accomplished swordsman, found it rather difficult to convincingly engage in duels with Power, who is obviously more at home doing a hat dance with leading lady Linda Darnell. With his chubby cheeks, his smarmy smile, his bulging basket, and his Cesar Romero moustache, Tyrone is, as always, cute.

Mask of the Musketeers
(Italy 1960 Released in color. Shown on TV generally only in b&w)

"A soft and frivolous dandy . . ."

"There's no one quite as . . . *mincing* as he is."

Can it be that these contemptuous words are actually intended to describe . . . Gordon Scott?! Well, yes, as a matter of fact, they are. The film is *Mask of the Musketeers* and, for once in his career, he's portraying an effeminate type, instead of merely getting drooled on by one (his more customary cinematic position). The movie might better have been called *The Three Musketeers Meet Zorro*. Gordon is featured in the latter role: the dashing hero who poses as a pansy in order to ward off suspicion regarding his secret alter ego. The action transpires in seventeenth-century France and Spain, which means that his bulging biceps and hairy, voluptuous pectorals are swathed in capes and cloaks and velvet finery. Gesturing flamboyantly with a foppish plumed hat in one hand and a huge hankie in the other, his eyebrows dancing, a sappy grin plastered on his face, Gordon sighs, "I'm a romantic soul and I always look at things from the sentimental point of view." Isn't he sweet?

Without a beard, he looks surprisingly avuncular. Also rather lantern-jawed. His fussy, fruity little moustache only worsens the already unflattering effect. At times it almost seems as though the presiding male glamourpuss is co-star Giacomo Rossi Stuart, cast as Aramis, the cutest and most amorous of the Three Musketeers. But he isn't able to swish and camp it up the way Gordon does. I mean, Gordon may look a teensy bit less hunky than usual, but there's nonetheless something appealingly poignant, something adorably vulnerable about a beefcake star forced by narrative circumstances to keep his manhood under wraps. We actually get to see him dance a minuet at court—bowing and smirking, clutching a lace handkerchief, with one hand archly poised on his hip. How the mighty have fallen! (Don'tcha *love* it?) Whoever was responsible for the choreography must have had a simply delightful time training him to assume such airs and graces.

---

*Mata Hari** (U.S. 1932 B&W)

A gong is struck. So begins *Mata Hari*, starring Greta Garbo as the notorious dancing spy of World War I. Her "dance" mainly consists of moving very slowly and deliberately while trailing gilded draperies behind her. Her costumes (by Adrian) are fabulously ornate and extravagant. And her target for tonight is Ramon Novarro. He's cast as a Russian aviator, but his accent is clearly Hispanic. "What people you Russians are!" Garbo enthuses. "What charming savatches!" Before they make love, she compels him to extinguish the holy lamp which burns before his sacred icon of the Virgin. (His mother walked a hundred miles to fetch it for him, and made him swear on the altar that he'd never let the light go out.) All this high heterosexual passion is, of course, an ironic charade; in real life, Novarro was gay.

Mata Hari's undoing is a Russian general played by Lionel Barrymore. His crazed, eyeball-rolling fit of jealousy is ham acting at its most hilarious. I was, however, quite taken with Novarro. His eyes smolder appealingly, especially after he's blinded in a plane crash. When Garbo visits him in the hospital, a patient with a violin is playing "Ave Maria." Later Ramon is brought to visit her in prison, where she's awaiting execution. Oh, the pathos! He's tricked into thinking it's a sanitarium. The morality of lying to blind people need not concern us here. I should point out, however, that all this sappy love stuff is very fictitious. The real Mata Hari was a pretty cool customer.

Mildred Pierce* (U.S. 1945 B&W)

As better eyes than mine have noticed, *Mildred Pierce* combines the visual conventions of the film noir with the thematic concerns of a melodrama geared toward a female audience. It also made a lot of money, won Joan Crawford her only Oscar, and revived her flagging career. The movies she made after *Mildred Pierce* were generally tougher, darker, and more hard-boiled than the ones she'd made before. The ones before were women's pictures; the ones afterward often attempted to duplicate the winning formula of *Mildred Pierce*.

Crawford, of course, plays the title role. The early scenes imply that Mildred has murdered her wealthy, sleazy second husband (Zachary Scott). Down at police headquarters, the suspects are grilled. As Mildred tells her story, the flashbacks begin. She was just a poor, sheltered housewife, unschooled in the ways of the world, when her first husband (Bruce Bennett) took a powder. (Actually, she throws him out.) God knows what she would have done if she hadn't found a job as a waitress. (The restaurant hostess who gives her a break is Eve Arden, any movie heroine's dearest chum.)

"My mother . . . a waitress!" sneers Veda (Ann Blyth), Mildred's spoiled, petulant daughter. The kinky, acrimonious love/hate relationship that these two share set a pattern that was to be repeated in subsequent Crawford vehicles about mothers with ungrateful offspring. (Repeated in real life, too. See Christina Crawford's book, *Mommie Dearest* for further reference.) Mildred courts Veda like a woebegone suitor, plying her with ever more expensive gifts while settling for progressively tinier scraps of the girl's affection. This situation culminates in an unbearably tense scene wherein Veda strikes her mother on a staircase, knocking her down against the bannister. Hatred, antagonism, potent and palpable, suffuse the screen like a bloodstain.

Always ambitious and practical, Mildred is just about ready to open a restaurant of her own when she first encounters Zachary Scott. (He's the owner of the property she wishes to convert to commercial use.) "No whistle?" she asks, the first time he sees her in a swimsuit. "I'd need a police siren," he replies. I'd need one, also, in order to do justice to the bathing briefs he's got on. Sleek, slick, and squirrel-eyed, he's alluring in his gracefulness and soft, decadent passivity. His aura of swishy mellifluousness could, in a more enlightened era, have made him a paragon of androgynous chic. Even Eve Arden says he's got "beautiful brown eyes." When Joan asks him what he "does," he tells her, "I loaf, in a decorative and highly charming manner." I've always been drawn to men who describe themselves as decorative and charming.

But this is Crawford's show, from start to finish. The plot differs from that of the James M. Cain novel on which the film is based, but at least the movie retains the mood and flavor of its source. The director, Michael Curtiz, punctuates the picture with jarring, fragmentary stylistic quirks: the clang of a cop's nightstick against a metal railing; the curt, clipped gesture with which Crawford pulls down her hemline over her knees. Still, it's a fusty, draggy, often ploddingly ponderous drama. Crawford made better films. She also made campier ones. But this is the key film for understanding Crawford's place in the camp pantheon.

Maurice* (G.B. 1987 C)

Maurice, a ravishingly pretty film on the topic of homosexuality, has a plot which may be summarized very briefly. A pair of British boys fall in love while pursuing their studies at Cambridge. (The time is just before the First World War.) One of them (Hugh Grant), frightened of society's disapproval, decides to get married and play it straight. The other is the title character (James Wilby). He assuages his grief by running off with a studly lad (Rupert Graves) from the lower classes.

The film is based on a novel by E. M. Forster, which, despite its exteme politeness, was far too scandalous to be published during his lifetime. The movie more than matches the discretion of its

JAMES WILBY (1958–   ), standing, and RUPERT GRAVES (1963–   ), shown here as the two lovers in the Cinecom/Merchant Ivory production of *Maurice*, a study of homosexuality in pre-World War I Cambridge University. Now becoming a gay cult classic likely to endure.

source. What emerges is a mildly interesting portrait of Edwardian hypocrisy and repression. Trouble is, the film gets smothered in its own good taste and winds up being a cup of rather weak tea, kind of like a gay version of a *Masterpiece Theatre* soap opera. A cult of sorts has already sprung up around this film, as if it were some kind of landmark in the history of gay cinema. However, with the passage of time, I suspect that *Maurice*'s exalted reputation will fade.

Mr. Skeffington* (U.S. 1944 B&W)

Mr. Skeffington is an extremely well-acted and well-written film about an ill-omened marriage. About the only thing wrong with the movie is its rather too bombastic music score. Claude Rains is the saintly husband, Bette Davis his vain and selfish wife. She gives a quite unusual performance, speaking in an oddly breathless voice, as if she were doing an impression of Billie Burke. The character Bette portrays is obsessed with a fear of growing old, which makes it fairly easy for gay men to relate to her. In which connection I should probably mention that the plot spans thirty years and that co-star Walter Abel, cast as Bette's unmarried cousin, never seems to age a whit, shows little or no interest in feminine companionship, and gets to utter all the bitchiest lines. However, this is definitely a gay cult film (with the ineffable Bette) rather than primary camp.

Mommie Dearest* (U.S. 1981 C)

Like many gay men, I'm a devoted Joan Crawford fan. Thus I'm almost inclined to disqualify myself from reviewing this movie, on the grounds that I didn't take kindly to her daughter's whiny, badly written hatchet job. Much of what Christina Crawford complains about in her book was fairly common practice among the stricter parents of the Forties and the Fifties. In those days people were

BETTE DAVIS (1908–1989) in a scene from *Mr. Skeffington* (Warner Brothers 1944). Arguably *the* pre-eminent gay camp/cult icon star: see the 22 Davis films reviewed in this book. "She would probably have been burned as a witch if she had lived two or three hundred years ago. She gives the curious feeling of being charged with power which can find no ordinary outlet."—E. Arnot Robertson.

much more worried that a privileged kid would be "spoiled," not abused. It's easy to write a book like *Mommie Dearest*; by concentrating on a handful of isolated incidents, distorting some things and leaving out others, anyone can make his or her parents sound like tyrannical monsters.

The film's Christina, from junior high school onward, is delineated by Diana Scarwid, who delivers what seems a heavily sedated performance. As Joan Crawford, Faye Dunaway is quite simply wrong for the part. With garishly painted eyebrows, a mouth like a scarlet slash, and costumes seemingly designed to make her resemble some she-creature out of an old horror picture, Faye can't help but look silly, grotesque, and artificial. In other words, she's ready-made camp.

Though the script is superficially faithful to Christina's account, the screenwriters have included a whole slew of rationalizations in hopes of explaining Joan's behavior and creating a more credible movie plot. Somehow this only serves to make the storyline fuzzier. The film seldom connects with Crawford's life as we know it. In the final analysis, the film isn't really about Joan Crawford; instead it's about Faye Dunaway portraying the declining years of some barely specified actress from Hollywood's Golden Age. (And were they really declining years? I've always felt that Crawford's most interesting movies were all made after, not before, M-G-M let her go.)

If this movie bores me (and it does), perhaps I should put the blame on Frank Perry's plodding direction. The flamboyant talents of Ken Russell are what it takes to do justice to the life and career of Joan Crawford. As for Christina, what Joan may or may not have done to her is nothing, compared to what she deserves: being ignored.

---

*Mondo Trasho** (U.S. 1969 B&W)

Mondo Trasho, a highly experimental film directed by John Waters, hastens to let us know it intends to offend. Waters starts right out by showing us chickens getting their heads cut off.

The heroine of the movie is Mary Vivian Pearce, who, for some obscure reason, is got up in the style of a Thirties glamour girl. We watch her take a bus to the park, where she feeds the bugs on the sidewalk with bits of raw hamburger. (Aboard the bus, she reads *Hollywood Babylon*.) Then she is set upon by a foot fetishist, who sucks on her toes while she dreams that she's Cinderella trying on the glass slipper.

On her way home, she gets hit by a car. The driver is Divine, who then wheels her all over town in a wheelchair (a gift from the Virgin Mary, who inexplicably materializes in a laundromat). The girls get dragged off to an asylum, where co-star Mink Stole does a topless dance and is promptly gangbanged. (These unseemly activities are disrupted by a second appearance of the Virgin Mary.) Pearce falls into the hands of a mad doctor, who cuts off her feet and replaces them with the hideous, oversized tootsies of a creature from some B-grade monster movie. No more glass slippers for *her*!

There's scarcely a scene in the film that doesn't run on too long, but this provides ample room for the wonderfully eclectic music score (featuring several golden oldies which I hadn't heard since my childhood). Divine is so young, she looks a little like Jayne Mansfield—not exactly fat, so much as charmingly chunky. The film contains no more than a bare minimum of dialogue and might as well be classified as a silent picture. Still, it's weirdly entertaining. I like it better than *Pink Flamingos*, which it predates by three years.

---

*Morocco** (U.S. 1930 B&W)

Gary Cooper is a French Legionnaire in *Morocco*. All the girls want to get in his pants. When he marches into town, the Arab women make eyes at him. One girl even doffs her veil, granting him a glimpse of her face. Another poses provocatively beneath a human skull that's perched on a post. All this attention greatly annoys his commanding officer, who seems, for some implausible reason, to want to keep Gary pure.

Marlene Dietrich sails into port looking desolate, her veil like a wisp of fog trailing across her face. She's come to entertain at the local night club. She appears onstage in a top hat, white tie, and tails. This causes Gary to sit up and take notice. When she kisses a female customer full on the lips, he applauds all the louder.

In one of the film's most erotic scenes, she goes through the cabaret peddling apples. Cooper sure knows his way around one of those. He and Marlene inhabit this movie so gracefully, we end up inhabiting it right along with them. *Morocco* is more than camp; it transcends its corniest plot developments by treating them as if they were freshly minted. Marlene agrees to marry a millionaire (Adolphe Menjou), but then walks out in the middle of his posh engagement party, because she's heard a rumor that Cooper's been wounded. She tracks Gary down, but he feigns indifference to her. Then she chances to notice that he's neatly carved her name in the wooden table where she found him seated. When his regiment goes out on patrol, she tramps along behind with the rest of the camp followers, kicking off her fancy high-heeled shoes to cross the burning sands barefoot. The director, Josef von Sternberg, decorates the picture with sultry patterns of tropical light and shade. Which means it really looks like a movie. And when it's over, we feel like we've really seen something.

*Motorcycle Gang** (U.S. 1957 B&W)

John Ashley wears a black leather jacket in *Motorcycle Gang*; that in itself signifies that the film is of more than passing interest. He plays a bad boy in this one. He's got a gift for such roles. And he's even able to look halfway natural pretending to ride a motorbike in process shots. (I also like the fastidious way he pronounces the "t" in "often.")

The plot of this opus is somewhat reminiscent of *Ben-Hur*, but with Harleys instead of chariots. Comic relief is provided by Carl "Alfalfa" Switzer, many years past the height of his fame as one of the Little Rascals and two years short of his premature demise. (According to Kenneth Anger's *Hollywood Babylon*, he was "shot to death in a dope burn.") At the climax, Ashley's "gang" (four cyclists) drunkenly terrorize the entire population of a town (roughly a half-dozen people). Yes, this is definitely a low-budget enterprise, but Ashley pretending to be in his cups is rather amusing. Just a whisper of swish, if you know what I mean.

Multiple Maniacs* (U.S. 1970 B&W)

Multiple Maniacs, a John Waters grungefest, is unusual in the sense that it makes an overt political statement. But the important thing is that the film made me laugh.

The opening scenes take place at a freak show known as Lady Divine's Cavalcade of Perversions. One of the star attractions is a pair of gay men French-kissing, the sight of which makes the audience of straight onlookers cringe with disgust. ("Eeuw! Look at them! Why can't they like women?!")

The plot gets underway when Divine discovers that her boyfriend has been untrue. (Edith Massey is the bearer of these bad tidings.) So, clad in a tight-fitting sweater and leopard-skin skirt, she sets out to settle his hash. On her way, she encounters the Infant of Prague, who leads her to a cathedral, where she prays for guidance. Her orisons, however, are interrupted by a lesbian parishioner (Mink Stole), who gives her a "rosary job" right in the church. (This may have been the inspiration for Linda Blair's famous crucifix scene in *The Exorcist*.)

Divine gets raped by a giant papier-maché lobster. (Or is it supposed to be a cockroach?) She also boasts about killing cops and claims to want to assassinate the entire Reagan family. (Mink, meanwhile, fantasizes about doing something dreadful to Tricia Nixon.) The murder scenes in this movie, however, are not at all convincing. Divine "stabs" people by waving a knife in front of them. A maniac of this sort is a danger to no one but herself.

The Music Lovers* (G.B. 1971 C)

The Music Lovers, Ken Russell's biographical film based on the life of Peter Ilyich Tchaikovsky, begins with Richard Chamberlain and Christopher Gable merrily tumbling into a cozy, blood-red bed. Chamberlain is the great composer, Gable his voluptuous, somewhat vulgar-looking male lover. We cut to the following morning. "Peter, you're getting too careless," his brother, Modeste, warns. "Your music will never be played! You'll be stigmatized for life!" And, sure enough, the great Nicolai Rubinstein (depicted in the film as being a pompous pettifogger) contemptuously denounces Tchaikovsky's music as being "Woman's stuff!"

As biography all this may sound too pat to be believable, yet it comes across as compelling drama. Credible, too—such as the scene wherein Gable implores Chamberlain to face reality and not embark on a (to say the least) unfortunate marriage to a raving nympho played by Glenda Jackson. Tchaikovsky, however, is seeking a "cure": the respectability of married life. Like his boyfriend, we know that no good can come of it.

Russell's direction captures the morbid essence of Russian romanticism. As expected, there are many bravura passages: audacious match-ups of music and phantasmagorical visual image. Most flamboyant of all is the climactic rendition of the 1812 Festival Overture, the cannon blasts of which are seen to decapitate most of the principal characters. We're reminded of the fact that this piece was performed at Nixon's second inauguration. In that case, the heads didn't roll till later on.

My Little Chickadee* (U.S. 1940 B&W)

My Little Chickadee is, at least technically, a western. And as westerns go, it is most unusual, since the star of the show is Mae West. In the opening scene we find her riding in a stagecoach. Margaret Hamilton (the Wicked Witch from *The Wizard of Oz*) is also on board. She is cast as a stuffy old prude, who frowns disapprovingly as Mae files her nails. The coach is held up by the Masked Bandit (Joseph Calleia), who kidnaps our heroine. She escapes. "I was in a tight spot, but I managed to wiggle out of it," she assures her Aunt Lou (Ruth Donnelly).

Margaret Hamilton sees the Masked Bandit crawling out of Mae's bedroom window. She leaps to lurid, but appropriate conclusions and gets poor Mae run out of town (until such time as she can return, "respectable and married," as the judge puts it). Mae travels to Greasewood City via train. Margaret Hamilton goes along, to stir up the Greasewood Ladies' Vigilante Committee against her. En route, the train picks up W. C. Fields, an actor

I have never liked (he's a great favorite of heterosexual males, however).

"Nice day," he says to Mae.

"Is it?" she replies.

In Greasewood she sings a song called "Willie of the Valley." She also encounters Dick Foran (looking portly, but pretty), whose voice trails off in a dither every time he looks her full in the face. He persuades her to accompany him on a visit to the local one-room schoolhouse. She steps in to teach the arithmetic class (the regular instructor had a nervous breakdown): "Addition is when you take one thing and add it to another and you get two, and two and two is four, and five'll get you ten, if you know how to work it." Earlier, Dick had exhorted her to stay out of the saloon: "It's a sordid place and full of temptations."

"I generally avoid temptation, unless I can't resist it," she brusquely replies. By the end of the film, she more or less conforms to community standards. She saves W. C. from being lynched, persuades the Masked Bandit to return his ill-gotten gains, and even suggests to the townsfolk that they use the money to build a church. This picture really isn't about sex; it's about Mae West taking everything that's anti-sex down a peg or two. I can relate to that.

Myra Breckinridge* (U.S. 1970 C)

In a public toilet I recently noticed the following bit of graffiti: "Myra lives! I am she!" The words were printed in letters so miniscule, I almost needed a magnifying glass to read them. At the same time, it occurred to me that I might almost have scrawled the message myself, since, like Raquel Welch, I am *Myra Breckinridge*.

Or, rather, I might as well be. As practically everybody knows by now, Myra was originally Myron, a homosexual film critic herein portrayed by Rex Reed. The ministrations of a surgeon (John Carradine) in the movie's opening scene transform him into Myra, a bitchy teacher of "Posture and Empathy" at a school of dramatic arts. (Reed, I hasten to mention, does not vanish from the film at this point; he continues on, functioning in the capacity of Myra's memory, alter ego, invisible second self, etc.) Myra's hidden agenda is the demasculinization of the American male; the continued reign of patriarchy, she fears, could literally bring about the end of the world. This movie has a lot of important things to say about "traditional family values" in an age of population explosion. One thing's for sure: there is nothing in this picture which could possibly lead to an increase in population.

The film was based on a bestselling novel by Gore Vidal. He disowned the movie, though it certainly hews to his narrative line with scrupulous fidelity. His name still appears in the opening titles, which, furthermore, assign top billing to Mae West for her smallish role as Letitia Van Allen, a talent agent who sleeps with her clients. When my best friend and I read Vidal's novel, we pictured a British actress (Hazel Court) in this part, but Hollywood didn't see it our way. Miss West, despite her advanced age, does have some memorable moments, one of them with Tom Selleck (an obscure bit player in those days). In her best scene, she sings a number entitled "You've Gotta Taste All the Fruit."

The most notorious scene in the book was Myra's rape (with a dildo, of course) of a muscular, ultra-butch pupil named Rusty Godowski. In the film, this sequence concludes with what has to be the screen's longest orgasm, completely interpreted in phallic symbolism and vintage film clips. I once ran this tape for some gay friends who actually viewed this scene in the spirit of pornography, even to the point of rewinding and obsessively watching it over again. For erotic stimulation, I much prefer an earlier scene: the one in which Rex Reed beats off while contemplating frankfurters, peanut butter, and whipped cream.

As for Raquel, her most memorable moment is a lesbian love scene with Farrah Fawcett, who, like Selleck, was not yet a star when this movie was made. *Myra Breckinridge* was, in many respects, a motion picture far ahead of its time. Bear in mind that it was released in the summer of 1970, and that *Life* magazine ran a Fourth of July editorial declaring the film to be representative of all that was wrong with America. I am able to conceive of no higher praise. It is my belief that the book which you hold in your hands could have been written by Myra Breckinridge. And it is my fondest wish that you, dear reader, will agree with me on this.

The Nanny   (G.B. 1965 B&W)

The concept of Bette Davis playing the title role in a movie called *The Nanny* sounds very ominous, indeed—especially considering that the film is from Hammer, a British company specializing in horror pictures. Davis looks appropriately drab in the part. She wears a frumpy uniform and has eyebrows that look like they've been pasted on her face. In the early scenes, we notice she has a knack for making adults as dependent on her as children—even more so, perhaps, since the only child in her care is a morbid little chap (William Dix) given to playing ghoulish pranks and generally expressing "an inborn antipathy towards middle-aged females." He's bitter towards Nanny because she accidentally drowned his little sister in the bathtub, and then allowed him to take the rap. Now she's fixing to do away with him, as well. Everyone (including the audience, at first) thinks he's just a lying little brat. Aunt Pen (Jill Bennett) slowly gets wise to Nanny's game, but has a heart attack before she can warn anybody. (This gives Davis a chance to replay her famous *Little Foxes* scene, withholding the medicine and refusing to be of assistance.) And why is Nanny so homicidal? Is it because she's afraid of being sacked or put in jail? Mercy, no. "I've never been one for self," she says. She just wants to safeguard the reputations of "all those nannies who have devoted their lives to taking care of other people's children. They're the ones I'm thinking about."

This is a very tidily constructed suspense film, with excellent performances from all concerned. Perhaps it's heresy to say so (this is, above all else, a Bette Davis film), but I would single out Bennett and Dix as the best. The cast also includes Pamela Franklin, one of my all-time favorite juveniles.

A Night in Paradise   (U.S. 1946 C)

A Night in Paradise is a typically elaborate Arabian Nights fantasy, steeped in exotic opulence, fairy tale lyricism, and plenty of lush, flamboyant color. As befits the film's title, the plot unfolds like a story told in a dream. The numerous anachronisms at first seem incongruously campy, but even they fit into the wild and whimsical scheme of things. Leading lady Merle Oberon is suitably vain, imperious, and haughty. She's got her Princess of Baghdad routine down pat, as if she's been taking lessons from Maria Montez. Merle's the betrothed of King Croesus, who, as embodied by Thomas Gomez, is strictly a comic opera monarch. "My gold!" he enthuses with lustful ardor. "I've guarded it all my life. We'll guard it together! We can take turns!" This litany of courtship leaves Merle unmoved. She's distracted by the presence of Turhan Bey, the Omar Sharif of the Forties, who hangs around the palace spinning fables in his role as the legendary Aesop. There are further complications: Gale Sondergaard, as a slinky sorceress, enticingly entreats both the male principals, appearing before them in puffs of smoke, in flickering flames, and in each and every reflecting surface available.

We learn something new every day. History would have us believe that Aesop was crippled, hideous, and hunchbacked. Turns out, however, he merely disguised himself thusly, supposing, quite rightly, that people would never take him seriously if they learned of his resemblance to Turhan Bey. This actor is seven different kinds of cute. Flared, curling lashes encircle his big, round eyes, which alternate between two expressions: a cool, calm, come-hither gaze and the look of an injured puppy dog. His smile (actually, it's more like a smirk) is full of ironic detachment and sensual self-confidence. This picture affords us ample opportunity to ogle his shapely ankles and well-formed forearms.

Like most early Technicolor extravaganzas, this one's a study in contrasts between hot and cold hues. This opposition's incarnated in Merle's bewitchingly beautiful person: pale skin, black hair, and blue eyes interact with ruby-red lip rouge, violet eye shadow, and a vast array of gaudy garments. Her thin, wispy voice has a deeper, darker register that's all atremble with passion. At the grand finale she and Turhan are being led at spear point to the brink of a precipice. (They've been condemned to death for exposing the Delphic oracle as a phony.) Just when all hope seems lost, the lovers inexplicably disappear; they're whisked out of harm's way by Sondergaard's magic. Presumably she's wafted them to her own enchanted realm, there to spend eternity peering seductively from out of TV picture-tubes.

---

*Now, Voyager** (U.S. 1942 B&W)

Now, Voyager is probably the most widely beloved Bette Davis film. It's clearly a cult favorite for Davis fans of any and every sexual persuasion. The film's credentials are impeccable: it's based on a novel by Olive Higgins Prouty, the author of *Stella Dallas*, and the director is Irving Rapper, who later had the honor of helming *The Christine Jorgensen Story*.

Davis is cast as a dumpy spinster, hopelessly dominated by her dragon of a mother (Gladys Cooper). Along comes a helpful psychiatrist (Claude Rains), whose therapy somehow transforms the ugly duckling into a swan. Then she promptly falls head-over-heels in love with a married man (Paul Henreid).

Davis gives one of her very best and least affected performances. Cooper, meanwhile, is appropriately formidable as the gorgon. For me, the real delight is in the supporting cast: Franklin Pangborn, very aptly cast as the social director on a cruise ship; Mary Wickes as a no-nonsense nurse; Lee Patrick, reeling off reams of exposition so smoothly, you hardly even notice. And I also spotted Reed Hadley, one of my favorite B-movie heartthrobs, in a bit part as one of Bette's many admirers (once she's a woman of the world).

Old Acquaintance   (U.S. 1943 B&W)

Old Acquaintance casts Bette Davis as a smart young thing who writes books that get brilliant reviews but really don't sell very well. Miriam Hopkins portrays a rival novelist: a pretentiously affected, effervescently melodramatic airhead who apparently wants to become the new Barbara Cartland. She succeeds all too well. This movie is so uproariously campy that I'd been laughing myself sick for about an hour before it suddenly dawned on me that maybe the comedy wasn't intentional. Hopkins doesn't have all that many scenes, but she steals the show, just the same. She huffs and puffs her way through the movie, rolling her eyes dementedly. The plot spans almost two decades. By the final scene, these girls are supposed to be forty-two. Davis, biting her consonants and smiling bitchily, is wearing glasses by this time and has a white streak in her hair, plus a handsome, devoted, decorative young suitor (Gig Young). As for Miriam, middle age has made her so outrageous that Bette finally has to grab her by the shoulders and shake her.

The Old Maid*   (U.S. 1939 B&W)

In this movie Bette Davis and Miriam Hopkins are fighting over George Brent, who's as puffy and corpulent as ever. When Miriam jilts him, he finds comfort with Bette, who, somewhat later, discovers she's pregnant. Owing to the strictures of the Production Code, we are unable to piece this narrative detail together till George is dead and the kid is five years old. Such extreme discretion does tend to garble the storyline, but what the hell. Anyway, Miriam brings the girl up and gives her a name. Bette grows old and bitter debating with Miriam as to whom George loved the most. The kid grows up to be Jane Bryan and remains quite ignorant of her actual parentage. The most surprising thing about this far-fetched soap opera is the fact that it's based on a novel by Edith Wharton. Bette's old age make-up isn't convincing. Indeed, the campiest moment

MIRIAM HOPKINS (1902–1972), shown here in a publicity release photo from *A Gentle-man After Dark* (Edward Small Prod. 1942). Her brittle style has aged into camp.

is when Jane says that Bette is "old and hideous and dried-up," whereas Bette, standing nearby, has seldom looked prettier, her hair upswept in a Gibson girl coiffure and with huge, liquid eyes like those of a waif in a Walter Keane painting.

The Outlaw* (U.S. 1943 B&W)

The Outlaw, directed by Howard Hughes, affords us a public glimpse into the private obsessions of a noted recluse. As an "auteur," he's pretty crude, but at least he's got a basic understanding of how a story should be told. As expected, he shows a strong grasp of macho behavior patterns. Surprisingly enough, he's also skilled at explicating more subtle psychological tensions. And, of course, he's remarkably firm and forceful in his portrayal of sexual implications. Anyone who knows anything about Jane Russell is well aware that this was her first picture, that it was banned for alleged indecency, and that her opening scene takes place in a barn. Her entrance is oddly fragmented. At first all we see is the glint of her eyes in the shadows. It takes a while before we even perceive that she's female. Twice she lunges at Billy the Kid (Jack Buetel) with a pitchfork. Then, for good measure, she lunges it at the camera, and at all those dirty-minded, slavering voyeurs out in the audience. Then she and her antagonist tumble into the hay, and the rest is left to our imagination. She and Buetel are constantly trying to kill one another, but they always seem to end up screwing, instead.

The director is preoccupied with the big bazooms on his leading lady. At one point she's bound and spread-eagled, her wrists secured with wet strips of rawhide, which grow more taut in the sun's heat, while she pants with thirst and heaves her chest. Later she falls into a pool of water. Anything, apparently, to give us a look at those tits. And, perhaps for an added touch of culture, her signature theme is taken from Tchaikovsky's "Pathetique."

Despite his reputation as a womanizer, Hughes ultimately shunts Jane off to the sidelines of the drama. The climax goes beyond machismo, into the realm of latent homosexuality. Doc Holliday (Walter Huston) and Billy the Kid square off for a duel. They've agreed to pull their pistols as soon as a nearby clock strikes the hour. When the time comes, the accompanying montage is so distractingly brilliant, we forget to count the cuckoos. Billy doesn't draw his gun. Doc attempts to goad him, even going so far as to nick the boy's ears. Still the Kid refuses to defend himself, having decided that Doc's the one he loves the most, after all. Arriving at this realization, Holliday undergoes a similar change of heart. Tchaikovsky's Sixth Symphony gives way to Tchaikovsky's Fifth Symphony, and it looks as though the two guys are going to ride off into the sunset together (Tchaikovsky would most certainly have approved). But wait! Pat Garrett (Thomas Mitchell), Doc's longtime buddy, has stood by and watched this scene unfold. Now he sees fit to intrude upon the proceedings, indulging in a grotesque display of jealousy. He carries on like a wife whose husband is fixing to ditch her for a younger woman. In what can only be called a fit of passion, he shoots Doc dead. Hell hath no fury, etc.

We had our suspicions well before this. Jack Buetel, who is not an actor, is presented as a homoerotic icon. He swings his hips a good deal more than Jane swings hers. His large, dark, liquid eyes are cool, yet they smolder. He wears tight pants that button along the side of one leg. The brim of his hat is curled in such a way as to suggest that he's one cocky dude. Arrogantly, he blows a smoke ring. He eyeballs his betters with impertinent disdain. While recovering from a gunshot wound, the dear boy catches a chill. In an effort to warm him, Jane takes off her clothes and gets into bed with him. First, however, she swipes the ring that he's wearing and slips it on one of her own fingers. Thus they are "married"; Forties community standards must needs be propitiated.

Outrageous! * (Canada 1977 C)

Despite its lack of surface polish, *Outrageous!* is a fairly engaging depiction of the loving friendship shared by a plump drag queen (Craig Russell) and a deinstitutionalized female schizophrenic (Hollis McLaren). This rough-edged Canadian-made feature became a cult item and was sufficiently successful to inspire a sequel (*Too Outrageous!*), made ten years later. Russell's an impressive impressionist, especially when impersonating female singers such as Channing and Streisand. As for McLaren, we can sure tell she's crazy, and not just because the screenplay says so. This is one disturbed woman, but at least she's always able to get all the Valium she needs. McLaren's performance is genuinely moving. Still, I've got to admit what interested me most were Russell's men friends.

Paris Is Burning* (U.S. 1990 C)

Though I live deep, deep in the Midwest, I subscribe to *The Village Voice*. And that's why I appreciated *Paris Is Burning*, a documentary about a dance craze called voguing. I had read about voguing in the *Voice*, and now, having seen the movie, I know what it is.

Voguing takes its name from *Vogue* magazine. The dance consists of striking a series of fashion model poses. Unlike most current dances, it can be performed to classical music (I heard a little bit of *Aida* in the movie). The practitioners are usually drag queens, mostly very young and from minority ethnic backgrounds. They group themselves into gangs named after Paris fashion houses. I am not making any of this up.

As documentaries go, this one's pretty dramatic. It's even got a surprise shock ending: the youngest and most beautiful of the drag queens turns out to have been murdered in the course of the filming. Along the way, ironies abound. At drag balls, prizes are given for how convincingly you can go back into the closet. Wearing straight attire is not enough; you have to actually seem that way. On the other hand, it transpires that some of the men are so good at being women, they give real women lessons in modeling and femininity. (Once again, I feel I must assure you I'm not kidding.)

A final word of caution: this movie should not be confused with the similarly titled *Is Paris Burning?* starring Leslie Caron and Charles Boyer. These kids have probably never even heard of Leslie Caron.

Pink Flamingos* (U.S. 1973 C)

In his recent work, John Waters eloquently celebrates the joys of being different. His is a benign philosophy with profoundly subversive implications. However, in one of his earliest features, *Pink Flamingos*, his extreme esthetic of sleaze and ugliness is presented in terms so crude and raw, viewing the film is like being clubbed repeatedly over the head. In this opus, his principal inspirations appear to have been drawn from porno and low-budget gore flicks. My main interest in the picture is historical: we get to see what members of the Waters stock company (many of them now late and lamented) were like, circa 1972. Divine was more feminine, more girlishly trashy, more content to merely do Mae West impressions. Edith Massey was sweet and charming, as always. To establish the contours of her character, Mink Stole relies upon superficial visual details, such as rhinestone-studded eyeglass frames and hair that's been dyed a decidedly unnatural auburn. David Locharie (a close friend and confidant of Waters in those days) is the only person present who gives what might be called a performance.

To put it briefly, the narrative depicts a competition for the dubious distinction of being "the filthiest family in the world." The contest is between a set of "good" murderers (Divine's funky gang of cannibals and grunge addicts) and a couple of "bad," hypocritical, avaricious dope-pushers (Locharie and Stole), who've also got a baby-selling racket going on the side. Toward the end, the movie touches heights (or depths) of dream logic and sublime irrationality. Divine and her sex-crazed son break into the home of their opponents, where they proceed to lick and drool on the furniture. Consequently, when Stole and Locharie come back, their chairs and sofa eject them; the cushions pop up and knock them to the floor. At the climax, Divine invites reporters from the various supermarket tabloids to watch and take pictures while she tars, feathers, and finally kills her two enemies.

But, let's face it, no one goes to see *Pink Flamingos* for the sake of its surrealism. Instead, they go for the grossness. For instance, they go to see a naked man perform tricks with his anal muscles, making his asshole purse and pucker like a pair of lips. There's also an onscreen act of fellatio: Divine goes down on the actor portraying her son. Thus she manages to simultaneously be both incestuous (in the context of the fictive plot) and homosexual (in the context of reality). And, of course, there's also the bizarre and famous denouement, in which Divine devours freshly-laid dog-shit, winks at the camera, and sticks out her tongue at us. Is she a good enough actress to convince us that it tastes good? The answer, of course, is no, but it's interesting to watch her try.

Please Don't Touch Me!* (U.S. 1959 C)

This movie begins with a pretty redhead in a gingham dress being attacked by a bearded stud wearing a sailor hat. *Please Don't Touch Me!* screams the opening title. The advertising copy from the poster art provides us with further information: "Why did marriage have to be like this? CRUEL! UGLY! Why couldn't it bring me the happiness I longed for?"

Well, honey, maybe it has something to do with that form-fitting silver lamé jumpsuit you've poured yourself into. Or maybe it's your age-conscious mom, who's terrified you might get pregnant and make her a grandmother. I don't want to hear a word against your husband, who buys you gorgeous Frederick's of Hollywood lingerie and keeps himself in a constant state of semi-undress, thereby adding immeasurably to the visual interest of the film. He's wonderfully patient as you keep on complaining of headaches and offering to get up and fix him a sandwich. I love the part where he gets frustrated and tears your black lace panties apart with his teeth. If only he had a little more hair on his chest . . .

Mom drags our heroine to a shrink, who dredges up memories of that rape we witnessed earlier. The seriousness of the moment is undercut by the harmonica music on the soundtrack. Turns out that no actual penetration occurred, after all. Hypnosis reveals Vicki's frigidity stems from the fact that her husband wears a ring just like the one worn by the would-be rapist. And, when hubby turns out the light, it reminds her of when the attacker put his hands over her eyes. The solution is two-pronged: Men should eschew jewelry. And make love with the lights on. I don't have a problem with that.

Polyester* (U.S. 1981 C)

Polyester is a satirical send-up of those tacky, deeply reactionary melodramas of sin and retribution which enjoyed a certain disreputable popularity in the Fifties and Sixties. Divine, the famous 300-pound transvestite, is cast in the sort of masochistic role which, once upon a time, would probably have been played by someone like Dorothy Malone or Susan Hayward. When first encountered, she's clad only in undergarments. We perceive that she is preoccupied with matters olfactory: we watch as she shaves her armpits and applies a deodorant spray. This is merely in keeping with the picture's promotional gimmick, which is called "Odorama" and consists of ten haunting fragrances preserved for posterity on a souvenir scratch-'n'-sniff card.

Divine delineates a noble heroine whose name is Francine Fishpaw: a decent, God-fearing Baltimore housewife who's been burdened with more than her share of earthly woes. Her husband operates a porno theatre which is currently presenting an opus entitled *My Burning Bush*. Her son is a sadistic foot-fetishist who stomps on the delicate tootsies of hapless female shoppers at the local mall. Her daughter earns spending money by performing lewd dances for the amusement of the boys at school. Worse yet, the misguided girl has been impregnated by her punk rocker boyfriend, who, with her help, makes a practice of hot-rodding recklessly down the street, swatting innocent pedestrians on the backside with a broom.

With the help of her dearest chum, a mentally retarded cleaning lady named "Cuddles" (Edith Massey) who's inherited a vast fortune from a former employer, Francine discovers that her beloved husband is carrying on with another woman: his slut of a secretary (Mink Stole). Cuddles spies the illicit lovers checking in at the White Gables Motel. "At first I thought he was walking a dog," she later clucks disapprovingly. Her marriage in ruins, Francine seeks solace in the arms of Todd Tomorrow (Tab Hunter). Though she meets him while they both are rubbernecking at the scene of a grisly auto accident, Todd is actually quite a classy catch. He owns a ritzy drive-in theatre which is featuring a triple bill of Marguerite Duras movies. The snack bar serves caviar, champagne,

TAB HUNTER (1931–   ), shown here in his 1950s incarnation of America's All-American boy, later played in such camp classics as *Lust in the Dust* and *Polyester*.

and oysters. Formal attire is de rigueur. Fauré piano music is played between shows. It's all so elegant, Francine just about swoons.

(Oh, Francine, if only you knew!)

Director John Waters is particularly cogent in his observations regarding right-wing pressure groups. Anti-smut crusaders are picketing on the sidewalk in front of Francine's home. Pitilessly, they pelt her with rocks when she begs them to leave her family in peace. Meanwhile, at the neighborhood abortion clinic, her daughter suffers similar abuse at the hands of fanatical right-to-lifers. "What if Mary 'n' Joseph had an abortion?" they ask rhetorically, as they pummel their pregnant victim.

Divine is absurdly compelling in her overplayed, hysterical reactions to disaster. At any rate, she hits all the notes. Mink Stole is another distinctive screen presence. With her hair arranged in undernourished Bo Derek cornrows, she resembles a crazily debauched Audrey Hepburn. However, it's Edith Massey who steals the show. She's a snaggle-toothed saint who, despite her utter lack of acting ability, somehow strikes a note of genuine pathos (the only one in the movie!), touching our hearts and winning our affection through her simpleminded sincerity, her dim-witted devotion and unswerving loyalty to poor, embattled "Fwancine." As for Tab Hunter: it's just too bad that they don't give Oscars for good sportsmanship.

The Private Lives of Elizabeth and Essex* (U.S. 1939 C)

Bette Davis as Good Queen Bess? Any film that offers such a spectacle is sure to be a lasting source of inspiration to female impersonators everywhere. And The Private Lives of Elizabeth and Essex more than fulfills its promise, at least as regards turgid, overripe dialogue. At one point Elizabeth thusly addresses a portrait of the Earl of Essex: "Robert! Robert! I don't know which I hate the most—you, for making me love you, or myself, for needing you so!" Meanwhile, Essex (portrayed by Errol Flynn) has this to say about Elizabeth: "I love her! I hate her! I adore her!" As for their "private lives," they are mainly spent talking politics. And the politics of these two are no more coherent than their emotions.

Davis gives a twitchy, fidgety performance. She looks almost monstrous, her cold, heavy-lidded fish-eyes balefully glaring from a face of chalky, corpse-like whiteness. (Stylized lighting effects are the main dramatic strength of the production.) Flynn is his usual dashing self in the role of a rather ambiguous hero. Essex, however, at least comes off looking better than Sir Walter Raleigh, who, far from being the chivalrous paragon of historical tradition, is herein portrayed by Vincent Price!

The Prodigal* (U.S. 1955 C)

The Prodigal, a Fifties Biblical epic derived from the parable of the prodigal son, has at least one significant distinction in its favor: it's the only film I'm aware of that's based on an original story by Jesus Christ. Too bad they couldn't get Him to write the screenplay, as well.

If that sounds blasphemous, my only excuse is that the film itself is more blasphemous still. In point of fact, the film seems inspired, not by theological concerns, but by purely commercial motives. ('Twas ever thus.) This movie plays a cynical, hypocritical game that's as old as Hollywood: condemning sex, while at the same time dishing it up in terrific abundance. This is the kind of picture that Jesse Helms and Jerry Falwell would no doubt like to see studios cranking out today. Little do they realize that it's a quintessentially homosexual film. Our enemies lack any feeling for camp, or for esthetic irony in any other of its various forms. This, I think, could prove to be their Achilles heel.

Jesus never specified precisely what it was that lured the prodigal son away from home. This movie hastens to inform us it was actually a pagan love priestess portrayed by Lana Turner in an assortment of hubba-hubba peekaboo gowns that she apparently inherited from Maria Montez. The very sight of Lana Turner strutting around with a ceremonial candlestick in each hand and a faraway look in her eyes is sufficient to cause a certain type of gay man (me, for example) to collapse in a paroxysm of helpless mirth. The film provides her with a prepubescent protégée who's ordained to succeed her as high priestess of Astarte. In one of the funnier scenes, Lana gives the child instruction in the fine art of applying eye makeup.

Lana is also in charge of the temple prostitutes (she's a sort of divine madam, as it were). For a Fifties flick, the film is surprisingly explicit with regard to what sort of activities temple prostitutes engaged in. It has always been my understanding that a sizable percentage of these people were boys, but the only male prostitute I noticed was in a street scene, at a marketplace where servants and "companions" may be purchased. He's cute, muscular, stripped to the waist, and we get to see him twice. Plus there's a studly blonde human sacrifice, also clad in revealing attire, whom Lana leads to a perch overlooking the temple fire pit. Good-naturedly enough, he dives right in.

The prodigal son, played by Edmund Purdom, can't keep his clothes on for very long at a time. In the opening reel we find him returning from a journey and eager to wash the dust of the road from his firm, yet supple body. In the concluding reel, he leads a rebellion. The mob breaks down the doors of the temple. Lana attempts to placate them by assuming a prayerful pose, but they promptly stone her to death, anyway. Like a prize in a shooting gallery, she's knocked from her pedestal, down into the aforementioned lake of fire, where she vanishes in a whoosh of roaring flame.

This is a movie that's interesting to look at and listen to, rigorously color-coordinated with a drop-dead sense of style on a succession of picturesque soundstages. There's scarcely an outdoor scene in the film that wasn't lensed indoors. It's a typically glossy M-G-M production, which means that even the dungeons are pretty. I blush to admit that I liked it. So sue me; I don't care.

Queen Christina* (U.S. 1933 B&W)

There are those who've tried to tell me that Queen Christina is Garbo's greatest film, but I knew I was in camp territory from scene one, wherein a soldier on a battlefield asks a fallen figure who he is and the dying man replies, "I *was* King of Sweden." Cut to his successor, a tiny little princess whom we know will become the title character. We are astonished that M-G-M didn't man-

GRETA GARBO (1905–1990), Swedish-born star of several memorable 1930s Hollywood films. Shown here disguised in men's clothes in *Queen Christina* (MGM 1933), playing the 17th century Swedish sovereign who abdicated her throne.

age to find a child actress with a Swedish accent. How can this clearly American kid possibly grow up to be Greta Garbo?

We are told that she was raised to be a boy. Garbo is constantly being mistaken for a male in this movie—an error she does absolutely nothing to correct. (Early on, she even seems to have a lesbian thing for one of her ladies-in-waiting.) When her chancellor warns that she'll die an old maid, she pertly replies, "I shall die a bachelor."

Garbo's leading man here is John Gilbert, whose career was supposedly scuttled by the advent of talkies and the unsuitability of his speaking voice. He sounds perfectly fine to me. In fact, he impressed me more favorably here than in any of his silent classics. Laboring under the misconception that he's dealing with a man, Gilbert avidly insists that Garbo should share his bed for the night, and is highly put out when Garbo turns him down. They end up sleeping together anyway. And, the following morning, Gilbert's valet (Akim Tamiroff) seems perplexed to learn that the "gentlemen" have made up their minds to stay in bed together all day. This is all very heterosexual romance, no doubt, but it has possibilities.

Queen of Outer Space* (U.S. 1958 C)

Queen of Outer Space sounds like it might be the title of a gay porno novel—something about hunky, well-hung astronauts exploring new frontiers with one another. Well, it's not porno, but it is pretty campy. And the rocketship does have an all-male crew.

The film stars Zsa Zsa Gabor as a lovelorn scientist on the planet Venus (naturally). The title monarch has declared war on men, drat the luck, so vot is a voman like Zsa Zsa to do? Especially when a bunch of handsome, horny American space jockeys land just outside the capital city? Vy, of course: foment a rebellion, dollink!

Emerging from their spaceship, the doughty heroes find that the atmosphere of Venus is so much like that of Earth, no pressure suits or breathing apparatus are necessary. (Which circumstance certainly helps to keep the production budget down.) The first indication that something may be amiss is when they hear strange noises which the wise old professor tentatively identifies as being electronic signals.

CAPTAIN: Electronic signals could only be made by humans!

PROFESSOR: Not necessarily humans, Neil. Intelligent beings, perhaps, yes, but who knows what form they may have taken?

Shapely form, indeed. Venus, they discover, is inhabited by a race of statuesque women wearing brightly colored miniskirts and Fifties hairstyles. Brandishing ray guns, they take the earthlings prisoner. A lieutenant who fancies himself a ladies' man attempts to reason with them as follows: "Why don't you girls knock off all this Gestapo stuff and . . . try to be a little friendly?"

Zsa Zsa is first seen hard at work in her laboratory. Trusted confederates bring her news that good-looking fellas have landed.

ZSA ZSA: Vot sort of men are they?

BEAUTEOUS BLONDE: They seem strong and brave.

And ready for action. But they've only got one thing percolating in their little minds and tight britches.

FIRST LIEUTENANT: What do you make of all this? There's nothing but women!

PROFESSOR: Perhaps this is a civilization that exists without sex.

SECOND LIEUTENANT: You call that civilization?

PROFESSOR: Frankly, no.

Zsa Zsa explains how the "kveen" came to power: "She said dat men caused the ruin of dis vorld and it vas time for vimmen to take it over."

PROFESSOR: How did she manage to overthrow the men?

ZSA ZSA: They didn't take her seriously! . . . After all, she vas only a voman.

LIEUTENANT: Then we're the only men on the whole planet?

ZSA ZSA: Yes.

LIEUTENANT: Wow!

ZSA ZSA: Vimmen can't be happy witout men.

LIEUTENANT: You're so right, baby!

The man she craves, however, is the rugged skipper played by Eric Fleming. Consequently, she's somewhat peeved when the queen demands a private audience with him.

ZSA ZSA: I hate dat kveen!

LIEUTENANT (to the other men): She's jealous! Twenty-six million miles from earth and the little dolls are just the same!

Zsa Zsa attempts to articulate her reasons for opposing the present administration: "Ve haf no life here, vitout luff." Furthermore,

ZSA ZSA GABOR (1919–   ), Hungarian-born actress, shown here as a rebel Venusian in *Queen of Outer Space* (Allied Artists 1958).

the queen is planning to annihilate Earth with her "Beta Disintegrator," a polka-dotted contraption that looks like a giant cardboard hatbox.

FIRST LIEUTENANT: Oh, come off it! How could a bunch of women invent a gizmo like that?

SECOND LIEUTENANT: Sure, and even if they invented it, how could they aim it? You know how women drivers are!

And, of course, he's absolutely right. Since the queen is merely a woman, she isn't able to get the machine to work. She presses the wrong button or something and it explodes before she even gets a chance to have a man come in and fix it. The good guys and their gals escape into the jungle. Deep in the bush, Zsa Zsa feels free to be plainspokenly provocative.

CAPTAIN: Is there any special reason for taking your friends along?

ZSA ZSA: Yes. Because, if we can't change the civilization here, I thought perhaps we can go someplace and start vun on our own.

PROFESSOR: She's straightforward about it, anyway. I hope you realize, Captain, this leaves you with a grave responsibility.

ZSA ZSA: I'm sure dat the Captain iss dependable in everything.

Any possibility of suspense is sabotaged by the sexism intrinsic to the plot. It's rather difficult to be intimidated by a bunch of incompetent-looking women running around in silly outfits and spike-heeled sandals. Especially when these babes are routinely presented as objects of sniggering male contempt. How can they be queens of outer space? They don't even know how to dress. They seem barely qualified to fulfill traditional Fifties female roles. Zsa Zsa could never be convincing as a housewife or a typist or a schoolmarm, let alone a scientist. And yet this film is probably her ideal vehicle, mainly because the script so eloquently catalogues all of the hoary precepts on which she based her career. To amuse the reader, I quote from the dialogue; the real joke, however, is simply the sight of such glamour girls as these trying to pass themselves off as a functioning military unit. A chorus line is where they all-too-obviously belong. That goes for the men, also; in terms of visual emphasis, their neatly packed posteriors get almost as much attention as the tits on the girls.

The Queen of Sheba* (Italy 1953 B&W)

In her title role as *The Queen of Sheba*, Leonora Ruffo delivers a leering, sneering, self-consciously sexy performance. Seldom have I seen an actress more aware of her own prettiness. "Why talk of tears?" asks this chorus-girl queen, with a haughty toss of her head. She has a milk bath scene that's quite extraordinary by Fifties standards (it would have been old stuff, however, to Maria Montez in the Forties.) The film also features an exotic dancer from Babylon, who performs to the accompaniment of some hilariously inappropriate cocktail music (by Nino Rota) that's approximately three thousand years too modern.

The Queen of Sheba is not above womanly desires. Heavily veiled, she attends a wrestling match. Furthermore, common jealousy compels her to lead her nation in combat against King Solomon of Israel, all because Prince Rehoboam, his son and her true love, has been promised in marriage to a princess of Tyre. The Bible is generally poor source material for a gay cult movie, but it's been my experience that no film with the word "queen" in the title can be entirely without interest.

Querelle* (Germany 1983 C)

Querelle, a strange blend of sodomy and homicide (derived from Jean Genet by way of director Rainer Werner Fassbinder), is alternately appealing, intriguing, and silly. Brad Davis is cast in the title role, that of a seagoing sexpot who's desired by all of the principal characters and by several of the minor ones, as well. The officer he answers to is a closet case played by Franco Nero. The action transpires on campy, blatantly artificial sets straight out of an M-G-M musical from the Forties. (The lighting, too, is garishly theatrical.) The soundstage is swarming with sweaty, seminude sailors. The mooring posts on the dock are unmistakably phallic. Even the swooping Art Nouveau ornamentation on the windows is obscenely suggestive. Anything, apparently, for erotic effect.

Davis isn't playing a human being; he's playing an emblem off the cover of a gay porno novel. It's hilarious to watch him and Franco Nero "act," mainly because they've so obviously been led to believe that they're doing something Cultural and Important. Jeanne Moreau sings "Each Man Kills the Thing He Loves." Nearby is a drag queen got up as Madame Butterfly. Meanwhile, Jeanne's husband is bragging to Querelle's brother about fucking Querelle up the ass. We get the feeling that, if they upped the decadence by one iota, the screen would start oozing fungus.

In the course of his brief career, Fassbinder directed several kinky and provocative films. Also worth your attention are *Lili Marleen* (1981), *Veronika Voss* (1982), *Fox and His Friends* (1975), and *The Bitter Tears of Petra von Kant* (1972).

Rain* (U.S. 1932 B&W)
Miss Sadie Thompson* (U.S. 1953 C)

Rain, based on the famous story by W. Somerset Maugham and starring Joan Crawford as the notorious Sadie Thompson, is a drama depicting the conflicts of a group of Americans temporarily stranded on a tropic isle. Crawford is given a most unusual entrance: she comes at us in bits and pieces. We see her tawdry rings and cheap, clanking bracelets, her high-heeled shoes and black-net stockings, before we've even been granted a glimpse of her face. Sadie Thompson, in case you haven't heard, is a certified slut and brazen hussy. She drinks, smokes, tells racy jokes, and dances on the Sabbath. In short, she's precisely the creature to raise the hackles on the neck of the Reverend Mr. Davidson (Walter Huston), a missionary determined to reform and redeem the heathen of every hue. When Sadie gets religion, he's still not satisfied. Having had his way with her spiritually, he proceeds to do likewise in the physical sense. Then, chagrined at his own precipitous fall from probity, he does away with himself.

This film was more than a little ahead of its time. It's practically a case study of a "lost soul" brainwashed into joining a cult. On an altogether different level, however, the narrative addresses itself to one of the eternal, unanswerable questions: what do W.A.S.P. heterosexual men want? Sadie the Whore elicits Davidson's heartfelt distaste, disdain, and disgust, but, once he's transformed her into a madonna, he promptly knocks her off her pedestal. Truth to tell, Sadie's conversion struck me as being scarcely credible. In the final scene, she reverts to her former free-and-easy self. This I found similarly difficult to swallow. On the other hand, I had no trouble believing that the Reverend could suddenly turn into a skulking rapist. This, I fear, tells a lot about me and not much regarding the movie.

Back in the Twenties, *Rain* had been a huge triumph for Jeanne Eagels on the Broadway stage. Crawford was evidently hoping for a comparable success. Unfortunately, her fans weren't buying. They didn't like to see her behaving that way—so common, raw, and naturalistic. And Joan always listened to her fans. She strictly adhered to the dictates of her public for the course of a career spanning almost half a century. Some might call this prostitution of a different sort, but it certainly made for a fascinatingly unpredictable body of work, full of contradictions and ambiguities. *Rain* is Crawford's picture, through and through, but mention should also be made of co-star Beulah Bondi, cast with pathetic appropriateness in the role of Davidson's wife, a purse-lipped apostle of smug self-righteousness.

Rain qualifies as a cult movie. The Technicolor remake, starring Rita Hayworth as *Miss Sadie Thompson*, is considerably campier, mainly due to its Fifties ambience. Though the script comes right out and calls her a prostitute, Sadie now is clearly nothing of the sort. As personified by Hayworth, she's just a breezy dame who enjoys a good time. Gone are her bangles and baubles, replaced by a couple of significantly scarlet dresses designed by Jean Louis. This time around, the plot machinations are even more absurdly perfunctory. Out of pure vindictiveness, the Reverend Mr. Davidson (José Ferrer) obliterates her every chance for happiness. She's got more than sufficient reason to loathe him and everything he stands for. Then he reads her a few verses of the 23rd Psalm and she abruptly becomes a Born Again Christian. Then he sees a couple of natives doing a sexy dance, so he immediately turns around and rapes her. The most impressive performer is on the sidelines: Aldo Ray, perfectly cast as the tough marine who falls in love with Sadie and then (briefly) ditches her when he learns of her past. He's a nice piece, if you like 'em crude (and who the hell doesn't?).

Rebel Without a Cause* (U.S. 1955 C)

Rebel Without a Cause is the most famous of all j.d. films, a genre notoriously rich in homoeroticism. Before this movie is ten minutes old, James Dean is offering his suitcoat to Sal Mineo (and resents the fact that Sal won't take it). Both have been hauled into their local police station, James for public drunkenness. Instead of answering questions, he sits humming "The Ride of the Valkyries." ("Don't hum, dear," says his mother, played by Ann Doran.)

The next day both boys are back in school. Sal has a pin-up photo of Alan Ladd on display in his locker. (In real life, they probably didn't know each other. But Dean was once a boy toy of Clifton Webb, rumor has it.) Both boys wear suits. Very uncool. Later, James reproaches his dad (Jim Backus) for wearing an apron. It *is* a pretty frilly one, at that.

Dad notices that the boy's chest is covered with little knife wounds (an altercation at school). James strips off his T-shirt to assess the damage, granting us a look at his remarkably scrawny, underdeveloped, and generally unappetizing body. (Maybe I'm just an old crab, but James Dean doesn't do much for me. I find that injured, sensitive look in his eyes kinda nauseating. His maniacal giggle doesn't turn me on, either.)

Sal would like James to stay overnight with him: "Hey, you wanna come home with me? . . . If you wanna come, we could talk and then in the morning we could have breakfast . . ." Where have I heard that line before? Mineo very probably used it in real life. (He ended up getting stabbed to death in 1976 in Hollywood.)

They *do* spend the night together, along with Natalie Wood. James gives his jacket to Sal, who nuzzles it like a pet. Shortly afterward, he gets killed and James goes home with Natalie. I realize that this movie, though not exactly camp, is regarded as a classic cult film, but I don't like it much. I prefer sleazoid B-grade j.d. epics. They, at least, don't dabble in ersatz existentialism.

Reform School Girls* (U.S. 1986 C)

Women's prison pictures can be hilarious fun, if they're done with wit and style. Unfortunately, Reform School Girls has neither. It does show some promise, however, when Pat Ast makes her entrance. She portrays Edna, the sadistic head matron, and she provides a leering, sneering, eyeball-rolling, lip-smacking, head-tossing performance. I haven't seen such a bravura display of bad acting since Divine first put on Capri pants. Aiding and abetting Ast is punk rocker Wendy O. Williams as a rather strident young hussy who wears a black leather brassiere and little else. These two put on a show, all right, but it grows monotonous surprisingly quickly. What we have here is basically a bad, unimaginative, uncredited, paint-by-numbers remake of Caged (1950). It's really very ordinary softcore porno, apparently designed for dirty old men who like to watch naked, pubescent girls get their anuses sprayed with DDT.

Risky Business* (U.S. 1983 C)

Risky Business is a very Eighties film (and I mean, very, very Eighties) which epitomizes the youth culture that spawned it. The star is Tom Cruise, a heartthrob of the teenybopper set. There are, of course, many others who like him, as well. Here and there, we perceive a fleeting nod in the direction of that "other" audience. For instance, there's a scene or two which finds him prancing around in his undies. I was more interested in the scene which finds him reading Architectural Digest. (See, I told you this was a very Eighties film.) The plot is something about high school boys cashing in savings certificates in order to spend time with prostitutes—the female variety, needless to say, though we do catch a glimpse of a black transvestite hooker. An aura of unreality pervades the entire production. I kept thinking it was all a particularly bad dream, and that Cruise (who looks rather geeky in this early stage of his career) would wake up at any moment. Perhaps this shows how far from the Reagan Eighties we've come. I hope so, anyway.

The Rocky Horror Picture Show* (G.B. 1975 C)

A lot of films attempt to be serious and wind up being camp. Such developments are invariably disappointing to the moviemakers involved. However, can anything be sadder than a film that deliberately sets out to be camp and fails? *The Rocky Horror Picture Show*, a rock musical that's become a major cult film, has little to offer, aside from Tim Curry's portrayal of Dr. Frank N. Furter, a bisexual transvestite from the planet Transsexual in the galaxy of Transylvania. With every squaring of his shoulders, toss of his head, arch of his brow, flare of his nostrils, curl of his lip, etc., etc., he etches and delineates an elaborate, meticulously detailed homage to Joan Crawford (despite the fact that he looks more like Faith Domergue and has a British accent that's pure Hermione Gingold).

The hero and heroine are Barry Bostwick and Susan Sarandon. They are cast as Young Republican types whose idea of rock music is probably the Carpenters. (On their car radio, however, they listen to a speech by Richard Nixon.) They fall, like ripe fruit, into the clutching hands of Dr. Frank N. Furter. "If you want something visual that's not too abysmal," he croons to them, "we could take in an old Steve Reeves movie." Later he seduces the both of them. "Admit it. You liked it, didn't you?" he tauntingly says to Barry, after their first embrace.

Though pleasingly decadent, the film falls flat both musically and dramatically. I've been told that there are people who have seen this movie literally hundreds of times. That saddens me. Think of all the vastly superior pictures that, in all likelihood, such people haven't even seen once!

The Roman Spring of Mrs. Stone* (G.B. 1961 C)

Older-woman-and-younger-man melodramas constitute one of my
very favorite film genres, mainly because the "older woman" is
usually standing in for a gay male. One of the best (and most fla-
grant) examples of this is *The Roman Spring of Mrs. Stone*. The
screenplay is by Gavin Lambert, working from a novel by Tennessee Williams. Really, need I say more?

Yes. I must. This movie seems so full of veiled references to the
homosexual experience (and to my *own* experience, as a matter of
fact), it is directly comparable to Tchaikovsky's "Pathetique" Symphony. (Indeed, this could have served as appropriate background
music for the film.) Early on a narrator tells us, "For more than
two centuries, the immense cascade of stone stairs descending from
Trinita di Monte to the Piazza di Spagna has been a favorite place
of assignation." Whereupon we are shown a virile, dark-haired
fellow in an unbuttoned shirt, bouncing down the steps to rendezvous with a bald and sweating businessman wearing glasses. And
then we cut to a gigolo handing his card to an old bag. The comparison is explicitly made, simple (and vulgar) as that.

Similarly, the script comes right out and calls the title character a "chickenhawk." This is a term which I personally have only
heard applied to men of a certain persuasion. Mrs. Stone is a wealthy American widow residing in Rome. She's portrayed by Vivien
Leigh, looking utterly exquisite in gowns by Balmain of Paris.
Along comes Warren Beatty, who is given a grand entrance: we
don't get to see his pretty face until she does. And she likes what
she sees. Oh, she has her pride, of course. But she ends up giving
him money, just the same.

After she and Beatty play their first game of hide-the-salami, we
see her come sweeping out of Elizabeth Arden, so radiant she's
positively twittering. It's the kind of brittle, intoxicating joy and
euphoria that cannot possibly last. (Believe me, dear. I know.) Once
she's gotten hooked on cock, no one or nothing can save her, not
even good-horse-sense-no-nonsense chums such as co-star Coral
Browne. And sure enough: there comes the inevitable decline and
fall. "Oh! Swallows!" Mrs. Stone innocently burbles, gazing up
into the hard, bright, dazzling Roman sky. "Is it true they have no

VIVIEN LEIGH (1913–1967) and a young WARREN BEATTY (1937–   ) in Tennessee Williams' *The Roman Spring of Mrs. Stone* (Warner Brothers 1961).

legs? That's why they stay in the air all the time?" It's the sort of silly, romantic notion Tennessee Williams might have had. "No," snaps Beatty impatiently. "They stay in the air because they don't want to mix with American tourists." It's the sort of caustic comeback Tennessee Williams might have heard from one of his European rent-a-boys.

I've seen this picture more times than I can count, and I always find myself wishing for a happy ending which I'm well aware is not possible. I identify with the heroine so fiercely, and for the simple reason that I know she's really not a woman. In this movie, we invariably can tell who the real women are: they're the ones who are always trying to come between her and Warren. She ultimately falls victim to a grotesque contrivance like something from the pages of Poe: she is watched, followed, hounded by a shabby, gaunt young man in an overcoat. He's a street kid, a "man of the crowd," a vulture with eyes for her alone. And when at last she finds herself bereft and abandoned, she tosses *him* the key to her apartment. We think of newspaper clippings: unmarried bus boys and male librarians found murdered in their beds; no sign of forced entry. It's an ending as thoroughly macabre, as downbeat and final as that of *Sorry, Wrong Number*. In a very real sense, this is a horror story.

Years ago, I was telling my Aunt Gert about a movie somewhat similar to this: *Of Love and Desire*. "Merle Oberon plays a rich tramp living in Mexico," I began. "Oh, I saw that!" my aunt enthused. "Then she meets Warren Beatty, right?" My aunt, of course, was confused; the movie she was thinking of was the Vivien Leigh picture presently under discussion. These melodramas do tend to run together somewhat. I've seen quite a number over the years. I've also seen times change. Back in 1961, when this picture was made, Beatty was a juicy young stud. Today we see him playing love scenes with Madonna and we notice he's become as withered and dried-up as Mrs. Stone. We all have to take our turn on the carousel, and only the good die young.

Salome* (U.S. 1953 C)

In 1953 Rita Hayworth was a little old to be playing *Salome*, but at least she's a good dancer, so I guess it's all right. Her famous Dance of the Seven Veils is performed in an elaborate Jean Louis concoction. The veils are multicolored and, by the grand finale, she's stripped down to little more than a bit of gossamer and a few strings of beads. Her campy dance is cut short when she catches a glimpse of the severed head of John the Baptist (Alan Badel), whereupon she shrieks—not at all convincingly, I'm afraid. In this movie, Salome dances to save John the Baptist, not to slay him. Other than that, the movie does not depart too outrageously from the Biblical text. Unfortunately, it's not remotely faithful to the Oscar Wilde version. Charles Laughton is cast as Herod; I had a bit of trouble believing him consumed with heterosexual lust. Still, this is not as tedious a film as it might have been. The makers of Fifties religious epics often used the genre as a pretext to indulge their penchant for gaudy colors and bizarre decor. Whatever else this film might be, I'll concede that at least it's interesting to look at.

Salome, Where She Danced* (U.S. 1945 C)

Salome, Where She Danced is a difficult movie to classify. Indeed, much of the film's charm resides in the fact that it doesn't seem to know what to be.

Yvonne De Carlo is cast in the title role. She makes her entrance arising from a giant clam shell, just like the Botticelli Venus. Of course, she isn't naked; she's wearing a white ball gown, and she prances (somewhat stiffly) to "The Blue Danube" amid a welter of champagne bubbles and stray wisps of dry-ice fog. Needless to say, she looks ridiculous, but the issue is complicated by the fact that she's supposed to be in Berlin circa 1865 and that, furthermore, this movie was made during World War II. Therefore, *all* the women have to look ridiculous, especially the German ones.

Yvonne's next number occurs about a half hour later, by which time the scene has shifted to the American West of cowboy films. She comes to the aid of Marjorie Rambeau, who is singing an aria from *The Bohemian Girl* and, to put it politely, "laying an egg the size of a beer barrel." Yvonne appears in a skimpy belly-dancer outfit encrusted with golden sequins. Grizzled old prospectors fall from the rafters just at the very sight of her. It's only a standard kootch dance, but Yvonne performs it with moderate flair. She may not be Pavlova, but, as Little Egypt, she'll pass inspection.

Yvonne is kidnapped by outlaws. The bandit chieftain (David Bruce) romances her under a blatantly theatrical sky of purple and lavender. Members of his gang serenade the lovers. Yvonne is moved to join in the music-making. She sings "O Tannenbaum" in German. Bruce is inspired to reform, and also to give back his ill-gotten gains. Moments like this, after all, transcend mere camp.

But you ain't heard nothing yet. In San Francisco she dazzles a Russian plutocrat played by Walter Slezak. With his derringer he shoots a heron feather from her hat and replaces it with an egret plume which he has just purchased for the sum of two thousand dollars. Next he buys her a Rembrandt. But her heart belongs to Bruce, for whom she performs an exotic Oriental dance, waving white scarves and wearing an elaborate headdress apparently borrowed from Anna May Wong.

I see why she likes David Bruce; he intrigues me, too. A man can be sexy without being truly handsome, and this guy proves my point. His eyes are dull and heavy-lidded. His characteristic expression is perpetually impassive, suggesting either boredom or melancholia. But that merely whets the curiosity, doesn't it? We long to see the sleeper wake. In the throes of orgasm, a bland face is often the one most dramatically transfigured.

Samson Against the Sheik* (Italy 1962 C)

Since the heyday of Rudolph Valentino, sheiks have had a lascivious reputation. There's even a brand of condom called Sheik. Thus, when a muscleman epic is entitled *Samson Against the Sheik*, one can hardly be blamed for thinking that the connotations of the word "against" are possibly more tactile than adversarial. This is particularly true when Samson is played by Ed Fury, darling of the Fifties beefcake magazines. Dauntingly adorable, Fury is a massive hunk of manly cuteness, with a chiseled physique and a sculpted hairstyle, a neatly trimmed fringe of beard and moustache, a wise-ass shrug and endearingly impudent eyes, plus a capped set of teeth and a pugnacious button of a nose. Furthermore, the guy's got a healthy, if somewhat lewd, sense of humor about himself. His big, hard tits are used as weapons. One assailant is overcome simply by running up against them. The effect could not have been more suggestive if the bosom involved had been that of Jayne Mansfield.

At any rate, Fury is rugged stuff. The Sheik is contrastingly smooth and slick, much like his prophylactic namesake. At one point, he enters a scene quite literally prancing. "I must admit you have succeeded in . . . really surprising me," Ed tells him, enhancing the already provocative line with a slyly insinuating smirk. Much of the film takes place in sixteenth-century Spain, but the Sheik is most impressive on his palatial home turf, feeding his swans and barking at his eunuchs. This film is bizarre, exotic, and sexy, but it's not exactly "good." The fight scenes are so badly done, they seem intentionally incoherent. In the grand finale, Fury contends with a virtual parade of bodybuilders. He defeats the lot of them, but the camerawork and editing are so wretched that we can't make out the gory details. Perhaps the director was secretly opposed to violence; in any case, he appears to have been more a master of mood than of action. The best scene is a vespers service in a nunnery. Then a bunch of horny Moors come crashing through the stained-glass windows, and chaos resumes its incompetent reign. The Moors have come to kidnap the heroine and bear her off to the Sheik, who wants her in his harem. The good guys hasten to rescue her, but, by the time they get to North Africa, she doesn't wanna come home. "I'm no longer a prisoner, but I don't wish to leave here," she informs her former fiancé (Samson's rather effeminate sidekick). "I have found things here that I have always desired," she adds, giving the Sheik a look that speaks erotic volumes. How's that for a sleazy little slut? Apparently, this is what comes of giving a girl a convent education. Not that the Sheik—and, more especially, Samson—couldn't tempt monastics of either sex to forget their vows of chastity.

Samson and Delilah* (U.S. 1949 C)

Victor Mature is a hardass in *Samson and Delilah*; I mean that literally. In his very first scene, his mother tries to whop him on the bottom with a soup ladle. His buttocks are so massively muscular, the ladle breaks.

Delilah is Hedy Lamarr. Before she turns his head, however, he's engaged to her sister (Angela Lansbury). That alliance, however, ends in disaster. The wedding feast turns into a riot and the bride gets impaled on a spear. Victor reproaches co-star Henry Wilcoxon: none of this would have happened "if you had not plowed with my heifer."

After the fracas, our hero hides out in the hills with a cute chicken (Russ Tamblyn of *High School Confidential!* fame). Three times I noticed him fondly tousling Tamblyn's hair. Should we read some significance in that, or not? Perhaps the director (Cecil B. DeMille) was merely working a variation on the hair motif so vital to the plot.

Delilah's motivations are sometimes difficult to fathom. Lamarr's performance—two parts Vera Hruba Ralston to one of Theda Bara—does little to explicate matters. At least she gets to rest her head against Mature's mighty chest. But so does Tamblyn.

Bear in mind that the story transpires in the palaces and temples of the Philistines. Under the circumstances, what one might call camp might, in fact, be historical accuracy. This is a garish picture, but, after all, one should not expect good taste from Philistines.

Samson and the Seven Miracles of the World*
(Italy 1963 C)

The opening scenes of *Samson and the Seven Miracles of the World* are like a homoerotic wet dream. A lithe and lissome Oriental prince is thrown by assassins into a tiger pit. Then a tiger falls down there, too. Whereupon Gordon Scott, clad in a very revealing loincloth, comes bounding out of the jungle, kills the assassins, hurls himself into the hole, slays the (ridiculously fake) tiger, and sweeps the dainty young man into his arms. The prince, his head nestled against Gordon's massive chest, is so overwhelmed, he goes into a swoon.

Casually slinging the prostrate youth over his brawny shoulder, Gordon brings him to the safety of a Buddhist monastery. When they arrive, the poor kid doesn't seem to wanna let go of Gordon. Can't say that I blame him. Later on, a wounded rebel leader is taken into Gordon's muscular arms, the better for him to hear the urgent news the injured man must impart: leading lady Yoko Tani has been kidnapped by the bad guys! For emphasis, this bearer of bad tidings puts his arms around Gordon's neck. Then he, too, passes out.

Gordon never once puts on clothing in this movie. All he ever wears are tight, red loincloths. It's also significant that he shows no romantic interest in Miss Tani. While she shares a tender moment with her beloved, Gordon is busy horsing around with her brother, the aforementioned prince. As I have indicated, the film is far more touchy-feely than most Gordon Scott vehicles, perhaps because it was directed by Riccardo Freda. (For further reference, consult my review of *Giants of Thessaly*, earlier in this volume.) Beats me what the "seven miracles" of the title are supposed to be; the various bumps and bulges of Gordon's body, I guess. Speaking of which: the most visually spectacular scene does not involve physical contact. In a collapsing cavern, Gordon holds back the boulders till his followers have all passed safely through. The pose and the camera angle combine to make the configuration of his cock and balls so clear, he might as well be naked.

---

*Samson vs. the Vampire Women** (Mexico 1961 B&W)

The bloodlusting ladies of the title have at their disposal a trio of musclemen flunkies. These guys have beautiful bodies, but rather unattractive teeth. Meanwhile, over at the hacienda, the heroine is fretting over the bat-shaped birthmark on her shoulder. Whatever can it mean? Her father puts in a special call to Samson, a Mexican masked wrestler who's known South of the Border as Santo.

But he's engaged in the ring at the moment. We get to watch the bout. Those Latins certainly love physical contact! (So does everybody else, come to think of it.) Samson wears a silver-colored hood and tight shorts. In civilian life, his attire is basically the same, though he does put on a sequin-studded cape when he goes outdoors.

The vampire action is mainly lesbian. Not all of it, however. The undead women maintain their beauty by kidnapping studs and using them as blood-cows. As for the hot and heavy mat action, it's like some violent symbolic representation of gay male sex. The film's most surreal moment, however, is of a musical nature: the scene wherein the heroine is discovered performing Beethoven's "Moonlight" Sonata. A bit of culture amidst the general mindlessness.

The Scarlet Empress* (U.S. 1934 B&W)

The Scarlet Empress, a useful lesson in political history, shows us how a glamour girl would administer the government of one of the world's largest countries. First, of course, a look at her childhood: is it any surprise that the future czarina's nursery should be crowded with movie stars? I spotted Jane Darwell, C. Aubrey Smith, and Edward Van Sloan, who reads to the prepubescent Catherine the Great an account of her illustrious predecessors. There follows a remarkable montage of whippings, beheadings, iron maidens, naked men being broken on the wheel, half-naked damsels being burned at the stake, and, finally, a trussed-up man hung upside-down and used as a bell clapper. For contrast, we cut from his back-and-forth agonies to Marlene Dietrich enjoying a graceful ride on a garlanded swing. She, of course, is Catherine, now sweet sixteen and about to be married to Peter the Third of Russia, who, she is told, is "sleepless because of his desire to receive you in his arms." This news is imparted by an ambassador portrayed by John Lodge, a very American-looking hunk with a shoulder-length, straight-out-of-the-late-Sixties hairstyle. He kisses Marlene as soon as he gets her alone.

"Why did you do that?" she innocently asks.

"Because I've fallen in love with you. And now you may punish me for my effrontery," he says, handing her a whip.

Arriving at the Russian court, she's chagrined to find her new home filled with doleful-looking statuary, and even more chagrined to find that her husband is Sam Jaffe (popeyed, twitchy, and with a lunatic grin). He hands her a music box, then makes a hasty exit. ("I'm in a hurry. I must witness an execution," he whispers, eagerly.) On their wedding night, every cathedral in Russia is full of loyal subjects praying that the bride will prove fruitful.

Lodge urges Dietrich to cheat on her spouse. She protests her devoted fidelity. "Don't be absurd. Those ideas are old-fashioned. This is the eighteenth century," he points out. Then she discovers he's also beefing her husband's aunt, the Empress Elizabeth (Louise Dresser). Honestly! How depraved can a royal family get?!

Dietrich, as usual, appears in male drag: a white Cossack's uniform which she dons before leading her troops in a victorious coup. They ride their horses right up the stairs of the palace and into the throne room. The production design is an apotheosis of crazy, delirious excess: doors so huge, for example, that it requires six of Catherine's ladies-in-waiting to push one of them open. The music score is an interesting battle of the classics: Tchaikovsky's Fourth Symphony vs. Mendelssohn's "Midsummer Night's Dream," with Wagner's "Ride of the Valkyries" as a climactic flourish.

The Seven Year Itch * (U.S. 1955 C)

The Seven Year Itch gets underway at Grand Central Station. A score or so of middle-aged men are seeing their families off on a summer holiday. Tom Ewell shepherds his wife and kid in the direction of a waiting train. The wife is Evelyn Keyes. The kid is a Captain Video space cadet who fires his ray gun at the porter who's assisting with the luggage.

Coming home alone to his air-conditioned flat, Ewell is excited to learn that his upstairs neighbors have sublet their apartment to a gorgeous airhead blonde (Marilyn Monroe). She earns her living demonstrating Dazzledent Toothpaste on television. When he tries to place her in a romantic mood by putting on a recording of Rachmaninoff's Second Piano Concerto, she coos, "This is what

MARILYN MONROE (1926–1962) and TOM EWELL (1909–   ) in a famous scene from *The Seven Year Itch* (20th Century Fox 1955). MARILYN has long been a cult icon for gays.

they call classical music, isn't it? I could tell because there's no vocal." To the intoxicating melody of this orchestral accompaniment, Ewell's febrile imagination concocts an assortment of outrageously campy, male-chauvinistic fantasies, one of which qualifies as a full-fledged rhapsody of paranoid irrationality: after a bungled seduction attempt, he envisions Monroe describing his disgrace to an audience of fifty million television viewers, including his wife and child, who are watching a portable out in the tall timber. Counterbalancing this absurd nightmare is a cinematic epiphany of sorts, when Marilyn opens the trap door connecting the two apartments and magically descends the previously unused stairway in her nightgown. And, speaking of epiphanies, the movie also features the single most iconic moment of Marilyn's career: when she's standing on the subway grating and the train passes beneath her and the wind from the train blows the skirt of her dress up in the air. (She's just come from seeing *Creature from the Black Lagoon*.)

It's implied that the main character is so horny because he's been married to Evelyn Keyes for seven years and has never stepped out of line in all that time. His entire lifestyle is steeped in temptation. Even his job involves sex: he helps design paperback book covers. And now he's alone in a building with Marilyn Monroe—except for the two guys (interior decorators, we're told) who share an apartment on the top floor. Of course, we never get to meet them. But it's reassuring to know that at least a few people don't buy into the heterosexual frustration and hypocrisy on display. Marilyn's movies often cast her opposite a homely jerk such as the character portrayed by Ewell. That's to enable the homely jerks in the audience to daydream about her more credibly. This picture gives the game away with a single line of dialogue: when co-star Sonny Tufts innocently asks Ewell about the blonde in the kitchen, he gets all defensive and snaps, "Wouldn't you like to know? Maybe it's Marilyn Monroe!"

Sextette* (U.S. 1978 C)

I have friends who adamantly feel that *Sextette* is a terrible film, but I just as stoutly maintain that, if you can only get past the fact that Mae West is way too old to be playing a sexually insatiable, internationally glamorous movie queen, there is really nothing wrong with this movie. In fact, it's a perfectly adequate example of the genre she invented and made her own. However, even I must admit that, since Mae is well into her eighties here, there is something vaguely surrealistic about this movie's habit of surrounding her with handsome, hunky young men who fall all over each other in pursuit of her favors. The film is a campy, corny, funny, smutty romp, just as one might expect. Furthermore, it's got all the suitably fruity trimmings: Timothy Dalton, who is cast as Mae's latest husband, spends most of the movie trying to disprove allegations that he's homosexual.

The humor is enhanced by the plot's inherent absurdity, which derives from the film's complete refusal to take any notice of Mae's advanced age. At least her singing voice still retains its tone of delicious innuendo. She wears a wig of cascading golden tresses and a neon-blue negligee. She resembles one of those amorphous Disney cartoon characters that are supposed to look human, but don't. More often, though, she seems like a salty old broad who's starting on her second childhood. There are times when the prevailing mood of innocent jest makes way for more ghoulish japery. At one point Mae is serenaded by a chorus that keeps telling her, "You've got the cutest little baby face." Another song terms her "the female answer to Apollo." Such moments carry chivalrous hyperbole into the realm of bad taste.

Oh, well. The film at least affords her the opportunity to repeat some of her most celebrated, tried-and-proven lines. Plus it gives her the chance to recite many outrageous new ones. ("I'm the girl that works at Paramount all day and Fox all night.") The supporting cast includes several well-known guest stars. In the role of a gangster, George Hamilton is easily the cockiest of our heroine's consorts. (Good grief! She's even got me doing it!) Whatever else it may be, the film is certainly one of cultural importance: a work of ready-made historical—and hysterical—value.

Shanghai Express* (U.S. 1932 B&W)

Shanghai Express begins precisely the way a movie called *Shanghai Express* might be expected to begin—with assorted passengers preparing, in their characteristic way, to board the train. There's the little old lady who wants to smuggle her dog on board. There's the ill-humored invalid who won't permit any windows to be opened. There's the stuffy Doctor of Divinity who questions the morals of everyone around him. There are camels at the station. There are cows and chickens on the track. But when that whistle blows, the train's gotta go. And we go with it, every mile of the way. We mostly wish to remain in the compartment shared by a couple of prostitutes. They are played by Marlene Dietrich and Anna May Wong. This is the film in which Dietrich delivers one of her most famous lines: "It took more than one man to change my name to Shanghai Lily." She is "the notorious white flower of China." The trip reunites her with pompous Clive Brook, her fiancé from the days when her name was Madelyn and she hadn't bobbed her hair. "I wish you could tell me there'd been no other men," Clive reproachfully tells her.

"I wish I could, Doc," Marlene replies. "But five years in China is a long time." (She is wearing his hat, by this point.) Unfortunately, he proves to be altogether unworthy of her. He's a gentleman and all that, but he never learned to trust . . .

Such paperback romance matters as these become sadly anticlimactic after Anna May Wong has used a knife to dispose of Warner Oland, the bandit chieftain who has dared to detain the Shanghai Express. Miss Wong, a major star once upon a time, deserves at least a minor place in the camp/cult pantheon. She is a subtle, silky, beautifully sinister presence. Her pale, impassive face is like an alabaster carving. A pair of huge, liquid eyes dominate her countenance: twin pools of moonlight, smoke, and opalescent cunning. Her movements are lithe, sinuous, cat-like. Her voice is low and throaty, her speech provocatively slurred, purring with a promise of mellifluous malevolence.

She Done Him Wrong* (U.S. 1933 B&W)

She Done Him Wrong affords Mae West her grandest entrance
ever: after seven minutes of listening to guys mainly go on about
how gorgeous she is, we see her twirling her parasol in a carriage
pulled by a pair of stallions. Earlier, we caught a fleeting glimpse
of her portrait—capturing her beauty au naturel, as they say. Her
current love, a tavernkeeper, proudly puts it on public display. "I
do wish Gus hadn't hung it up over the free lunch," Mae coquett-
ishly clucks.

There can only be one pretty goil in a Mae West picture; that
must be why we find co-star Rochelle Hudson sporting such a
dubious dress and hairstyle. She looks so downright peaked, we
almost wonder why the white slavers seem so set on carrying her
away to the Barbary Coast.

This is the film in which Mae says, "Why'ncha come up sometime 'n' see me?" to Cary Grant, who runs the mission next door.
She wants his cherry. Apparently she's never had a virgin male
(neither have I, for that matter). "You can be had," she tells Cary,
and we get the feeling she's right. (Only Randolph Scott knew
for sure.)

There's also a fugitive moment of explicit gayness. Mae pays
a call on a pal in the pen. On her way through the cell block,
she's greeted by a couple of cons who seem to have their arms
around each other; indeed, the two guys call to her in unison. "The
Cherry sisters," she explains (and a good thing she does, because
I couldn't believe my eyes).

In this movie she's constantly asking people what took them so
long. Thus it seems a turnabout when she sings that she prefers
"A Guy What Takes His Time." Cary looks slow and smooth
enough to suit her. He proves to be a cop and arrests all her cohorts.
(He frisks Gilbert Roland, who gives him a knowing look which
I found interesting.) He places Mae in special protective custody,
if you follow my meaning. "You bad girl," he chides.

"Mmmm. You'll find out," she chortles. You betcha.

The Silver Chalice* (U.S. 1954 C)

The Silver Chalice, a Biblical epic, features E. G. Marshall in a minor role as a wealthy Greek. In the opening scene, he asks a question which will surely sound familiar to wealthy "Greeks" the whole world over: "Where's the boy?" he thunders.

The fellow whose son he proposes to purchase expresses some reluctance: "You would soon tire of him. My older son . . . You would like him."

"My heart is set on the younger one," E. G. answers, inspiringly.

Before too long, the lad in question grows up to be Paul Newman, but he prances around in togas a lot, and his legs still look fairly boyish. Midway through the movie, he appears in a sheer nightgown which gives us a good idea of what his ass is like. We

PAUL NEWMAN (1925–) butching it up in his first film *The Silver Chalice* (Warner Brothers 1954), a film so badly directed and acted that it has been transmuted into camp.

might also have seen his tits, were it not for the shoulder straps which hold the garment up.

This movie is an exercise in wretched excess, particularly when the scene shifts to the court of Emperor Nero. Turquoise-skinned kootch dancers, clad in bright yellow, twirl around and wave their asses at the camera, just like a bunch of chorus girls from Las Vegas. The already overweight emperor is tempted with tray after tray of gold-plated delicacies. ("Aged grasshoppers, fried in honey to a light, golden brown.") Jack Palance, who seeks to become court magician (and wears an exotic outfit adorned with decorative little sperm-shapes), materializes bigger and bigger snakes for Nero, whose evident delight suggests a fondness for things phallic. As co-star Albert Dekker puts it, "There's no place like Rome."

Sincerely Yours* (U.S. 1955 C)

Sincerely Yours, the one and only starring vehicle of Liberace's screen career, is the sort of film where you don't know whether to laugh or throw up. The opening scene finds him performing a concert in Chicago, where an obnoxious little girl asks him to play "Chopsticks" as an encore. (He wows 'em with it!) The scene shifts to San Francisco, where Lee confers with his manager, portrayed by crusty old William Demerest. Demerest is taking a bubble bath at the time. (He never struck me as being the bubble bath type. Perhaps he simply wanted to feel safe from inquisitive eyes.) Joanne Dru is hoping Lee will take her to the fights. Silly girl! Demerest advises her not to give up on Lee. "I can't just throw myself at him!" she protests. "He'll only step over me on his way to the piano!" Lee, meanwhile, is meeting with Dorothy Malone, a beautiful blonde from Banff who also wants to marry him. Lee warns her that the life of a pianist's wife is no bed of roses. "It's not easy, competing with a concerto."

A scene where he's supposed to be playing at the Top o' the Mark is almost a capsule summary of Liberace's image. See, there's this whole table full of fat little old ladies, ogling him and giving him that "oooh-isn't-he-wonderful?" look, so he marches up to the fattest, most goggle-eyed one and oozingly asks her, "Do you wanna touch me?" These ladies are later crestfallen when they spy him kissing Dorothy. She seems oddly peeved and out of sorts throughout the picture. This may have been the fault of her leading men. She ultimately falls in love with Alex Nicol, who plays a composer desirous of writing an opera based on Longfellow's "Evangeline."

The script has Lee going deaf, just like Beethoven. He mopes a while, and then decides to devote his life to good works. See, there's this little crippled kid (Richard Eyer) who goes to the cathedral every day to pray that he'll grow up to be a football hero, so Lee pays for an expensive operation that will cure him. (Of wanting to play football? No.) And then there's this dumpy old Irish-washerwoman/bag-lady-type (Lurene Tuttle) whose daughter (Lori Nelson) has married into high society and is ashamed of her. So he buys Lurene a fancy gown and pays to get her hair fixed, then

LIBERACE (1919–1987) in a blatantly heterosexual publicity release photo from his only film *Sincerely Yours* (Warner Brothers 1955).

brings her to a posh charity function being given by the "Colonial Daughters," where she meets Lori's new family and wins them over by dancing with Lori's father-in-law while Lee pounds out the "Beer Barrel Polka." There's an orchestra there, too, and Lee invites them to join in the fun: "Say, you boys in the band! If you're not busy, jump in!"

Dorothy and Alex go off together, with Lee's blessing. Then he regains his hearing. For the grand finale, he goes to Carnegie Hall, where he performs the Tchaikovsky First Piano Concerto. (I'd been wondering when that one was coming up.) When last seen, he is locked in a passionate embrace with Joanne Dru. Now that's what I call acting!

The Sinister Urge* (U.S. 1962 B&W)

The Sinister Urge, written and directed by Edward D. Wood, gets off to a far more spectacular start than we'd normally expect this less than reputable auteur to be capable of conceiving. A pretty blonde, dressed only in a bra and half-slip (just like Janet Leigh in the opening scene of *Psycho*) dashes frantically down a country lane. She finds her way to a telephone booth, but, in her state of seminudity, she doesn't have a dime on her and therefore can't call for help. Then a darkly handsome sex fiend grabs her, rips off her brassiere, and stabs her to death.

Turns out that both the girl and her murderer were depraved and corrupted by their involvement in the "smut picture racket." This is a film full of paradoxes and contradictions. It's a dirty movie that pretends to self-righteously condemn dirty movies. The hero is a middle-aged police detective (Kenne Duncan) who inveighs against pornography. Early on, he makes an impassioned speech that, in its level of sophistication and knowledgeability, reminds us of a certain widely disseminated Reagan era report on the subject: "The dirty picture racket can be directly connected to a good percentage of the major crimes in this city. . . .We'd need a psychiatrist to explain it to you. . . . You know what pictures like this can cause? Sex maniac headlines! Murder! Some characters will steal or kill just to get this stuff! It's worse than dope for them!" He blusters to a crescendo worthy of Attorney-General Meese himself: "Show me a crime and I can show you a picture that coulda caused it!"

Owing to the social constraints of its time, the only "dirty pictures" that this movie can show us are innocuous cheesecake photos of typical pin-up sirens attired in swimwear. Despite the very moral tone, Wood's heart was probably with the pornographers. There are numerous tell-tale signs of this. For example, a director of smutty movies has an office lined with posters advertising previous Edward D. Wood productions. It's extremely likely that Wood identified himself with the dirty old cameraman who participates in a couple of scenes, making half-assed esthetic decisions as he tells the various "models" where and how to recline. There's a subplot about an innocent would-be starlet who ends up posing nude. Wood's tender concern for womanhood, however, doesn't ring true, since the vast majority of women in this film are stupid, greedy, crooked, overdressed sluts. Furthermore, there's a scene wherein a male police patrolman serves as a decoy to nab the killer by strolling through a park while dressed in female clothing. No more than we'd expect from the director of *Glen or Glenda?*.

"Pornography!" Duncan thunders as the movie draws to a close. "A nasty word for a dirty business!" At this point, I think I should mention the fact that, in later years, Wood supported himself by writing novels with titles like *TV Lust* and *Diary of a Transvestite Hooker*. (I think I might actually like to read that second one.) His hypocrisy was poignantly tragicomic. I mean, even he must have known that pornography leads, not to murder, but to masturbation. The "sinister urge" of the title is left unspecified, but we may safely take for granted that it's the urge to jack off. And, if this had really been a film about jacking off, it might have been a much less tedious (and more truly pornographic) motion picture.

Sitting Pretty   (U.S. 1948 B&W)

Sitting Pretty aspires to be a parody of smug suburban folkways. Maureen O'Hara is cast as a housewife who engages Clifton Webb to mind the kids and help her keep house. Most of the parents I know are not liberal-minded enough to let a prissy old queen like Clifton Webb give their little boys a bath. I should also point out that the children in this movie grow rather overattached to their new guardian. "I think he's kind of cute," simpers Junior. "Me, too!" little brother chimes in. Amazed and astounded by his vast range of expertise and experience, Maureen asks Clifton "Is there anything you haven't been?" and the first thing that popped into my twisted mind was something involving sex orientation. In fact, it turns out that she hired him because she thought he was a woman. An understandable error; far more comprehensible than the mistake made by co-star Robert Young (her husband herein), who, along with the rest of the community, suspects that Maureen and Clifton are balling every time his back is turned.

As if Mr. Webb were not sufficient, the cast also includes Rich-

CLIFTON WEBB (1893–1966) was often cast in acerbic roles (with thinly disguised gay overtones) in such films as *Laura* and *Sitting Pretty* (20th Century Fox 1948); he is shown here in a publicity release photo from the latter film.

ard Haydn as a bitchy horticulturalist who lives next door with his mother. You'd think he and Clifton would get along really cozy. Indeed, you'd think that Clifton could even go so far as to room at the Haydn residence, since it's located so conveniently close, and also because such an arrangement would put to rest all those obscene rumors about Maureen. But no. Hissing like a couple of alley cats, Webb and Haydn get into a spat every time they lay eyes on each other. Whereas, if I had been in charge of this production, they would have joined forces and discovered they had interests in common.

The Sisters* (U.S. 1938 B&W)

The Sisters has plenty to offer the camp enthusiast. It's got Bette Davis, Lee Patrick, Mayo Methot, Laura Hope Crews, and the San Francisco earthquake. In the opening reel, Bette Davis is practically engaged to Dick Foran, but we know she's never going to marry him. After all, Errol Flynn's the one who has top billing. So Dick is wed to one of Bette's sisters: prim and proper Jane Bryan. Her other sister is pretty Anita Louise, who marries Alan Hale, mainly because he'll buy her fancy clothes and take her to New York.

Mayo Methot goes to prizefights and drinks. Lee Patrick wears a feather boa and smokes. Neither one is a lady by 1905 standards. Laura Hope Crews is cast as Patrick's mother; I'm not positive, but I think she's supposed to be a madam. Her establishment in Oakland is where Lee and Bette repair to, when the walls, ceilings, and chandeliers of San Francisco come crashing down upon them.

Demon rum is the eventual ruination of all three sisters' husbands. It kills Alan Hale. It causes Flynn to lose his newspaper job and then sign on as a hand aboard a China clipper. Foran steps out on prissy Miss Bryan. This, too, is probably not the act of a sober man.

The period costumes are by no means flattering to everyone. Davis, however, seldom looked better, and Max Steiner backs her up with a perfectly scrumptious love theme.

Slander   (U.S. 1957 B&W)

Slander begins with a schematically rendered view of the New York City skyline, over which are superimposed the covers of magazines with titles like *Smut, Lurid, Real Dirt,* etc. Steve Cochran, flashing those big, dark, piercing eyes of his, is cast as "H. R. Manley," the notably effeminate publisher of a periodical which specializes in exposés of show business personalities. Cochran plays this smoothie soft as satin, with overly precise diction, too-too careful pronunciation, and just a hint of a lisp. On the basis of his cultured demeanor, you'd never guess that H. R. started his career on the sordid fringe of the entertainment industry, working as a press agent for "a stable of broken-down strippers." In Fifties movie parlance, this may mean that he was a pimp; I'm not certain. In any event, H. R. is a shrewd businessman. He knows that a smug, self-satisfied, holier-than-thou society requires a steady diet of gossip over which to cluck. "A rotten world full of rotten people" is how he so colorfully puts it. He drags the general public down to his gutter level and manages to turn a tidy profit in the process. Now he's got a plush Park Avenue apartment for himself and his dipso mother (Marjorie Rambeau), to whom he is ever so dotingly devoted. Displayed on the walls of his huge, swanky office are paintings by Degas and a motto: "Ye shall learn the truth, and the truth shall make you free."

But what is truth? "There's something dirty in everyone's background!" Cochran crows. "The cleaner the surface may appear, the more dirt is hidden underneath." Case in point: "Mary Sawyer," celebrated star of Hollywood religious epics, wife of a doctor and mother of a sweet little girl, had either an abortion or an illegitimate child during her misspent youth. The only one who knows for sure either way is her former neighbor, an up-and-coming puppeteer (Van Johnson) presently hosting a children's television program sponsored by Sterling Breakfast Foods, the makers of products with names like Korn Krinkles and Wheat Wallops. Diametrically opposed to tattletale Cochran, Van inhabits a world of sentimental falsehoods, a charade of wholesomeness and purity. Determined to get the goods on his clay-footed movie goddess, Steve puts the screws on Van. Ensuing scenes prove the accuracy

STEVE COCHRAN (1917–1965), shown here in a publicity release photo, played macho roles in Hollywood films of the 40s–50s. In the late 1940s he co-starred with Mae West in the Broadway revival of *Diamond L'il*.

of Cochran's most pessimistic opinions regarding the human race. Turns out that Van did time in prison for armed robbery, having severely wounded his victim with a knife. There are, of course, the inevitable mitigating factors: he only wanted the money in order to purchase medicine for his ailing mother. As for Van's wife (Ann Blyth), she is so eager for his success (and the suburban ranch house it will buy) that she urges him to betray the actress's secret. She deserts him when he refuses to be bought by Cochran's promise of silence regarding the term in jail. Just to make everyone's misery complete, Van's young son (Richard Eyer) gets run over by a truck while fleeing the abuse of unkind schoolmates.

The film concludes with an orgy of Fifties self-righteousness. Van appears on a prime-time network panel show entitled "What Do You Read?"; there he recites his own personal version of the Nixon "Checkers" speech, passionately imploring the viewing audience to stop shelling out their two bits for Cochran's scandal sheet. It seems unlikely that anyone would actually watch a program called "What Do You Read?", but perhaps there was nothing worthwhile on the other channel that evening: suffice it to say that the tide of public opinion turns in Van's favor. Indeed, the besotted Rambeau, regretting the trail of tears and tragedy that enables her to eat breakfast in bed every morning, is so deeply moved by the telecast that she grabs a gun and blows Cochran's brains out.

Poor, dead Steve. His bad-natured Mama's boy, obviously intended as a caricature of Robert Harrison, the editor of the now-defunct *Confidential*, nowadays looks more like Kenneth Anger, the relatively inoffensive author of *Hollywood Babylon*. Fact is, Cochran's a macho stud who is somewhat miscast in the role of a prissy, nouveau riche closet queen. I'm afraid that, in this instance, his overabundance of swarthy sex appeal merely gets in the way of his otherwise excellent performance.

---

*Some Like It Hot** (U.S. 1959 B&W)

The kinkiness of *Some Like It Hot* has made it a favorite with gays all over the world. Tony Curtis and Jack Lemmon portray a pair of musicians who, having witnessed a mobster massacre in Chicago, escape with their lives by disguising themselves as flappers and joining an all-girl band that's headed for sunny Florida (Anita, where are you?). Prior to their transformation, our heroes are very buddy-buddy: living together, all touchy-feely, and even holding hands on occasion. However, after they've donned dresses and become "Josephine" and "Daphne," they start to carry on like lesbians, loudly decrying the shortcomings of the male sex and seemingly unable to tear their eyes off their fellow females. The sexual confusion reaches its zenith when Lemmon accepts a marriage proposal from Joe E. Brown, a very wealthy dirty old man who has conceived an affection for him.

The opulently endowed Miss Marilyn Monroe, a sainted icon of fag fandom, herein resembles a pulchritudinous cartoon image of herself. As for the other leading ladies, Lemmon unsurprisingly shows promise as a screwball comedienne in the tradition of Marion Davies and Lucille Ball. Miss Tony Curtis, much like Jackie Curtis (no relation) and Holly Woodlawn, is more the glamour-puss type. With his dark, ripe, dewy good looks, his pouty lips and his fruity falsetto, Tony could easily have become the new Joan Crawford if he'd stayed in costume. He looks, if possible, even more fey and pretty in his guise as a suave and bespectacled millionaire. Curtis is forever switching sexes in this movie. Toward the end, he gets confused and kisses Monroe on the lips while still in drag. How explicit can a gay subtext get?!

The blend of mistaken identities and frenetic, nonstop action is rather like a French bedroom farce—but one played out in a semi-tropic world of palm trees, resort-hotels built like wedding cakes, and leisure clothes that look like they're made of spun sugar and vanilla ice cream. This comedy of the absurd concludes with a glorious triumph of irrationality: everyone learns the actual sex of everybody else, and no one gives a damn. Brown, in fact, seems downright pleased ("Nobody's perfect," he shrugs) to learn that he's engaged to a transvestite male. There's at least a chance that he knew all along.

Son of Samson* (Italy 1961 C)

Son of Samson is a veritable wet dream of half-naked sadists locked in orgasmic frenzies of ancient torture, bloodlust, and cruelty. (Do I hear you panting already?) This is the sort of picture in which both good guys and bad guys say things like "Feed him to the crocodiles!" and "Punishing you will be a pleasure!" The plot (downtrodden Egyptians vs. brutalizing Persians) is so extremely alienating (and crudely filmed), it may as well be transpiring on another planet. Or maybe in hell.

Son of Samson, also known as Maciste (Mark Forest), kills people so adeptly and with such alacrity, he might as well be Son of Sam. He carries himself with the confidence of a king, or a queen, or, at any rate, some kind of royalty. Slave girls automatically kneel down before him, or, to be more specific, before the huge, phallic-looking knot perpetually jutting and dangling from the front of his loincloth. To idly pass the time, he pulverizes rocks with his bare hands.

Maciste befriends the Prince of Egypt (they rescue each other when attacked by big cats of indeterminate gender). The Prince tells Maciste to look him up when he's in town, then sets off for the capital city, where he's distraught to discover that his father, the Pharaoh, is dead. Pharaoh was assassinated by order of the Queen, the Prince's wicked stepmother, who now invites the Prince to marry her. Since his dad is scarcely cold in his tomb as yet, the Prince is understandably reluctant to comply. So she gives him a magic necklace; he dons it, and then immediately looks at her with a horny leer.

Meanwhile the body count multiplies. In one of the nastier scenes, a chariot with wheels adorned with whirling, poison-tipped knife-blades is driven through an arena crowded with stumbling, blindfolded women. A man is accidentally scratched; screeching in agony, he clutches his crotch as he dies. The film's finale is interesting for its demonstration of the ethical niceties involved in killing off the bad guys. Villains may, with impunity, be gruesomely and summarily put to death. A villainess, on the other hand, must die either by accident or by her own hand. The evil queen, for example, is such a monster of vanity that, when faced with the pros-

pect of being branded, she impulsively hurls herself into the crocodile pool. His work done, Maciste heads for greener fields which,
presumably, he'll soon turn crimson with gore.

The Son of the Sheik* (U.S. 1926 B&W)

Rudolph Valentino, a Twenties obsession, is a figure of glossy
glamour and ambiguous sexuality. His eyes have an almost rep-
tilian cool, despite their insistent smolder. He's particularly good at
conveying horniness. Whenever engaged in something that, in those
days, was generally considered erotic—say, for instance, kissing a
lady's forearm—he exceeds the bounds of mere concupiscence and
seems to be having an orgasm. All the dramatis personae in *The
Son of the Sheik*, men and women both, seem to regard Rudolph
as a male sexpot. Men kidnap him, lash him to a grating, open his
shirt, and whip him. Men come to his rescue and nurse him back
to health with tender loving care. Of course, he's the hero; that's
why we're meant to excuse it when he rapes an innocent dancing
girl (Vilma Banky) as punishment for a supposed betrayal. At one
point we're shown a pair of unclad men tied up together in a cozy
bundle. They pinch and bite one another. If I ever found myself
in such a situation, I'm sure I'd find a far more interesting way
to pass the time.

Springtime in the Rockies* (U.S. 1942 C)

It would seem, with regard to *Springtime in the Rockies*, that the
critic's first order of business would be to determine what the hell
Carmen Miranda might be doing in the Rocky Mountains. Turns
out that she was transported there by John Payne, ever the light-
weight Forties pretty boy. She's supposed to be his secretary. He
also brings along all of her brothers, even though she has six of
them. "They're very cute," he explains. But even a sextet isn't
enough for John; he's also got a hired companion and valet por-

trayed by Edward Everett Horton (who, Payne tells us, took advantage of him in a bar; no need to wonder what kind of a bar).

Payne is ostensibly a down-on-his-luck Broadway song-and-dance man who's come to Lake Louise in the Canadian Rockies to confer with Betty Grable, his former leading lady. She, meanwhile, has hooked up with Cesar Romero to form a dance act known as Victor and Victoria. Together with Harry James and his orchestra, they entertain at a resort, before an audience of what seem to be tourists, Indians, and Royal Canadian mounties. Carmen flirts with Edward Everett Horton in a hotel room, while, downstairs, Betty and Cesar trip the light fantastic. The latter pair announce their engagement. Payne, however, seriously doubts the sincerity of Cesar's passion for Betty. The critic, knowing a thing or two about Cesar Romero, is inclined to agree.

"Nice for you to make my acquaintance," says Carmen, when introduced to Grable. There's a certain degree of cattiness between these two, and it's not at all hard to see why that should be. Betty has top billing in this frothy concoction. Carmen, however, is the señorita who steals the show. The final number surrounds her with lavender-clad chorus boys. Just in case we failed to notice the color of their tights, they turn and shake their tushies at the camera. I don't know if the Greeks had a word for this, but I can sure think of a few. Camping, I might add, is still a popular pastime in the Canadian Rockies.

Spy Smasher* (U.S. 1942 B&W)

Kane Richmond was the homoerotic icon of the chapterplays. Spy Smasher, his most famous serial, doubles our viewing pleasure by giving us two Kane Richmonds for the price of one.

This is a World War II cliffhanger. We are able to discern this immediately; the musical accompaniment for the opening titles is Beethoven's Fifth Symphony. Shows like this don't mess around. The opening scene transpires in occupied France. Spy Smasher (Kane, of course) is captured by the Gestapo, stripped to the waist, and flogged. Film scholars will surely want to note that it's his chest that tastes the lash (the back is more customary).

KANE RICHMOND (1906–1973), star of low-budget Hollywood films and serials of the 1930s–40s.

The scene shifts to the U.S. of A. Kane Richmond #1 meets Kane Richmond #2 aboard a train. They're brothers—identical twins (and you know what they say about identical twins). Of course, they're both good guys. In a serial, the bad guys are always unattractive, droopy-assed men wearing business suits. Good guys, meanwhile, are well-muscled hunks dressed in fairy suits. When not thus attired, Kane is partial to leather jackets.

Speaking of clothes, have you ever noticed how frequently men in serials exchange outfits with one another (always ostensibly under the pretext of tricking and misleading the bad guys)? Have you ever wondered if switches like these involve hanky-panky the camera doesn't show? If guns are phallic symbols, what is the sexual significance of a machine gun? Kane has an engagingly crooked smile. What is it about a crooked smile that makes it so much more sadistically sexy than the regular kind? *Spy Smasher* raises all of these questions and more.

Richmond's ass, though somewhat fuller than it was in *The Lost City*, is just as photogenic, if not more so (when that darn cape isn't in the way). He gets it into some pretty tight scrapes (and some pretty tight trousers, too). As always, there's a girl in the case (Marguerite Chapman), but she doesn't have much to do. Richmond's the one who functions as the damsel tied to the railroad tracks.

The Smasher and his twin share a motorbike at one point. I've always believed that brothers should share. It's a bouncy ride, and they seem to be making the most of it. Unfortunately, they suffer a spill. Perhaps the one at the wheel wasn't paying proper attention.

However, the most interesting and hilarious thing about this serial has nothing whatsoever to do with sex or gender. As I've already indicated, the music consists of derivations and outright quotations from the opening movement of Beethoven's Fifth. So why do the titles make absolutely no mention of Beethoven and attribute the entire score to someone called Mort Glickman?

Staircase (G.B. 1969 C)

Staircase, with its chillingly squalid, relentlessly maudlin portrayal of an aging gay male couple, is rather heavy going, even for me. Lord knows how it would strike a younger homosexual, let alone the occasional misguided straight. Not that straight people have anything to fear from this film. In fact, it caters to their most cherished prejudices. Harry and Charlie, the pair under consideration, are seething with guilt, shame, regret, and above all, self-loathing. Both wish they were straight. One of them even tries to convince himself that he might be. Ironically enough, he's the one who faces a possible prison sentence as punishment for (get this) appearing in drag at a local pub. The film is laced with religious references, which now seem so out of place as to be downright bizarre. Said notations, however, no doubt seemed perfectly appropriate to the pious, judgmental hypocrites who made this film. When, in the end, Harry and Charlie at last admit that they need one another, even this is portrayed as a sign of their weakness.

Ordinarily, one would be justified in saying that such a pathetic exercise as this has no place in a book on gay camp. Once again, however, the ludicrous casting is what makes all the difference. The stars are Richard Burton and Rex Harrison, both of them veritable icons of heterosexuality. Indeed, Dick was married to Liz when he made this film. However, it's Sexy Rexy who cuts the finer figure, since he's cast as the one who's managed to hang on to his looks. The acting is generally good, but there's an underlying tension, as though both stars are worried we might start thinking they actually are "that way." This movie was made just prior to Stonewall. If nothing else, it vividly illustrates that the time for gay liberation was way past due.

The Star* (U.S. 1953 B&W)

Bette Davis once claimed that she modeled her performance in *The Star* on Joan Crawford. This makes the picture seem like a particularly cruel form of caricature. Filmed in a heavily realistic style that would seem to preclude camp, the movie depicts what it's like to be a has-been in Hollywood. It's sort of like a *National Enquirer* where-are-they-now story come to lurid life.

Davis is cast as Margaret Elliot, an Oscar-winning actress who has fallen on hard times. She's first seen skulking around outside of an auction hall where her personal belongings are being sold to pay off her creditors. She goes to the palatial mansion of her ex-husband, now a successful director, to see if she can cadge some ready cash. Instead, she gets a lecture on Fifties morality from her ex's second wife ("You *deserved* to lose him!"). When she gets home to her seedy little bungalow, she's met by her no-good relatives, who want to mooch off of her. She throws them out. If anyone's being imitated in this scene, it's Bette Davis, not Joan Crawford. ("Now! I want you BOTH to-get-out-of-here. Get OUT!")

So then she gets sloshed and goes for a ride and gets picked up for drunk driving. ("Take your hands off me! You don't seem to know WHO I AM!") When she gets out of jail, she finds she's been locked out of her apartment for non-payment of rent. Before the movie shudders to a close, she's even reduced to shoplifting.

This could have been a perfectly delirious picture, if only it wasn't so much a propagandistic product of its time. The Davis character's desire to continue with her career is portrayed as a form of mental illness. The cure, of course, is the love of a good man (Sterling Hayden). Can anybody believe Bette Davis (or Joan Crawford) would be happy to give up acting in favor of housewifery?

A Star Is Born* (U.S. 1954 C)

At the time of its release, A Star Is Born was perceived as a major comeback for Judy Garland. The premiere was a great event, attended by precisely the sort of celebrities one might expect: Liberace, Raymond Burr, Cesar Romero, etc. Lee showed up with his mother. Butch was squiring Joan Crawford. Burr attended with a soldier just back from Korea. Momentous occasions call for hyperbole; on this one, George Jessel called Judy a combination of Helen Hayes, Al Jolson, Jenny Lind, and Sarah Bernhardt. You can see why the poor girl must have been rather nervous about measuring up.

As for the film itself, it's a garish epic of tragedy in Tinseltown. The phantasmagorical Technicolor, quirky photography, and subtly unsettling editing techniques are intended to underscore the phoniness, the superficiality, bad taste and just plain ugliness that once was, and probably still is, Hollywood. In his role as Norman Maine, an alcoholic matinee idol, James Mason provides what is probably his most abrasively brilliant performance. When first seen, he is livening up a charity benefit with a disruptive display of drunken debauchery. He is hustled home by a watchfully solicitous press agent (Jack Carson), who hovers vampirically at Mason's bedside till finally the troublesome star feigns sleep.

I hasten to point out that Mason is not the star to whom the title refers. Far from it. That distinction belongs to Judy Garland in her role as Vicki Lester, would-be Queen of the Hit Parade. She announces her stellar ambitions on a balcony while, in the background, an ersatz, studio-manufactured dawn is breaking. Garland's face is fascinatingly fragmented by the magnifying lenses of the men in the make-up department. They transform her into a slash-browed harpy in a pink evening gown, with auburn hair and clashing red lipstick. "I've been sitting in that chair since six o'clock this morning!" she complains, referring to her bout with the cosmeticians. And Mason bitchily replies, "You sat an hour too long, honey." He wipes away their gaudy handiwork moments before Judy faces the cameras for her screen test.

Somewhat later on, James and Judy are wed. In many respects they resemble a male homosexual couple. He is the fussy old auntie, complete with a Mayfair accent; she, with her short haircut, is the pompadoured pretty boy. Several of her musical numbers present her in male attire. Whenever she commences to sing, my eyes are inexorably drawn to the chorus boys behind her and I find myself wondering which of them are gay (probably all). I could have sworn that I saw transvestites backstage in the final scene at the Shrine Auditorium.

Her star rises while his is eclipsed. *Black Legion* is the ominous title of Norman Maine's final film. A billboard promoting it is replaced with one advertising Vicki Lester in a musical trifle called *Happiness Ahead*. Oh, the irony of it all! Mason is reduced to keeping house at their mansion by the sea, where windows open on waves which lap soothingly on the sands. To cheer him up, Judy performs a feverishly energetic production number, making do with props which happen to be lying around their living room. Her improvisation is unappreciated: at the Cocoanut Grove, Mason makes an excruciating spectacle of himself right in the middle of Judy's Oscar acceptance speech. He is consigned to a sanitarium for a drying-out period. Upon his release, however, he finds that society will not permit him to stay sober. And so, in a paroxysm of self-sacrifice, he is last seen shambling down the beach to set off on the long swim to China, while Judy, his movie-star wife, busies herself in the kitchen, singing sweetly while preparing soup 'n' sandwiches.

But even this isn't the ultimate. *A Star Is Born* is the rare camp classic that saves its most melodramatic line for the very end, when Judy, her husband dead and gone, her voice full of tears, and millions—yes, millions—of devoted fans hanging on her every breath, announces herself with the immortal words, "Hello, everybody. This is Mrs. Norman Maine!"

A Stolen Life* (U.S. 1946 B&W)

In all too many of her major films, Bette Davis found herself working with sexless wonders like Paul Henried and George Brent. This is why *A Stolen Life* comes as a refreshing change: her leading man is the preternaturally cute Glenn Ford.

As in *Dead Ringer* (q.v.), Bette is cast as identical twins. Kate is the sweet, quiet, introverted sister, who tries, none too successfully, to keep Glenn away from Pat, the predatory, man-hungry sister. Matters are complicated by the presence of Dane Clark as a struggling, ill-humored artist. "I bet you're not even a woman," he says to Bette. (Who does he think he's talking to? Craig Russell? Possibly so. Later he tells her, "Don't go female on me.")

Ford is wed to the wicked Pat. She later drowns in a sailing mishap. So then, of course, the good sister, still deeply in love with Glenn, tries to pass herself off as the bad sister and take her place in his bed. I couldn't help wondering how she proposes to succeed in this deceit. I mean, she's all too obviously a virgin, whereas the dead woman had been married for several months. Isn't Glenn going to notice something's different the first time they have sex? I realize this is an indelicate question, but it's nonetheless pertinent.

Storm Center (U.S. 1956 B&W)

"Your boy is not just an average boy. He is different. Value that difference! We put far too much stress on conformity in this country!" says Bette Davis, the freethinking lady librarian of *Storm Center*. "The ball park isn't the only place a person can be a hero." Them's fightin' words, especially since this movie takes place in the McCarthy era Fifties and Bette is addressing Joe Mantell, the film's presiding anti-intellectual, who's terrified that his bookworm kid (Kevin Coughlin) might be a pansy.

Bette has worries of her own. Brian Keith, a young right-winger on the city council, insists that she remove a Communist book from the shelves of the library. When she resists, he accuses her of being a fellow traveler, has her sacked, and appoints his girlfriend (Kim Hunter) to be librarian in her place. (At this point, I feel I should mention that I've been employed by a public library for the past twenty-two years. And I've seen my share of dirty deals.) A whispering campaign is soon underway. Bette is the target of malicious gossip. "It's a comfort to know my children aren't subjected to her influence any longer," says one worried mother. "I think she was a danger to the community."

Which brings us back to Joe Mantell, who now has just the

ammunition he needs to make a man out of poor little Kevin. "Books that stir people up give 'em nightmares. That can be pretty bad stuff," Joe contends. Kevin concurs, a mite too vehemently. The child makes an ugly scene, publicly denouncing Bette as a Communist at the dedication of the library's new wing. That night he burns the whole building down. Which goes to show that a poisonous political climate can turn a bibliophile into a bookburner. (As if that hadn't already been proven.)

I love Fifties movies; everything is always spelled out so clearly. This movie may seem insanely naive and simplistic, but I like the way it draws a firm correlation between intelligence, humane impulses, and femaleness. (Maleness, on the other hand, is made to seem blatantly destructive.) And yet the film's most hysterical witch-hunters are all women. At any rate, even though there's not a trace of sex in this movie, sex is nonetheless a tacit issue underlying everything else.

Strange Fascination   (U.S. 1952 B&W)

Strange Fascination begins with a classic camp tableau: a skid row derelict (Hugo Haas) standing outside of Carnegie Hall, listening to a piano concerto that he himself used to play back in the days before he was brought to grief by a cheap, trashy, no-good woman!

She is portrayed by Cleo Moore, a frequent Haas leading lady. The film takes the form of a flashback, telling us the whole sorry saga from the beginning. Cleo's a night club dancer who has it in for Hugo because he dares to order dinner while she's doing her number. (It's hardly a show-stopper. As a matter of fact, at first I thought she and her partner were just a couple of customers who happened to be dancing.) She attends one of his recitals, with the intention of hacking and coughing all the way through. But then, in the middle of the concert, she is overcome by a . . . strange fascination. As she listens to Hugo perform Chopin, she suddenly realizes that she is in the presence of Art.

"Art who?" one might reasonably inquire. Cleo goes to Hugo's dressing room, asks for his autograph, and invites him out for a drink. She gives off neurotic vibrations that spell trouble, but he's oblivious to them. In fact, he gives her his phone number.

The trouble doesn't start till after they're married. Financial reverses. Jealousy. Alcoholism. Missed engagements. The usual downward spiral. He can't even hold a job playing piano in a bar. Turns out he's the one who feels a strange fascination, though masochistic obsession would be a better term. He's got his hands insured for a hundred thousand dollars, so he sticks one of them in a printing press. She walks out on him, anyhow. The insurance company, meanwhile, sees right through his claim and refuses to pony up. So that explains why he's last seen playing boogie-woogie at a Salvation Army mission.

Hugo Haas must have been extremely fond of this plot; he used variations on it in several of his vehicles. He wrote, produced, directed, and starred in a whole series of these low-budget efforts, many of them featuring Moore, a pudgy blonde who later ran for governor of Louisiana. All of their collaborations are orgies of hopelessness and degradation. *Strange Fascination* is surely the most excruciating.

A Streetcar Named Desire* (U.S. 1951 B&W)

I'm skating on thin ice with this film. It's an established classic, based on a Tennessee Williams play that's considered an even greater classic. A lot of gay men identify with Blanche DuBois (played by Vivien Leigh), the central protagonist of the piece. She's a wilted flower of Southern gentility who pays a disastrously overextended call on her married sister (Kim Hunter), who resides in a squalid two-room flat with her husband, a working-class brute named Stanley Kowalski (Marlon Brando). Blanche is vague, vaporous, fluttery, and ever so oversensitive. She would never deign to admit that she finds Stanley a teensy bit attractive (this is the main point where she differs from her male homosexual fans).

Late in the film, there's a reasonably sordid sex scene: Stanley, clad in a sleazy dressing gown, finds himself alone with Blanche and rapes her. She has a nervous breakdown and has to be put away. Powerful stuff, ain't it? Yet Stanley never really comes into focus as being a villain, mainly because we know that, underneath it all, he's lovable Marlon Brando. Indeed, the Brando sex appeal is the principal commodity that the picture is selling. The camera is indecently preoccupied with his musculature. I guess I'm just immune to his charm: every time he started to shout in someone's face, I couldn't help but think about how bad his halitosis must be. His sweaty, mumbling, rough-edged brand of Method acting was considered High Art back in the days when this film was made. The passage of time, however, has reduced it to something resembling camp.

An amusing footnote: the very same year that Warners brought out *Streetcar*, this same studio released a vulgar, lurid, immensely entertaining carbon copy of its plot. The title of the imitation is *Storm Warning*, starring Ginger Rogers as Vivien Leigh, Doris Day as Kim Hunter, Steve Cochran as Marlon Brando, and Ronald Reagan as the brave, heroic good guy Tennessee Williams somehow neglected to include in his play.

---

*Suddenly, Last Summer** (U.S. 1959 B&W)

When Vito Russo wrote *The Celluloid Closet*, he was taken to task for being literal-minded in his approach to *Suddenly, Last Summer*. Establishment critics complained that he willfully ignored the poetry and symbolism of the Tennessee Williams drama on which the film is based. I'm not much into poetry, either. What I like about *Suddenly, Last Summer* is the way it taps into the lurid imagery of campy B-movie genres, most notably vintage horror and women's prison flicks. Not that the all-star cast ever realized they were making something lurid and campy. In 1959, the film was simply considered "daring" and "adult." The irony is that, in the intervening years, the cast itself has become the film's most supremely campy component.

The film begins at a state asylum for the mentally ill. The state is Louisiana, the year is 1937, and there's no money to keep the place from sliding into disrepair. Montgomery Clift performs a lobotomy in a makeshift operating theatre where even the lights malfunction. That very afternoon he's sipping tea with Katharine Hepburn, a rich New Orleans lady with a tropical garden straight out of a Charles Addams cartoon (it's all Venus flytraps and statues of the Grim Reaper). She'll give the hospital a generous endowment, if only Clift will agree to lobotomize Liz Taylor, an inconvenient niece who says dreadful things impugning the moral character of Hepburn's son, Sebastian, who, as the title says, died suddenly, last summer. From chance remarks here and there, we gather that Sebastian was a flaming queen, but the doctor appears to be ignorant of such things. (You may rest assured that, in real life, Montgomery Clift was not unacquainted with homosexuality.)

We first encounter Liz at a Catholic sanitarium. The nuns are all frustrated sadists dressed in downright medieval habits. (Their wimples resemble the carnivorous birds about which the screenplay interminably natters.) Liz is desperate for a cigarette. When she lights one up, a particularly grumpy sister demands that she fork it over, so she crushes it into the palm of the woman's outstretched hand. We see right away that she's perfectly sane, but "violent" acts such as this soon land her in the even grimmer loonybin where Monty plies his trade. Twice she wigs out on a catwalk. First time, it's the one over the men's ward and poor Liz is screaming and hollering while sex maniacs jump up and grab at her ankles. She doesn't make that mistake twice: next time, she wanders along the gallery over the women's ward, and nearly throws herself down when the inmates laugh at her. (A handsome blonde intern grabs her, just in time.)

With sodium pentothal and a little bit of hypnotism, Monty helps Liz recover her memory of Sebastian's untimely death. She was vacationing with him in Europe when it all happened. He forced her to wear an immodest swimsuit and used her as bait to draw horny peasant boys. Ah, the perils of cruising for chicken! The exploited youngsters, starving and penniless, got out of hand one day and literally ate him alive. We see this in a hallucinatory flashback sequence (which includes an animated skeleton). The cannibalism, though brutally explicit, is also symbolic: both a religious sacrifice and an obscene parody of fellatio. Anyway, the truth comes out, at which point Hepburn loses her mind.

I saw this movie when I was twelve years old. At that age, I didn't know much about abnormal psychology, but I *did* know that this was the neatest horror film since *The Blob*. Today my sole complaint is the lack of Depression era atmosphere. The only period notation I noticed was an old issue of *Look* in the solarium of the asylum. And even that might merely be a comment on how old the magazines are in the waiting rooms of hospitals.

Superargo and the Faceless Giants* (Italy 1966 C)

Superargo and the Faceless Giants, a film about a masked wrestler who dresses in neon red tights, is an esoteric masterwork of homo-erotic art and, perhaps, a midnight cult movie waiting to happen. The wrestling scenes alone are so—shall we say—*intense* that, with the addition of some full frontal nudity and a bit of hardcore genital action, this could have been a porno flick to reckon with. Such hairy chests! Such pumping buttocks! Such nasty moves! Such suggestive contortions! The subject matter of this fiction is friction, in all its most intimate and delectable forms.

Our hero (Ken Wood) is "in training" with a bearded East Indian mystic who wears a white turban. These two exotic dressers don't even need to touch each other to get it on: a typical scene has the Hindu yogi reclining on the floor while Superargo levitates in mid-air directly above him. The two are in perfect position for Super-argo's mentor to give him a rim job—or, at any rate, they would be, if they didn't have their clothes on.

Superargo's mat action is considerably less cool—as witness the orgiastic screeches of his opponent. The ringside announcer claims that Superargo has this match "in the bag." To me it looked, how-ever, as if the contenders would prefer to be in the sack. "Don't tell me the great Superargo believes in fairies!" someone comments at one point. If he doesn't, why does he wear a fairy suit?

The cast includes one of the great beauties of yesteryear: Guy Madison, in his mid-forties and slipping fast, although, wearing a conservative business suit and a pair of horn-rimmed glasses, he nonetheless manages to make a favorable impression. He portrays a mad scientist who's kidnapping well-proportioned athletes and turning them into soulless zombies, for what fell purpose no one knows (though we certainly might hazard a guess, mightn't we?). His name in the film is "Dr. Wond," which is pronounced "wand," as in magic. I find this apt. Maybe even provocative.

But perhaps all this smut is just in my mind. Perhaps it's all merely a figment of my perverted imagination. Even so, the Indian mystic does see fit to remark, "The imagination often has more truth than reality itself."

"I guess you're right," Superargo agrees. He wouldn't dream of disputing the point. For that matter, neither would I.

Sunset Boulevard* (U.S. 1950 B&W)

Sunset Boulevard is one of the many movies that's both a bona fide film classic and, at the same time, a classic of camp. Modern viewers have problems with this wallow in Hollywood decadence, and with the flamboyance of Gloria Swanson's performance in it. I presume that, in 1950, few people noticed that her acting has more than a whiff of the drag queen about it. Still, this is undeniably appropriate to the nature of her role: she's cast as Norma Desmond, a has-been movie actress whose star ascended in the silent era and declined with the coming of sound. Now, while the postwar prosperity of 1950 L.A. bustles all about her, she huddles in the shadows of her Gothic mansion and feeds off her own faded glamour. Her life is so swaddled in illusion and artifice, it's become a series of expressionistic gestures. We are therefore missing the point if we try to dismiss Swanson's acting by calling it "unreal."

The film is a character study: Norma is nothing if not a character. But she's only half the story; the other half is William Holden, who plays her kept man. The pretext for their relationship is that he's a struggling young writer who's helping her polish a screenplay in preparation for her big comeback. They play it this way for a while, but then, on New Year's Eve, he beds her. First she has to slit her wrists, though, to show that she means business. Holden also has a girlfriend his own age: a wholesome type played by Nancy Olson. He eventually ditches crazy old Norma, who then goes berserk and shoots him (three times). Straight men (and even, I fear, the younger generation of gays) tend to sympathize with the Holden character, wishing that he could break free of stud hustling and lead a normal, productive life (yuck). Old queens like me, however, can't help but identify with Norma all the way through the movie, even up to and including her final, mad writhe toward

GLORIA SWANSON (1897–1983) and ERICH VON STROHEIM (1885–1957) in a scene from the cult/camp classic, *Sunset Boulevard* (Paramount 1950).

the camera ("Mr. DeMille! I'm ready for my close-up!").

The supporting cast is studded with Hollywood right-wingers (Jack Webb, Hedda Hopper) who would no doubt hasten to assure us that obsessive/excessives like Norma are merely phantoms from Tinseltown's florid, exaggerated past; that the entertainment industry of a new and squeaky-clean decade has purged all grotesquery from its system. But we know better: their presence is counterbalanced by that of co-star Erich von Stroheim, the laconic, sardonic incarnation of Hollywood as Babylon.

Tarzan and the Trappers* (U.S. 1956 B&W)

In his role as the jungle hero of *Tarzan and the Trappers*, Gordon Scott is utterly devoid of body hair. We are, of course, curious as to just how thoroughly he's been shaved, but that troublesome loincloth of his is sufficiently elaborate to keep his most personal charms concealed, even during his most acrobatic moments. When the camera angle is right, however, we are at least able to plainly discern the ripely sensual curve of his buttocks.

There's quite a bit of bondage on display in this opus. Boy gets kidnapped by ruffians who, at one point, keep him penned up in what looks like a chicken coop. What we're yearning for the most, however, is the spectacle of Gordon all tied up. In this film he even gets spread-eagled. (And, yes, his armpits have also been shaved.) Seeing him rendered helpless, one of the trappers (Saul Gorse) gloatingly intones the following: "A hunter can do two things. He kills his prey or he tames it. I think I shall get great pleasure in taming you." And I would have taken great pleasure in watching. Gordon, unfortunately, bursts his bonds before anything really provocative transpires.

GORDON SCOTT (1927–   ) starred in numerous Tarzan films and muscleman epics of the 50s–60s. Shown here in a publicity photo as Tarzan.

Tarzan's Hidden Jungle   (U.S. 1955 B&W)

Gordon Scott is once again cast as Tarzan in *Tarzan's Hidden Jungle*. I took the title to be a probable reference to the tangle of pubic hair concealed beneath his loincloth. Early on, he shinnies up a tree while the camera remains below, thereby granting us a fairly unobstructed look beneath said garment. Of course, he's wearing a jock of some sort, protecting his privates from prying eyes, but we nonetheless feel like we're stealing a peek at something we're not intended to see.

Gordon is boyishly, breathtakingly gorgeous. I particularly like the way his muscles glisten when wet. He is kind to animals and conveys what seems to be a genuine fondness for them. This comes as a blessed relief, since jungle films tend to be full of bad men who hurt animals. (If you watch enough Tarzan movies, you start to talk like him.) Unfortunately, he proves quite incapable of investing his dialogue, however monosyllabic, with anything resembling conviction. Furthermore, the movie contrastingly pairs him with Vera Miles, who always seems to know precisely what she's doing, even when sinking into quicksand. He rescues her from the quicksand and, in a remarkably erotic scene, washes the muck from her shapely limbs. He also carries her in his arms quite a lot. In real life, they wed. (It is good to know that at least someone was allowed to explore the hidden jungle.) Both careers outlasted the marriage, and her career outlasted his. Gordon's husbandly endowments appear to be the only part of him that had any impact on the history of film: Vera's pregnancy prevented her from playing the Kim Novak role in *Vertigo*. I trust that he was livelier in private than when attempting to emote.

Tarzan's Magic Fountain   (U.S. 1949 B&W)

Tarzan's Magic Fountain, a routine jungle opus full of bad guys getting shot with flaming arrows, is distinguished by its campy, oddball plot and by the presence of Lex Barker in the role of Tarzan. The details of his breathtakingly gorgeous physique are abundantly displayed herein. His face is impossibly pretty, his loincloth skimpy, and his long blonde locks have been tousled by the best hair stylists Hollywood has to offer.

The ludicrously sexist script involves a fountain of youth. "There isn't a woman anywhere in the world that wouldn't pay any price to remain young," says co-star Albert Dekker. Men, of course, have no vanity whatsoever. Tarzan is faced with a minor domestic rebellion: Jane, going against Tarzan's wishes, agrees to guide Evelyn Ankers to the magic fountain. (Poor Miss Ankers is obliged to spend much of the film wearing old-lady make-up.) But girls are so darn klutzy in the jungle. Jane can't find drinking water or a decent place to sleep, let alone a fountain of youth. Whenever she screws up too badly, Tarzan steps in to save the day. The age-defying waters, by the way, glow in the dark. Looks radioactive to me.

Major stardom eluded Barker in America, but he was hugely successful in European westerns. In the Fifties he was briefly married to Lana Turner, whose daughter, in her autobiography, accuses him of molestation. She states that, in their initial encounter, he forced her to watch him jack off. Now an avowed lesbian, she was unimpressed by Tarzan's magic fountain.

Tarzan pictures constitute a hardy and durable genre, and many of them contain gay camp elements. The three movies reviewed above are representative examples.

Taxi Zum Klo* (Germany 1982 C)

Tazi Zum Klo (which translates as "Taxi to the Toilet") is a gay slice-of-life cult film about a schoolteacher who's into drugs and casual sex. He's not much to look at with his clothes on, but he's got a big dick and he's very good at finding hot-looking men. His life is about what you'd expect: water sports, drag queens, correcting test papers, etc. True to the title, at one point he does take a cab and make the rounds of his favorite public toilets. He's played by Frank Ripploh, who also wrote and directed the movie.

I could readily relate to this film. For one thing, I studied to be a teacher, although (thank God) I never actually went into the profession. Furthermore, I noticed Mr. Ripploh has a Tom of Finland stroke book which is also in my own personal collection. Speaking of porn, I should mention that this film does feature sexually explicit scenes.

The movie also has an appearance by Liberace: he's seen in a television broadcast. So you might say that *Taxi Zum Klo* was Lee's last film. Somehow I think he would have wanted it that way.

The Ten Commandments *
(U.S. 1923 B&W with one color sequence)

Cecil B. DeMille's silent version of *The Ten Commandments* must've really wowed 'em back in 1923. The film has crowd-pleasing elements to spare: epic spectacle, religious pageantry, sex, violence, pietistic moralism, special effects, and even a primitive attempt at color tinting, all choreographed to the accompaniment of the mighty Wurlitzer pipe organ. The first hour or so is devoted to a brisk retelling of the Biblical account: Moses, Pharaoh, the parting of the Red Sea, and the handing down of helpful hints to live by. The Golden Calf, as depicted herein, is an idol of unmistakably phallic design. Its high priestess, moreover, is a wanton hussy. But she gets leprosy. Religious fundamentalists invariably picture the ultimate evil as being feminine (or effeminate) sexuality in the thrall of a male organ (and I don't mean Wurlitzer).

The film shifts gears midway through. There's a fade from ancient days to contemporary (Jazz Age) San Francisco. A dour and severe old woman (Edythe Chapman) is reading the Book of Exodus to her grown-up sons. One of them, a devil-may-care type portrayed by Rod La Rocque, scoffs thusly: "All that's the bunk, Mother. The Ten Commandments were all right for a lot of dead ones—but that sort of stuff was buried with Queen Victoria!" In the narrative which follows, he breaks almost all of them. First off, his mother banishes him from the house for dancing with his ladylove (Leatrice Joy) on the Sabbath. He marries Leatrice and becomes a successful contractor. Then he builds a vast cathedral, lining his pockets by using shoddy material. His proud mama tours the unfinished structure, which collapses on top of her, crushing her to death.

At this point Rod has a twinge of conscience. It's merely a fore-taste of punishments to come. He's seduced by a beauteous Eur-asian leper-woman (Nita Naldi) who has sneaked into the United States by concealing herself in a sack of the Bombay jute with which he adulterates his concrete. Ah, poetic justice! When he learns of her leprosy, he shoots her. Then, attempting to flee the country in his motorboat (aptly named "Defiance"), he perishes in a squall. Leatrice fears that she too is infected with leprosy, but is soon convinced otherwise by her husband's God-fearing brother (Rich-ard Dix).

The screenplay contains some clever examples of parallel plot-ting. In both stories, God in His heaven finally takes notice of the immorality down below when one of the good guys gets crushed to death. Then the person responsible gets drowned (in the Red Sea or in San Francisco Bay). Or else gets leprosy. This disease (which, by the way, is not contagious) is used herein as a virtual emblem of divine retribution for sexcapades. And this antediluvian moral-ity play gives us a hint as to what sort of movie the Religious Right would make on the subject of AIDS.

Cecil B. DeMille's sumptuous remake of The Ten Command-ments* (1956) *also has its share of camp: Charlton Heston's pon-derous seriousness as the Savior Moses; Edward G. Robinson's manic worship of the Golden Calf (complete with orgy) while Charlton-Moses is magisterially communing with the Divine up the mountain; the parting of the Red Sea, etc.* —Editor

---

The Terror of Rome Against the Son of Hercules*
(Italy 1963 C)

In *The Terror of Rome Against the Son of Hercules*, Mark Forest comes striding into the arena, looking the very picture of voluptu-ous pagan decadence. His loincloth is cut disconcertingly short. Leathern straps crisscross his otherwise naked chest. At the victory banquet, he wears an essentially identical outfit, except that the straps are of cloth. (Looks rather like a toddler's playsuit.) He's somewhat stocky of build, but nonetheless quite fetching, no doubt owing to the coyness of his costumes.

At one point there's an orgy, remarkably well-clothed. The action is sedately heterosexual, except for the part where a drunken soldier attempts to detain his male comrade by grasping him by the shoulder and saying, "Oh! Don't go away!" Paradoxically, Forest wears more clothes in this scene than in any other part of the movie. One must bear in mind, however, that by now he's under the influence of a pious Christian maiden. Indeed, his Christianity causes some rather obscene improbabilities of plot: since our hero is no longer allowed to kill people, the clumsy bad guy is obliged to accidentally stab himself to death in the crotch!

SABU (1924–1963), adolescent star (born in India) of such classics as *The Thief of Baghdad, The Jungle Book, Drums.* Shown here in a pensive scene from the otherwise manic camp classic, *Cobra Woman* (Universal 1944).

The Thief of Bagdad* (G.B. 1940 C)

The Thief of Bagdad, the apex of Technicolor Arabian Nights fantasy, is dazzlingly imaginative, phantasmagorical, and rather psychedelic. It's aswirl with ornate barges, veiled houris, flying horses, magic carpets, turreted cities, and blue roses of forgetfulness. In other words, this is very serious stuff.

Take, for example, its historical significance. This 1940 release obviously served as a prototype for all those exotic Maria Montez vehicles which so brightened the balance of the decade. No Maria here, however. John Justin, a romantic swashbuckler type, is cast as the handsome prince whose throne has been usurped by a lecherous wizard (Conrad Veidt). Justin's devoted servant is the thief of the title, played by Sabu, whose goal in life is to run off with Sinbad the Sailor: a healthy impulse which, unfortunately, is frustrated as soon as Justin lays eyes on June Duprez, the beauteous princess. He'll need the help of Sabu to get her away from Conrad's clutches. The wizard reduces our princely hero to a blind beggar and also transforms Sabu into a puppy dog. What had been a master-slave relationship is now a master-canine one. Kinky.

This is a very pretty film to look at, as well it should be, since it's devoted to "the beauty of the impossible." Veidt makes an imposing villain. His bearing and the way he bulges his eyes tend to remind me of Joan Crawford. His turbans, furthermore, would not have looked out of place on her head. In her equally regal role, Miss Duprez consistently manages to maintain her dignity. Sabu and Mr. Justin both show plenty of skin. At the film's conclusion, Sabu finally puts on a shirt. Seldom have I seen a lad look more uncomfortable.

The Third Sex* (Germany 1958 B&W)

Veit Harlan will forever be reviled for having directed *Jud Suss*, the notorious Nazi anti-Semitic film. In a very real sense, *Jud Suss* was a contributing factor in the Holocaust. In 1958, almost two decades later, Harlan directed a film called *The Third Sex*, wherein he attempted to do for homosexuality what he had already done for Judaism. Although it was made several years after the fall of the Hitler regime, I believe it is nonetheless fair to designate *The Third Sex* as being a Nazi film. It not only makes use of former Nazi film personnel (both behind and in front of the cameras; more about that later); it also employs favorite Nazi propaganda techniques. Guilt by association, for example. In this movie, homosexuals are uniformly portrayed as being connoisseurs of electronic music, blank verse, and abstract expressionist painting. Homosex, in other words, is used to smear any form of non-traditional art, no matter how mild the unconventionality. As always, homophobia merely plays a part in a larger and more extensive cultural agenda. When Jesse Helms uses homoerotic art as an excuse to declare war on the avant-garde in general, he's carrying on a right-wing tradition that served the Nazis well.

In light of his consistently hate-mongering works, one naturally feels inclined to dismiss Veit Harlan as being a man of somewhat limited interests and capabilities. In fact, however, his films might be said to have wide-ranging appeal. An irony occurs to me: neo-cons such as Norman Podhoretz, who would no doubt like to see every print of *Jud Suss* consigned to the flames, would, on the other hand, probably consider *The Third Sex* a fair and accurate appraisal of a serious "problem." Midge Decter (Mrs. Podhoretz) has bemoaned, in the pages of *Commentary* magazine, the tendency of homosexual males to be alienated from their fathers and from bourgeois family life in general. She deems us disgusting because we don't procreate. Her bitter and resentful vituperations might have come straight (that word!) from the screenplay of this equally mean-spirited movie.

The picture doesn't waste much time letting us know what it's all about. Klaus (dark, lithe, lissome) is late for his mother's birthday party. He's too busy holding hands at the bedside of a sick boyfriend named Manfred. Papa fumes when Uncle Max reminds him that Klaus is a talented prodigy. "Praise helps nothing. I wish he were more normal," Papa grouses. Mama, meanwhile, has put on her reading glasses and is studying up on "deviational behavior." A helpful psychiatrist advises her to get Klaus some pussy before it's too late. She prevails on her comely young housekeeper to seduce the boy. (Beats washing windows.) Klaus, intent on doing a sketch of this strumpet, visits the girl in her room. A strategically placed mirror while she's changing into something more comfortable purges him of any last vestige of perversion. Indeed, he becomes a raging incarnation of horny hetero lust, pursuing the girl through the garden and taking her by force. Mama is well-pleased by this rather abrupt turnabout, but her satisfaction is short-lived. Her chickens come home to roost when she's hauled into court for contributing to the delinquency of a minor. The judge sentences her to six months in the slammer. A fine how-do-you-do for a good German mother who simply wanted to save her son from "unsuitable companions."

This melodramatic storyline is rather like a Nazi version of *Tea and Sympathy*. Harlan, by the way, is not above catering to the very same group that he's castigating: the film includes a fairly hot scene of seminude boys engaged in a wrestling match. It's highly significant, however, that the only sex in this film occurs between a boy and a girl. Without intending to, Harlan ends up implying that homosexuals don't have sex. The gay men in this movie never go beyond holding hands and patting one another on the shoulders. We get the distinct impression that the "gay world" which fundamentalists are constantly frothing about is really just an innocuous trade school where handsome young men go to prepare themselves for a career in the arts. Cocksucking? What's that? Is it anything like flower arranging?

Movies about homosexuality were pretty uncommon in 1958; nonetheless, this must have seemed like old stuff to Paula Wessely, the actress awarded the plum role of the masochistic, self-sacrificing mother. In the course of the film she refers to gays, variously and disparagingly, as "them," "that crowd," "criminals," etc. The term her character most prefers is "sick," since that implies a "cure" may be possible. Like Harlan, Wessely was no stranger to the realm of hate propaganda. In the days of the Third Reich, she was probably the most famous and celebrated of Austrian film stars. *The Third Sex* is by no means her most notorious film; that distinction is reserved for *Heimkehr*, a Nazi flick depicting the plight of German ethnics residing in Poland. In that film also she was preoccupied with endemic ailments and weaknesses. "At home in Germany they're not weak any longer," she enthuses in *Heimkehr*'s most stirring scene. "Just imagine how it will be when there are only Germans around us. You won't hear Yiddish or Polish spoken in the shops. You'll hear German." Kind of helps you put *The Third Sex* into its proper perspective, doesn't it?

Thirteen Women   (U.S. 1932 B&W)

In *Thirteen Women* Myrna Loy is made up to play a beautiful—
but deadly—half-caste Indian who's got a fiendish fate in store
for each member of the sorority that snubbed her back in the days
when they all attended finishing school together. There's more than
one way to finish somebody, and Myrna's chosen method is rather
chancy: she accomplishes her evil ends by mailing extremely inauspicious horoscopes to the thirteen women in question. She lets their
imaginations do the rest; in most cases, that's all that's necessary.
The trapeze artist gets butterfingers. The happy housewife stabs
her husband to death at the breakfast table. ("I must have lost my
mind," she explains later.) The grieving mother shoots herself.
Myrna, her eyes very slinky and slanted, resorts to hypnosis when
the powers of suggestion fail her. In extreme cases, she's willing to
commit outright murder. She wants to hurt Irene Dunne by killing her kid, so she mails him poisoned chocolates. Irene intercepts
them, so next she arranges to give him a big rubber ball with a
stick of dynamite concealed inside it.

The film is unusually brief, but stylishly elegant, suspenseful, and
highly entertaining. It qualifies as camp because the entire plot is
based on the ridiculously sexist assumption that a bad horoscope
can manipulate a woman into doing virtually anything. Then again,
maybe in those days gals actually were that suggestible. Case in
point: one of the thirteen women is Peg Entwhistle, who, in honor
of this film, committed suicide in real life by hurling herself off
the thirteenth letter of the big old HOLLYWOODLAND sign in the
hills of L.A.

Thor and the Amazon Women*   (Italy 1963 C)

I'll admit it; I like films about the involuntary servitude of half-
naked men. There are plenty on hand in *Thor and the Amazon
Women*. In fact, at one point we see approximately a hundred
seminude guys, all sleeping together in one big heap.

The film's presiding bodybuilder is Joe Robinson as Thor, who is first seen frolicking in a mountain stream. Then those nasty Amazons attempt to abduct him. Fortunately, he is rescued by an Afro-American muscleboy who carries him bodily to the safety of a cave. This husky young fellow, clad in a bright red loincloth, arranges the prostrate demigod on a bed with more care than his wounds would seem to require. He calls him "Master," affectionately squeezing the inner side of Thor's naked thigh for emphasis.

This houseboy (or whatever he is) gets captured by the Amazons, who steal his pretty gold necklace, place him on a pedestal, and, in a remarkably blatant scene, force him to pose, display himself, flex his muscles, and generally show himself off. The queen, who is also black, orders him to go to bed with her. "Me?!" he asks incredulously. Fortunately, Thor arrives in time to break things up. ("Come away and leave this woman," he orders.)

Most of the film, not so fortunately, is devoted to lesbo-sado action among the female gladiators of the arena. This movie refers to matriarchy as "the most frightful and horrible form of government." Despite the plethora of gay notations, we should bear in mind that the people who made this picture probably actually believe that.

Thoroughbreds Don't Cry* (U.S. 1937 B&W)

In *Thoroughbreds Don't Cry*, Sophie Tucker runs a boarding house for jockeys. She's got eight of 'em in her stable, but Mickey Rooney's the star boarder. If this doesn't have the makings of camp, I don't know what does. Furthermore, the star of the film is Judy Garland (as Sophie's niece). And Frankie Darro is cast as a jockey named "Dink," who, when introduced to a dainty British lad (Ronald Sinclair), mockingly addresses him as "Butch."

Sinclair wants to learn how to ride in races, and Mickey agrees to teach him. This means they end up together astride the same mount. It's educational, you see. And, when you put them in motion, it's also a little obscene. ("How're you coming?" asks an observer.) After the lesson, Mickey gives the dear boy a rubdown.

"I think that's enough," Ronald protests demurely, as Mickey roughly paws him.

"Whaddaya mean it's enough?! I just got started! After the oil, we'll give you the alkie. And hold still."

"I *am* holding still."

Judy tries to intrude ("Can't I come in for just a minute?" she plaintively inquires), whereupon Ronald hastens to pull his pants up, but Mickey just yanks them down again ("No! We're busy!"). Boys have all the fun.

The notoriously foul-mouthed Sophie cleaned up her act for the movies, but she's still adorable. It's rather odd to see the likes of her interacting with the veddy dignified C. Aubrey Smith, who's cast as Ronald's grandfather. So here's the plot: Mickey's no-good dad, pretending to be critically ill, prevails on Mickey to throw a race and thereby get money for an iron lung. When Mickey complies, the loss of the race causes Ronald's grandpa to have a fatal coronary. And Mickey gets barred from the race track for keeps! I won't tell you how it all comes out. I'll merely say that (sniffle, sniff) thoroughbreds don't cry.

---

*Till the End of Time** (U.S. 1946 B&W)

Till the End of Time is a title rather cruel in its irony, since the leading man is beautiful Guy Madison, whose stardom was more like a flash in the pan. Didn't take very long for the powers-that-be to notice he couldn't act. This postwar melodrama finds him cast as a marine who's just been mustered out of the service. All I can say is that he certainly walks like one: he's got a gait which can best be described as assholish, not only for its pretentious butchness, but also because it seems to be centered on that particularly fundamental part of his anatomy.

A sense of feverish desperation pervades and permeates the entire film. It might have been a shrewd idea to surround this Guy with a cast of non-actors, in which case his woeful ineptitude would not have been so glaringly apparent. But no: instead he's surrounded with excellent actors, all of them emoting their little hearts out, and there he stands, front and center, in all his studly glory, barely able to string ten words together in a way that sounds like a sentence. At one point he gives a highly dramatic speech in a tight close-up, and a fly lights on his cheek, utterly spoiling the whole shot. "Why didn't the director order a retake?" I wondered. Then it suddenly occurred to me that there were probably twenty or thirty retakes, and this one happened to be the best, fly or no fly.

His romantic interest is Dorothy McGuire, who looks dowdy and dumpy and generally awful. But that's all right; unlike Groucho Marx, I'm fond of movies where the boy is prettier than the girl. She's a war widow; he's having trouble readjusting to civilian life. Just a couple of unhappy kids in love. "If you're laughing at me, I don't like it," he warns her, and, for a single uncanny moment, I was scared that he might have heard me. "I'll remember that," he says later on, when she tells him the name of her hometown. "You've got enough to remember," she replies oh-so-sweetly, which sounded to me like a subtle jab at his lack of histrionic experience. Finally he hits the nail right on the head: "It's me that's wrong. I guess I just don't fit anyplace yet."

He never did find his niche. In this whole movie, he has only one good, convincing scene: it's the one where he nearly comes to blows with his foreman at the factory where he works. (It kind of gives you a taste of how matters must have stood between him and the director, Edward Dmytryk.) Toward the end of the film, he has a bathing suit scene. At last he gets to show off the chest and shoulders which, together with his beautiful eyes and engaging smile, constitute the principal reason why he was ever even allowed in front of a movie camera.

Torch Song Trilogy* (U.S. 1988 C)

In *Torch Song Trilogy* an unattractive, fortyish drag queen (Harvey Fierstein) is romantically besieged by good-looking men. He makes a deep emotional commitment to a bisexual Robert Redford lookalike (Brian Kerwin), who eventually ditches him in favor of a woman. Next he's pursued by a gorgeous male model (Matthew Broderick) approximately fifteen years his junior. The two settle down together and share several happy years. Then one night the model heroically attempts to rescue an elderly man who's been set

HARVEY FIERSTEIN (1954–   ), seated and MATTHEW BRODERICK (1961–   ) in a publicity photo for *Torch Song Trilogy* (New Line Cinema 1988).

upon by gaybashers; he ends up getting bludgeoned to death himself. Then the Redford clone comes back on the scene, all contrite and remorseful. He's seen the light and knows he can only be truly happy in the arms of the drag queen—who, meanwhile, is in the process of adopting a troubled gay teenager. The film concludes with the clear implication that the kid, the queen, and the bisexual hunk are going to form an unconventional family unit and live happily ever after.

I love it.

The proceedings are indeed highly charged but they do reflect reality, being derived from Fierstein's actual life experiences. In its exposure of homophobia, its exploration of new ways of relating, the film is a gay liberation document for our times. Director Paul Bogart does give it the cozy, ingratiatingly reassuring veneer of a TV movie. Still, it took guts to release this film in 1988. Harvey Fierstein seemed an incongruous concept at theatres dominated by the likes of Sylvester Stallone and Arnold Schwarzenegger.

Trash* (U.S. 1970 C)

The opening scene of Trash (a self-explanatory title, if ever there was one) finds Joe Dallesandro getting a blow job. He has really unsightly blemishes on his butt. Administering the blow job is a naked young woman with big, pendulous tits. At this point, we might just as well be watching a Russ Meyer movie. But we're not: Joe, you see, is a junkie and he's unable to get a hard-on.

As the film continues, we notice other tell-tale signs that this is not a Russ Meyer picture. The cast, for example. There's this Jewish actress named Andrea Feldman who apparently thinks she can pass for a late Sixties British "bird" of the Julie Christie type. Her presence (she's also in Heat) marks the movie as an Andy Warhol production, as does that of Holly Woodlawn, noted transvestite superstar glamourpuss. Holly is cast in a (very) female role: a typical New York sophisticate who brings home high school boys from the Fillmore, pumps them full of drugs, and then sucks them off.

The real star of the show is Joe's cock, and a huge star it is—with the potential of getting bigger at any moment. Which brings us to the pivotal question: is *Trash* really camp, or is it just a porno experiment that didn't come off? Camp is, by definition, entertainment, whereas this film consists of seemingly interminable conversations involving people with gratingly abrasive voices.

The sole exception is Holly, and her scenes do indeed qualify as camp. (Gay camp, if you will, since she's a drag queen.) She is indubitably the best actress in the film. (There's no competition, frankly.) In the scene where she masturbates with a beer bottle, we almost believe that she's a woman. It may seem weird to say so, but she and Dallesandro actually do achieve moments of emotional truth together, most notably when they talk about going on welfare and how it will make them "respectable." (Unfortunately, their social worker turns out to be a fag who won't cooperate unless she gives him her Joan Crawford pumps so that he can make a lamp out of them.) What's more, she doesn't have pimples on her ass.

Trog   (G.B. 1970 C)

"In an age when man can launch an expedition to the moon, I think we should clarify the history of man's origin," enthuses Joan Crawford in *Trog*. With that as their excuse, she and her daughter (did Joan ever play the mother of a son?) commence detailed study of the troglodyte which Joan encountered on a spelunking expedition down a London sewer! The film is a blunt, unrefined, minimum-budget actioner, to which Joan somehow manages to add some subtlety. Her strength is overpowering (if not totally convincing), whether she's marching crisply across the sunny moors, firing tranquilizer pellets at Trog's advancing hulk, donning smock, mask, and rubber gloves to implant an artificial larynx, or mincing through a cave to rescue a child from the creature's clutches.

Michael Gough, a British obscurity and one of my favorite actors, is Joan's perfect foil as a woman-hating ("That female quack has made herself the star of the whole show!"), anti-evolutionist ("That's the talk of a heathen!"), faggy ("Don't you *dare* touch me!") old crank, who objects to the presence of a troglodyte in the neighborhood because it might lower property values. It's a ridiculous part, but it permits him and Joan to wrangle like alleycats, with him earning dozens more hisses than the leading lady and her monster (which is lovable as a housepet, once Joan has stared the thing down). They even take their feud to court (where they argue their own cases; any lawyers on hand are mute).

It's a gory tale: when Trog loses his temper, his very touch means death. The camera lovingly follows every rivulet of blood, waxing ecstatic when our furry friend hangs the village butcher on one of his own meat hooks. Trog himself winds up impaled on a stalagmite. This was Joan's last film, and it's a bathetic (if campy) close to a great career.

The Tyrant of Lydia Against the Son of Hercules *
(Italy 1963 Released in color. Available in video generally only in b&w)

If you rub the Tyrant of Lydia against the Son of Hercules, some high-voltage friction is likely to be generated, especially since neither one of these dudes wears much in the way of clothing. Both have perfectly gorgeous physiques, provocatively semiclad, and, furthermore, their garments grow much skimpier as the film progresses. Remarkably enough, the villain is the more undraped of the two. The good guy, however, is Gordon Scott, who's got considerably more than mere muscles (though they do catch the light rather fetchingly). Nice legs, nice thighs, nice buns, and his costumes, cut shorter than the average pair of bathing briefs, display everything to excellent advantage.

Various other wonders of the ancient world are also intriguingly glimpsed. One scene, for instance, presents us with a slave dealer offering to sell a precocious, rather impudent-looking little boy. "What's he for?" a prospective buyer inquires, somewhat ingenuously. "To steal the neighbors' chickens," replies the dealer, unconvincingly. (And, speaking of chicken, . . .)

As in so many of his gladiator vehicles, Gordon is seen consorting with a known homosexual. This time it's Alexander the Great. "You're the strongest man I ever saw in my life," Alexander drools when they first meet. "You keep this," he says, handing Gordon an armband of gold. "I want it to be a token of my great esteem and profound admiration. Now come with me. We've many important matters to discuss." Like, for instance, who's got the longer salami. Later on, this pair exchange knowing looks while drinking a toast. The plot is confusing. Several of the characters are hard to tell apart. Many of them meet with exceedingly gruesome fates. The body count is exceptionally high. All ends happily, however, with Gordon grasping (or should I say caressing?) Alexander's naked biceps while bidding him a fond farewell.

Untamed Youth   (U.S. 1957 B&W)

Untamed Youth takes place on a penal farm. The film gets off on the right foot with a young escapee being manhandled by cops behind the opening titles. Cut to Mamie Van Doren and Lori Nelson skinny-dipping. These girls are sisters on their way to California, but they get arrested for hitchhiking. The sentence is thirty days of hard labor on the plantation. The owner of the farm is John Russell, one mean-looking stud, as ornery as he is horny. He's dark and dangerous, with the kind of cruel, squinty eyes that give some men a hard-on. (Not me, of course. I'm not a masochist. Not much.) "You look real pretty in lipstick," he says to one young man. "I hate tramps, male or female." John's got a limitless supply of convict slaves, all because he's beefing the local judge (Lurene Tuttle). Every time he takes the old bag in his arms, he looks like he's gonna heave. His prisoners, meanwhile, are heaving for real; he feeds them a diet of Alpo.

In the end, of course, Lurene discovers that she's been had. Lori spills the news to her that John's been messing around. At this point the film could have really gotten interesting. The judge is on hand to supervise John's arrest. "Search him, Mitch," she says to her deputy.

"If you don't, we will," drools a male inmate nearby.

"Yeah, man!" chimes in another.

I do hate to see opportunities missed.

Victor/Victoria* (U.S. 1982 C)

Victor/Victoria stars Julie Andrews (cornball as ever) in the role of a coloratura who can't find a job in jazz-age Paree. In the opening reel artificial snowflakes filter down upon her, while she presses her nose against a restaurant window to droolingly watch a fat man consume an éclair. Julie is saved from starvation by the ministrations of Robert Preston, who portrays a gay cabaret entertainer. "How long have you been a ho-mo-secks-you-ull?" she inquires, her diction as impeccably British as always. Soon she's posing as one herself. Preston makes her a show biz sensation by presenting her to Parisian cafe society as the world's greatest female impersonator. This masquerade is a stunning success, but then Julie has the misfortune to fall in love with a Chicago gangster (James Garner) who's attracted to her in spite of himself. Garner's discarded moll, incidentally, is Lesley Ann Warren, whose delineation of a predatory, nasal-voiced Jean Harlow type is easily the comic highlight of the picture.

One of the best scenes is that in which Julie makes her debut as a drag queen. With eerie solemnity, she takes off her wig, revealing her apparent "manhood" (short hair), while the camera treats us to a panoply of reaction shots. Earlier, at rehearsal, a covey of gay chorus boys give her some provocatively appraising glances. They think she's sexy because they think she's male. Garner isn't so certain. However, when he thinks he spies Julie making love to Preston, who's notorious for only going to bed with guys, Garner gets so horny, he immediately makes a caveman lunge in Lesley's direction. Then, embarrassingly enough, he proves impotent.

The film seems to say that being a homosexual is no worse than being a mobster. In my opinion, this isn't a very liberating, uplifting message. But *Victor/Victoria* is far more concerned with Women's Lib than with Gay Lib. The picture is particularly preoccupied with the cozy charm of the Andrews/Preston relationship. I realize it's considered chic for heterosexual women to have gay male friends. Heterosexual moviemakers may consider this concept fascinating, but I think it's devastatingly dull. Furthermore, I feel it's extremely significant that Garner never shows or expresses any affection for Julie till he's absolutely sure that she's a girl. If he hadn't waited so long, this could have been a much more campy film.

What Ever Happened to Baby Jane? * (U.S. 1962 B&W)

In the autumn of 1962, when we were fourteen years old, my best friend and I were utterly obsessed with *What Ever Happened to Baby Jane?* At the time, it never occurred to me that this meant we were both homosexual. Today it seems a dead giveaway. It is reasonable to ask why this is so.

In the Sixties, director Robert Aldrich made four similarly-titled films dramatizing the misfortunes of celebrity. *What Ever Happened to Baby Jane?* was the first; the other three were *Hush . . . Hush, Sweet Charlotte, The Legend of Lylah Clare,* and *The Killing of Sister George.* All four are demonstrably camp. The last two actually deal with homosexuality (lesbianism, to be exact). Only *Baby Jane*, however, has become a gay cult film.

The title character is an alcoholic harridan (Bette Davis) who was formerly a top vaudeville child star. She resides with and cares for her sister, Blanche (Joan Crawford), a former Hollywood movie queen. Blanche is confined to a wheelchair. At the height of her career, she was crippled in an automobile accident. Rumor has it that Jane, a has-been by that time, may have been to blame for this mishap. Indeed, she is said to have deliberately injured her sister out of spiteful jealousy. Jane can't remember; she'd been drinking (as usual). Now the two of them, aging and forgotten, are penned up together in a gloomy, decaying mansion.

Obviously, there are limitless possibilities here for bitchy theatrics. The film can't seem to make up its mind whether it's serious drama or a horror flick; the end result is bizarre, pulpy camp. Jane's mental condition, we gather, has been deteriorating for quite some time. Now she's decided to do away with Blanche, starving and terrorizing the helpless invalid by serving her a macabre assortment of meals (roast rat, for example, and a parakeet salad). She also plans to attempt a comeback, reviving her old "Baby Jane" song-and-dance act. The sight of Bette Davis, clad in a frilly white organdy tutu, her face caked with clownish make-up, prancing around like Shirley Temple and singing "I've Written a Letter to Daddy," virtually defines a certain kind of low Sixties camp.

It is, to say the least, an attention-getting part. In horror movie terms, Baby Jane is comparable to the Frankenstein monster: she gets to be sympathetic and unsympathetic simultaneously. My friend and I were devastated when Bette didn't win the Oscar that year. She was nominated, but Anne Bancroft won for *The Miracle Worker*. And, since Bancroft was performing on Broadway at the time, Joan Crawford made arrangements to pick up the statuette for her. This was Crawford's vengeance for not being nominated—for having been slighted in favor of Davis. Her resentment was perhaps understandable: according to some sources, Crawford was the driving force that got *Baby Jane* produced in the first place. In *Bette and Joan: The Divine Feud*, Crawford is quoted as saying she read the novel on which the film is based and then promoted it to appropriate directors. She bought three copies of the book and mailed one to Alfred Hitchcock, one to Nicholas Ray (who had directed her in *Johnny Guitar*), and one to Robert Aldrich (who had directed her in *Autumn Leaves*). Aldrich optioned it, and the rest is camp history.

When *What Ever Happened to Baby Jane?* finally came to our town, my friend and I sat through it twice. He's gone now. AIDS, of course. Back in 1962, he and I thought *Baby Jane* was the greatest movie ever made. I no longer feel that way. Neither would he, I suspect. But I know he'd agree it's an absolutely essential movie for gays.

---

*Wicked Stepmother** (U.S. 1988 C)

Wicked Stepmother, the final film of her career, casts Bette Davis as a witch who marries into families and then demolishes them from within. As a Davis vehicle, the film has lots of things wrong with it. (1) She's wizened and shriveled and virtually unrecognizable. (2) She's had a stroke and is barely able to say her lines. (Her face is partially paralyzed.) (3) She fought with the director and walked out of the production midway through. (He then rewrote the script and gave much of her dirty work to dazzling Barbara Carrera, cast as her much younger alter ego. Perhaps I'm a sexist pig for saying so, but this is not exactly a drawback.) Though flawed, the film does manage a few campy cinematic in-jokes. Like, for instance, when the wimpy stepdaughter (Colleen Camp) addresses a portrait photo of her late and lamented natural mother. "Oh, Mom!" she gushes. "If I only knew, I would have been so much nicer to you when you were alive. You were so good!" The picture is of Joan Crawford.

Wild Mustang* (U.S. 1935 B&W)

Wild Mustang, a low-budget western from the Depression era, is best understood as an unintentional allegory of homosexual rape and seduction. The bad guys are a bunch of maniacal outlaws who have a habit of hogtying and then placing a brand upon every good-looking guy they encounter. Once marked in this way, a fellow becomes a kind of frontier pariah, rejected by "decent citizens" (women in particular) and therefore left with no alternative but to join the gang that scarred him. We will ignore the weird sociological implications of this, and, in keeping with the title, concentrate instead on the homoerotic symbolism involved. That there is hanky-panky going on we may readily surmise from the fact that this rather large group of "marked men" hole up in an incredibly tiny, cozy cabin where their wicked leader (Robert Kortman) announces lights-out by saying, "All right, boys, you can turn in or do anything you want to." We can safely assume that at least some of them "want to" get their rocks off.

The Wild One* (U.S. 1954 B&W)

The Wild One, wherein a motorcycle gang utterly terrorizes a town, is a virtual blueprint for all the juvenile delinquency pictures that came afterward. I should note, however, that the hoodlums aren't particularly juvenile, nor is the town an innocent victim (its citizens seem to be eagerly awaiting an excuse to form themselves into lynch mobs). But the movie certainly does convey a sense of how alien and how terribly threatening the new Fifties youth culture must have appeared when it first manifested itself.

The movie also conveys how Marlon Brando came to be a cult figure. Leering, sneering, insolently mumbling, clad in a black leather jacket and voluptuously formfitting blue jeans, he is blatantly homoerotic. (The mumbling has aged, forty years later, into camp.) The plot context supplements this impression: seems that he split off from his gang and formed his own all-male contingent as a reaction against the infiltration of trashy, hardcase motorcycle mamas. But, of course, all he needs is to meet a "nice" girl—in this case, attractive Mary Murphy, who, at the end of the movie, finally coaxes a genuine smile out of him.

Will Success Spoil Rock Hunter?   (U.S. 1957 C)

Will Success Spoil Rock Hunter? starts out as a spoof of Madison Avenue. In its evocation of Fifties consumer mindlessness, it seems less like a 1957 movie release and more like a 1957 issue of *Mad* magazine. But that's cool: I was a big fan of *Mad* in 1957, and this film is like taking a walking tour of my own childhood world.

The plot is simple to a fault: Rock Hunter (Tony Randall), a writer of TV commercials, wants screen star Rita Marlowe (Jayne Mansfield) to endorse Stay-Put Lipstick, his major account. Mansfield's presence guarantees a bumper crop of bosom jokes. This is the film in which she squeals with delight when someone declares her the "titular" head of a production company. In one scene a movie theatre has a life-size cardboard cutout of Rita Marlowe out front on the sidewalk. Someone bumps into it and knocks it face forward, but it pops right back up again, as if it had landed on something bouncy. I think I even heard it go "Boing."

All this harmless joshing is rather morbid, in light of later events. Rita's pet poodle is practically a duplicate of the one killed in Jayne's fatal car accident. Rita's boyfriend, a TV Tarzan with phony hair on his chest, is played by Jayne's musclebound husband, Mickey Hargitay. Clad in naught but a skimpy—though suitably bulging

237

—leopard-skin loincloth, Mickey gloats that "Rita will come crawling back to me on her hands and knees." A provocative line, especially for those of us who enjoy spending time on our knees. But co-star Joan Blondell is the one who gets to deliver the smuttiest line, when she tells us about a woman she knew who ran away with a milkman: "She must have liked his brand of cream."

Improbably enough, the film is preoccupied with Tony's sex appeal, not Jayne's or Mickey's. In the movie, Jayne and Tony become an item, a circumstance which brings him worldwide celebrity (hence the title). It's all very jolly, but I swear that poodle haunts the movie like a ghost: an intimation of mortality amidst the frivolity.

The Wild, Wild World of Jayne Mansfield* (U.S. 1968 C)

The Wild, Wild World of Jayne Mansfield is a leering, mind-boggling, obscenely tacky compilation of what appear to be Jayne's home movies, mainly taken in the course of a trip to Paris and Rome. Mostly she just parades around with her pet chihuahua, making a public spectacle of herself and fervently hoping that the public will notice. She also provides narration, breathlessly going on about "my studio," as if she still had one (Jayne was briefly under contract to 20th Century Fox in the mid-Fifties). As a travelogue, the film is almost poignantly bad. Jayne visits the Eiffel Tower ("Do you know it's the most famous monument in the entire world?"). She also visits a gay bar ("Oh, it was just too darn confusing!"). She cringes at the sight of lesbians groping one another ("Oh, no! This is too much!"). She also watches a queen fumble a pass ("In a way, I hoped the poor jerk would make it."). Of course, due attention is paid to the famous Mansfield bosom. She flaunts her naked tits every chance she gets, at the same time piously pretending that she doesn't want us to look ("Gee, I hope no one sees me like this!"). Her disingenuousness is really quite obnoxious. Perhaps we should take her at her word and close our eyes.

JAYNE MANSFIELD (1932–1967). Hollywood sex-icon of the 50s–60s.

The Witch's Curse* (Italy 1962 C)

Initially, *The Witch's Curse* seems to be just another Gothic horror thriller, perhaps more ineptly made than most. The setting is seventeenth century Scotland. A rash of suicide attempts take place at a site where, a century earlier, a witch was burned at the stake. When a pretty girl who happens to have the same name as the witch comes to town on her honeymoon, the panic-stricken citizens form a lynch mob and seize her.

So far, so bad. At this point, however, the movie blossoms into utterly outrageous, full-blooded camp. A muscleboy in a very skimpy loincloth appears out of nowhere to rescue the threatened heroine. He's Kirk Morris, and you'd think his inappropriate attire would cause him to catch cold in this damp northern climate. The poor laddie looks a mite confused, as if he's wandered off the set of another movie, as well he might have. His appearance is a source of consternation to the superstitious townsfolk, who presumably believe that he's a witch, too. No one thinks to ask him why he doesn't put some clothes on. Perhaps they're enjoying the view as much as I am. His labors, feats, and straining muscles are photographed for maximum homoerotic impact.

Much of the film is devoted to Kirk's exploration of Hades, which is depicted as an Hieronymus Bosch vision come to life. Perhaps he goes there to get warm. He eases the sufferings of Prometheus, who's as naked as he is, and so grateful, he can hardly keep his hands off Kirk's muscles. At the climax Kirk is almost trampled by a herd of bulls. Why are they in hell? Because they have horns?

This ludicrous attempt to blend horror with peplum is the work of Ricardo Freda, a director noted for his contributions to both genres. Perhaps he thought he could start a ridiculous new trend.

The Wizard of Oz*
(U.S. 1939 Color, with opening and closing scenes in b&w)

There can be no denying that *The Wizard of Oz* must be categorized as a gay cult film. It is, however, reasonable to ask why. Is this not, after all, what's known as a "family classic," beloved by wholesome—and prolific—heterosexuals?

As usual, one must look to the subtext. By definition, *The Wizard of Oz* is in touch with the sexual subconscious. The film, after all, consists mainly of an extended dream sequence, and the script makes a credible stab at giving it Freudian plausibility. It's the dream of a young girl, but it could just as easily be that of an old queen. I refer not only to the garish Technicolor decor; nor do I base my case entirely on the presence of Saint Judy, Our Lady of the Garlands. What interests me here is Margaret Hamilton, cast in the dual role of (Miss) Elvira Gulch and her dream counterpart, the Wicked Witch of the West.

In the real world of rural Depression-era Kansas portrayed in the opening scenes, Miss Gulch comes off as a sour old maid, bent on having Toto, Judy's cute little dog, destroyed by the county sheriff. Miss Gulch is a veritable icon of Protestant rectitude, repression, reaction, and drab respectability. She is, in short, the very incarnation of everything the American male homosexual flees the Midwest in order to escape. There is piquant irony here, since the character may also be "read" as a frustrated lesbian. Her costume is that of a nineteenth-century bluestocking. Though the script says she owns half the county, she only travels via bicycle. Judy has a dog and is therefore healthy and normal. Miss Gulch, on the other hand, has a cat and is therefore bitter and neurotic. When dream logic transmogrifies Miss Gulch into a witch, the homosexual viewer is able to have his cake and eat it, too: he can "love" poor, defenseless Judy Garland, while letting Margaret Hamilton bear the brunt of his misogyny.

Christian fundamentalists, by and large, disapprove of *The Wizard of Oz*. For precisely the wrong reason, I might add. The born-againers don't focus on Miss Gulch, even though, in both her incarnations, she is the perfect caricature of their own narrow-minded bigotry. Instead they object to the character played by Billie

Burke: Glinda, the Good Witch of the North. (The very concept of a "good" witch is a no-no in "Christian" circles.) In my contrary opinion, Miss Burke deserves credit, if only for making a line like "Toto, too" sound like something besides a tongue twister. In the fairy-tale land of Oz, the Wicked Witch melts into a slimy puddle. Back in Kansas, however, we never find out if Miss Gulch succeeds in snuffing poor Toto. This movie gives us plenty to chew on. Unfortunately, we can't avoid glimpses of the film that "normal" viewers are seeing. And *that* film is a tedious, ponderous bore.

A Woman's Face* (U.S. 1941 B&W)

A Woman's Face, an absurd collection of melodramatic clichés, has only a feeble glimmer of original thought behind it; its only inspiration is to cast Joan Crawford in the role of a hideously scarred criminal. The film takes place in Sweden—or, rather, some queen's idea of what Sweden must be like. (The director is George Cukor.) It's a courtroom drama, consisting mainly of flashbacks as the witnesses are testifying. Famous character actors virtually pop right out of the paneling. Joan's lawyer is George Zucco. The prosecuting attorney is Henry Daniell. And Connie Gilchrist turns up as one of the most Irish-looking Swedes I've ever seen.

Joan is the hard-bitten proprietress of a string of after-hours bistros which she exploits as a source of potentially scandalous information with which to blackmail wealthy ne'er-do-well customers. Then she meets Conrad Veidt, who finds her attractive despite her facial deformity. We instantly know he's depraved: he's first encountered at a party where a pair of women are dancing with each other.

Melvyn Douglas delineates the movie's only likable character: a plastic surgeon who thinks he can make Joan beautiful. He succeeds, whereupon she goes running right back to Conrad. At this point the movie misses a perfect chance for sublime irony: I would have had him regretfully announce that he can only get it up for women with scar tissue. Instead he cajoles her to aid him in a murder plot. He wants her to kill his four-year-old nephew, whose inheritance he covets. "No! No! No!" says Joan. "Yes! Yes, my darling! Yes!" enthuses Conrad.

And so she hires on as the child's governess. Upon the occasion of their initial meeting, he greets her by pelting her with a big, wet snowball. You'd think she'd be happy to send him hurtling over a waterfall. But no: now that she's got the face of a beautiful woman, she discovers that she's developed the soul of one, also.

At this point the film becomes a predictable Gothic romance, executed with routine competence. (Cukor, after all, directed *Gaslight*.) This movie was released in 1941, and the setting is supposed to be contemporary, which amazes me, since both the milieu and the psychology seem to date from sometime before the First World War. The plot is given some ersatz topicality by having the villainous Veidt turn into some sort of would-be Hitler.

This fascinatingly awful film is an excellent example of how even the most lurid, melodramatic material gets flattened out when subjected to the "classic" M-G-M treatment. When elderly ladies ask, "Why don't they ever make *good* movies anymore?," crap like *A Woman's Face* is probably what they're referring to.

The Women * (U.S. 1939 B&W with one color sequence)

The Women features an entirely female cast (directed by that notorious bitch, George Cukor) yammering and blabbering incessantly and interminably, till the very act of listening becomes literally exhausting. A catfest like this could be fun, theoretically, but only in very small doses. *The Women*, unfortunately, runs two hours and thirteen minutes.

Like a fundamentalist tract, the film is a virtual anthology of anti-feminist attitudes: anti-career women, anti-divorce, and stopping just short of an endorsement of wife-beating. Worse yet, such bitter poison sits side by side with a sweetly sentimentalized depiction of the upper classes. The plot revolves around Norma Shearer in her customary role as a paragon of virtue. She's cast as an embattled high society housewife whose husband is being filched by Joan Crawford, a fickle, grasping, conniving homewrecker from "the wrong side of Park Avenue." The Crawford character is presented as being hideously beyond the pale. To amuse herself, she "plays solitaire with the radio on." How very common! Basically, what we've got here is a hate letter addressed to proletarian women, warning them to know their place and not go poaching on upper-class turf. One can't help wondering: What's to be done about uppity lowlife types who refuse to accept their lot? Then again, maybe we needn't wonder. This film fails to offer any final solution, but the script does contain one dire hint. Extolling the joys of the single life, co-star Lucile Watson enthuses, "It's marvelous to be able to spread out in bed like a swastika!"

---

*Women on the Verge of a Nervous Breakdown**
(Spain 1988 C)

Pedro Almodóvar's *Women on the Verge of a Nervous Breakdown* stars Carmen Maura as a television actress going through a painful breakup with her married lover. The coincidences, the cruel tricks of fate so typical of conventional women's pictures are herein carried to the tenth power. Of course, the effect is farcical, sort of like an R-rated *I Love Lucy*. The subject matter isn't gay, but the sensibility certainly is. For instance, before the film is even ten minutes old, the director sees fit to show us a clip from *Johnny Guitar* starring Joan Crawford.

   The plot grows more and more madcap as it progresses. Toward the end, poor Carmen can't throw an object without it hitting somebody. At the climax she saves her lover's life (his jealous spouse was about to shoot him). Then she realizes that she's no longer in love with him. It's all very Joan Crawford, but with more of an ironic edge. (Crawford would probably have taken the bullet herself.)

   For many artsy moderns, Almodóvar virtually defines gay camp. If he's your cup of tea (he isn't mine), you might want to look at some of his other pictures, including *Labyrinth of Passion* (1982), *Dark Habits* (1984), *What Have I Done to Deserve This?* (1984), and *Law of Desire* (see review of this last film elsewhere in this book).

The Wrestling Women vs. the Aztec Mummy* (Mexico 1964 B&W)

The Wrestling Women vs. the Aztec Mummy is rightly regarded as a camp curiosity item. No doubt it was taken somewhat more seriously by the Mexican audiences for whom it was originally intended. The film is rock-bottom bad, but I must admit I was mildly frightened when the mummy at last came shambling and shuffling onscreen.

Ruby and Loretta, the hammerlocking heroines of the title, spend most of their time contending with the Black Dragon, a Fu Man-chu type whose henchmen have embarked on a campaign of murder and torture in an effort to locate the whereabouts of the Aztec treasure which the mummy is guarding. Of course, as soon as this treasure is plundered, there are sinister stirrings from a nearby sarcophagus. Chaos ensues. ("That monster is supernatural!" "There's something in this situation that's terrifying!") The late film scholar Parker Tyler once pointed out that movie monsters who walk stiffly invariably symbolize the erect phallus. Someone connected with this film evidently took this observation literally, since, at one point, one of the good guys expresses an incongruous concern with regard to the monster's sexuality: "Maybe that stupid mummy has fits and undresses! Who knows what he has beneath his clothes?" The fact that it's one of the male characters who frets over this unseemly possibility is, I believe, extremely significant. Wrestling women are too butch to care whether a mummy has balls; their men, on the other hand, are sufficiently weak and passive to worry about getting raped.

Young Frankenstein* (U.S. 1974 B&W)

Young Frankenstein, an affectionate send-up of old Universal monster movies, is most successful when it plays things (almost) perfectly straight. After all, why camp up something that's pretty campy already? Unfortunately, the tone is mostly farcical and the subtleties are few and far between. The film could have been forty-five minutes shorter if they'd left out all the schtick, all the skits and routines. Gene Wilder, Peter Boyle, Marty Feldman, Madeline Kahn, Kenneth Mars, and Cloris Leachman are no better than adequate at meeting the demands of roles which, in a happier time, would have been filled by Basil Rathbone, Boris Karloff, Dwight Frye, Valerie Hobson, Lionel Atwill, and Gale Sondergaard. The film's best moment plays off of the innocence, discretion, and restraint of Golden Age moviemaking. Wilder, questioning Leachman, the Mrs. Danvers-like housekeeper, about her relationship with his infamous ancestor, hesitantly asks, "Then you and Victor were . . . ?"

"Yes! Yes! Say it!" she hysterically hollers. "He was my . . . *boyfriend*!"

Ziegfeld Girl* (U.S. 1941 B&W)

Ziegfeld Girl, as its title indicates, is a film about showgirls in weird-looking headdresses walking up and down stairs. This movie means to show us how ordinary girls become Ziegfeld girls, as if there was ever anything remotely ordinary about Judy Garland, Lana Turner, and Hedy Lamarr, the stars on display herein. Mr. Ziegfeld is never seen; he's sort of like Christ in an old-fashioned Biblical epic. Apparently the girls are mainly selected by his right-hand man, played by Edward Everett Horton. It's no more than appropriate that one of "our kind" should be a judge of feminine pulchritude. We, at least, are able to be objective about such things.

As far as I'm concerned, the real stars of this show are buried so far down in the supporting cast, they don't even have billing. I spotted Eve Arden and Rose Hobart as a pair of over-the-hill Follies veterans. And also Dan Dailey, who is rather miscast in the role of a champion prizefighter (he slugs Lana, at one point). Hedy mainly just stands around looking beautiful. Judy's big moment is the "Minnie from Trinidad" number, which finds her wearing hoop earrings and a discreet skin darkener. She's got a phony parrot perched on her shoulder and what looks like the trunk of a palm tree jutting out of the top of her head. As for Lana, the glamour girl she portrays has a painfully protracted decline and

JUDY GARLAND (1922–1969), one of the pre-eminent gay cult stars, shown here in the colorful "Minnie from Trinidad" number from MGM's *Ziegfeld Girl* (1941).

fall. The part is good practice for an up-and-coming soap opera queen. And that pretty well sums up what's wrong with this picture: the cast is star-studded (I didn't even mention Jimmy Stewart as Lana's beau), but everyone seems to be biding their time till something better comes along.

Zorro's Fighting Legion* (U.S. 1939 B&W)

Zorro's Fighting Legion, a twelve-chapter serial, is incoherent pseudo-history about a masked hero who runs around scrawling the last letter of the alphabet all over the place. He's portrayed by skinny, delicate-looking Reed Hadley, who is far more convincing in his delineation of Zorro's alternate identity: a foppish, sissified bon vivant. In that effeminate guise he minces and flutters, gushes and preens. This gay caballero is undeniably likable, though his facial features remind us of a scared rabbit.

The mise en scène is made to seem surrealistically fluid: stone walls part like curtains; a water-gate is opened to cataclysmically flood a cave. The long, low, rambling haciendas all look like Fifties motels. The men all wear tight-fitting, gaudy outfits embellished with fancy embroidery. They also wear sideburns with spit curls. The principal villain wears a silly, clanking golden suit and helmet to disguise himself. The Yaqui Indians think he's a god and let themselves be manipulated. Later, when they see him without his grimacing false face, they kill him for being merely human.

As is the case with all good American juvenile trash, the homosexual content is almost as plentiful as the sadism. "Men of Zorro are we!" sing the good guys, endlessly. As usual, a bad guy was the one who won my heart. Named Manuel and portrayed by John Merton, he is short, stocky, plump, and elegantly bearded. Unfortunately, just as I started responding to him, he got shot in the back with a golden arrow let fly by a Yaqui assassin. The plot logic is seemingly governed by the violent poetry of a homoerotic dream. A slender, doe-eyed Indian prince, with coy pigtails framing his pretty face, exchanges sappy grins with Hadley while seminude warriors get impaled on swords and, shrieking with agony, topple into lava pits. Orgasmic adventures such as this qualify as all-male porno, even though they are products of a distant era's naïveté.

INDEX OF PRINCIPAL PERFORMERS
(not all necessarily with camp roles)

Acquanetta
  Jungle Woman
Allen, Steve
  College Confidential
Alonso, Chelo
  Goliath and the
    Barbarians
  Son of Samson
Andrews, Dana
  Laura
Andrews, Julie
  Victor/Victoria
Arden, Eve
  Mildred Pierce
  Ziegfeld Girl
Ashley, John
  Beach Blanket Bingo
  Dragstrip Girl
  Frankenstein's Daughter
  High School Caesar
  Hot Rod Gang
  Motorcycle Gang
Ast, Pat
  Heat
  Reform School Girls
Astaire, Fred
  Flying Down to Rio
Astor, Mary
  The Maltese Falcon
Avalon, Frankie
  Beach Blanket Bingo
Backus, Jim
  Rebel Without a Cause
Barker, Lex
  Tarzan's Magic
    Fountain
Baxter, Anne
  All About Eve
Beatty, Warren
  The Roman Spring of
    Mrs. Stone
Berger, Helmut
  The Damned
Bey, Turhan
  Ali Baba and the Forty
    Thieves
  A Night in Paradise
Blaine, Vivian
  Doll Face
Blondell, Joan
  Will Success Spoil
    Rock Hunter?

Blyth, Ann
  Mildred Pierce
  Slander
Bogarde, Dirk
  The Damned
  I Could Go on Singing
Bogart, Humphrey
  The Maltese Falcon
Boyer, Charles
  All This, and Heaven
    Too
  Conquest
Brando, Marlon
  A Streetcar Named
    Desire
  The Wild One
Brent, George
  Baby Face
  In This Our Life
  Jezebel
  The Old Maid
Brian, David
  Beyond the Forest
  Flamingo Road
Broderick, Matthew
  Torch Song Trilogy
Bruce, David
  Salome, Where She
    Danced
Bryan, Jane
  The Old Maid
  The Sisters
Brynner, Yul
  The Magic Christian
Buetel, Jack
  The Outlaw
Buono, Victor
  Hush . . . Hush, Sweet
    Charlotte
  What Ever Happened
    to Baby Jane?
Burke, Billie
  In This Our Life
  The Wizard of Oz
Burton, Richard
  Staircase
Calleia, Joseph
  Gilda
  My Little Chickadee
Canale, Gianna Maria
  Colossus and the
    Amazon Queen

Hercules
Carey, Roland
  The Giants of
    Thessaly
Chaney, Lon (Jr.)
  Cobra Woman
Clift, Montgomery
  Suddenly, Last
    Summer
Coburn, Charles
  Gentlemen Prefer
    Blondes
  In This Our Life
Cochran, Steve
  I, Mobster
  Slander
Colman, Ronald
  Lost Horizon
Conried, Hans
  The 5,000 Fingers of
    Dr. T
Cook, Elisha
  College Confidential
  The Maltese Falcon
Cooper, Gary
  Morocco
Cotten, Joseph
  Beyond the Forest
  Hush . . . Hush, Sweet
    Charlotte
Crawford, Joan
  Autumn Leaves
  Chained
  Flamingo Road
  Johnny Guitar
  Mildred Pierce
  Rain
  Trog
  What Ever Happened
    to Baby Jane?
  A Woman's Face
  The Women
Crews, Laura Hope
  The Sisters
Cruise, Tom
  Risky Business
Curry, Tim
  The Rocky Horror
    Picture Show
Curtis, Jackie
  Flesh

Curtis, Tony
  Some Like It Hot
Dallesandro, Joe
  Andy Warhol's
    Dracula
  Cry-Baby
  Flesh
  Heat
  Trash
Dalton, Timothy
  Flash Gordon
  Sextette
Darling, Candy
  Flesh
Darnell, Linda
  The Mark of Zorro
Davis, Bette
  All About Eve
  All This, and Heaven
    Too
  The Anniversary
  Another Man's Poison
  Beyond the Forest
  Dead Ringer
  Hush . . . Hush, Sweet
    Charlotte
  In This Our Life
  Jezebel
  The Little Foxes
  Mr. Skeffington
  The Nanny
  Now, Voyager
  Old Acquaintance
  The Old Maid
  The Private Lives of
    Elizabeth and Essex
  The Sisters
  The Star
  A Stolen Life
  Storm Center
  What Ever Happened
    to Baby Jane?
  Wicked Stepmother
Davis, Brad
  Querelle
Dean, James
  Rebel Without a
    Cause
De Carlo, Yvonne
  Salome, Where She
    Danced
De Havilland, Olivia
  Hush . . . Hush, Sweet
    Charlotte
  In This Our Life
Dekker, Albert
  The Silver Chalice

Suddenly, Last
  Summer
Tarzan's Magic
  Fountain
Del Rio, Dolores
  Flying Down to Rio
Depp, Johnny
  Cry-Baby
Dietrich, Marlene
  Blonde Venus
  Dishonored
  Morocco
  The Scarlet Empress
  Shanghai Express
Divine
  Female Trouble
  Hairspray
  Lust in the Dust
  Mondo Trasho
  Multiple Maniacs
  Pink Flamingos
  Polyester
Donahue, Troy
  Cry-Baby
Donnelly, Ruth
  Autumn Leaves
  My Little Chickadee
Douglas, Melvyn
  A Woman's Face
Dunaway, Faye
  Mommie Dearest
Dunne, Irene
  Thirteen Women
Duryea, Dan
  The Little Foxes
Evans, Dame Edith
  The Importance of
    Being Earnest
Evans, Linda
  Beach Blanket Bingo
Ewell, Tom
  The Seven Year Itch
Farrell, Timothy
  Glen or Glenda?
  Jail Bait
Fawcett, Farrah
  Myra Breckinridge
Faye, Alice
  The Gang's All
    Here
Fields, W. C.
  My Little Chickadee
Fierstein, Harvey
  Torch Song Trilogy
Fleming, Eric
  Queen of Outer
    Space

Fleming, Rhonda
  Bullwhip
Flynn, Errol
  The Private Lives of
    Elizabeth and Essex
  The Sisters
Fonda, Henry
  Jezebel
Foran, Dick
  My Little Chickadee
  The Sisters
Ford, Glenn
  Affair in Trinidad
  Gilda
  A Stolen Life
Forest, Mark
  Son of Samson
  The Terror of Rome
    Against the Son of
    Hercules
Fuller, Dolores
  Glen or Glenda?
  Jail Bait
Fuller, Lance
  The Bride and the
    Beast
  Girls in Prison
Fury, Ed
  Colossus and the
    Amazon Queen
  Samson Against the
    Sheik
Gabor, Zsa Zsa
  Queen of Outer Space
Garbo, Greta
  Conquest
  Mata Hari
  Queen Christina
Garland, Judy
  I Could Go on Singing
  A Star Is Born
  Thoroughbreds Don't
    Cry
  The Wizard of Oz
  Ziegfeld Girl
Garner, James
  Victor/Victoria
Geray, Steven
  Affair in Trinidad
  Gilda
Gilbert, John
  Queen Christina
Gough, Michael
  Trog
Grable, Betty
  Springtime in the
    Rockies

Grant, Cary
  Blonde Venus
  I'm No Angel
  She Done Him Wrong
Graves, Rupert
  Maurice
Greenstreet, Sydney
  Flamingo Road
  The Maltese Falcon
Hadley, Reed
  Doll Face
  Now, Voyager
  Zorro's Fighting
    Legion
Hagen, Jean
  Dead Ringer
Hall, Jon
  Ali Baba and the Forty
    Thieves
  Cobra Woman
Hamilton, George
  Sextette
Hamilton, Margaret
  My Little Chickadee
  The Wizard of Oz
Hargitay, Mickey
  Bloody Pit of Horror
  The Loves of Hercules
  Will Success Spoil
    Rock Hunter?
Harrison, Rex
  Staircase
Harvey, Laurence
  The Magic Christian
Hayden, Sterling
  Johnny Guitar
  The Star
Haydn, Richard
  Sitting Pretty
Hayes, Gabby
  The Lost City
Hayworth, Rita
  Affair in Trinidad
  Gilda
  Miss Sadie Thompson
  Salome
Hearst, Patty
  Cry-Baby
Heatherton, Joey
  Cry Baby
Henreid, Paul
  Now, Voyager
Hepburn, Audrey
  Breakfast at Tiffany's
Hepburn, Katharine
  Suddenly, Last
    Summer

Hobart, Rose
  Ziegfeld Girl
Holden, William
  Sunset Boulevard
Holloway, Sterling
  Blonde Venus
  Dancing Lady
Hopkins, Miriam
  Old Acquaintance
  The Old Maid
Horton, Edward Everett
  The Gang's All Here
  Lost Horizon
  Springtime in the
    Rockies
  Ziegfeld Girl
Hudson, Rochelle
  She Done Him
    Wrong
Hunter, Kim
  Storm Center
  A Streetcar Named
    Desire
Hunter, Tab
  Lust in the Dust
  Polyester
Huston, Walter
  The Outlaw
  Rain
Jergens, Adele
  Girls in Prison
  Ladies of the Chorus
Johnson, Van
  Slander
Kier, Udo
  Andy Warhol's
    Dracula
King, Perry
  Mandingo
Lake, Ricki
  Cry-Baby
  Hairspray
Lamarr, Hedy
  Samson and Delilah
  Ziegfeld Girl
Lansbury, Angela
  Samson and Delilah
La Rocque, Rod
  The Ten
    Commandments
Laughton, Charles
  Salome
Leachman, Cloris
  Young Frankenstein
Leigh, Vivien
  The Roman Spring of
    Mrs. Stone

A Streetcar Named
    Desire
Lemmon, Jack
  Some Like It Hot
Liberace
  Sincerely Yours
Lisi, Virna
  Duel of the Titans
Lodge, John
  The Scarlet Empress
Lorre, Peter
  The Maltese Falcon
Louise, Anita
  The Sisters
Loy, Myrna
  Thirteen Women
Lugosi, Bela
  Glen or Glenda?
Lynde, Paul
  Beach Blanket Bingo
Lynn, Peter George
  The Adventures of
    Captain Marvel
Madison, Guy
  Bullwhip
  Superargo and the
    Faceless Giants
  Till the End of Time
Mansfield, Jayne
  The Loves of Hercules
  The Wild, Wild World
    of Jayne Mansfield
  Will Success Spoil
    Rock Hunter?
Marshall, Herbert
  Blonde Venus
  College Confidential
Mason, James
  Mandingo
  A Star Is Born
Massey, Edith
  Desperate Living
  Female Trouble
  Multiple Maniacs
  Pink Flamingos
  Polyester
Mature, Victor
  Samson and Delilah
Maura, Carmen
  Law of Desire
  Women on the Verge
    of a Nervous
    Breakdown
McCambridge, Mercedes
  Johnny Guitar
  Suddenly, Last
    Summer

251

Meadows, Jayne
  College Confidential
Menjou, Adolphe
  Morocco
Methot, Mayo
  The Sisters
Miles, Vera
  Autumn Leaves
  Tarzan's Hidden
    Jungle
Mineo, Sal
  Rebel Without a Cause
Miranda, Carmen
  Doll Face
  The Gang's All Here
  Springtime in the
    Rockies
Mishima, Yukio
  Black Lizard
Mitchell, Thomas
  Lost Horizon
  The Outlaw
Monroe, Marilyn
  All About Eve
  Gentlemen Prefer
    Blondes
  Ladies of the Chorus
  The Seven Year Itch
  Some Like It Hot
Montez, Maria
  Ali Baba and the Forty
    Thieves
  Cobra Woman
Moore, Cleo
  Strange Fascination
Moorehead, Agnes
  Hush . . . Hush, Sweet
    Charlotte
Moreau, Jeanne
  Querelle
Morris, Kirk
  The Witch's Curse
Neal, Patricia
  Breakfast at Tiffany's
Nelson, David
  Cry-Baby
Nelson, Lori
  Sincerely Yours
  Untamed Youth
Nero, Franco
  Querelle
Newman, Paul
  The Silver Chalice
Noonan, Tommy
  Gentlemen Prefer
    Blondes
  A Star Is Born

Norton, Ken
  Drum
  Mandingo
Novarro, Ramon
  Ben-Hur
  Mata Hari
Oberon, Merle
  A Night in Paradise
O'Hara, Maureen
  Sitting Pretty
Oland, Warner
  Dishonored
  Shanghai Express
Palance, Jack
  The Silver Chalice
Pallette, Eugene
  The Gang's All
    Here
  The Mark of Zoro
Pangborn, Franklin
  Flying Down to Rio
  Now, Voyager
Park, Reg
  Hercules and the
    Captive Women
Patrick, Lee
  Now, Voyager
  The Sisters
Pearce, Mary Vivian
  Mondo Trasho
Peppard, George
  Breakfast at
    Tiffany's
Power, Tyrone
  The Mark of Zorro
Price, Vincent
  Laura
  The Private Lives of
    Elizabeth and Essex
Purdom, Edmund
  The Prodigal
Rains, Claude
  Mr. Skeffington
  Now, Voyager
Ralston, Vera Hruba
  Jubilee Trail
Rambeau, Marjorie
  Salome, Where She
    Danced
  Slander
Rampling, Charlotte
  The Damned
Randall, Tony
  Will Success Spoil
    Rock Hunter?
Rathbone, Basil
  The Mark of Zorro

Redgrave, Michael
  The Importance of
    Being Earnest
Reed, Rex
  Myra Breckinridge
Reeves, Steve
  Duel of the Titans
  The Giant of
    Marathon
  Goliath and the
    Barbarians
  Hercules
  Hercules Unchained
  Jail Bait
Rettig, Tommy
  The 5,000 Fingers of
    Dr. T
Richmond, Kane
  The Lost City
  Spy Smasher
Ripploh, Frank
  Taxi Zum Klo
Robertson, Cliff
  Autumn Leaves
Robinson, Joe
  Thor and the Amazon
    Women
Rodann, Ziva
  College Confidential
  The Giants of
    Thessaly
Rogers, Ginger
  Flying Down to Rio
Rogers, Roy
  Eyes of Texas
Roland, Gilbert
  She Done Him
    Wrong
Roman, Ruth
  Beyond the Forest
Romero, Cesar
  Springtime in the
    Rockies
Rooney, Mickey
  Thoroughbreds Don't
    Cry
Roth, Lillian
  Madam Satan
Ruffo, Leonora
  The Queen of
    Sheba
Russell, Craig
  Outrageous!
Russell, Jane
  Gentlemen Prefer
    Blondes
  The Outlaw

Russell, John
  Jubilee Trail
  Sitting Pretty
  Untamed Youth
Rutherford, Margaret
  The Importance of
    Being Earnest
Sabu
  Cobra Woman
  The Thief of
    Bagdad
Sanders, George
  All About Eve
Scott, Gordon
  Duel of the Titans
  Gladiators of Rome
  Hero of Rome
  Samson and the Seven
    Miracles of the
    World
  Tarzan and the
    Trappers
  Tarzan's Hidden
    Jungle
  The Tyrant of Lydia
    Against the Son of
    Hercules
Scott, Zachary
  Flamingo Road
  Mildred Pierce
Sellek, Tom
  Myra Breckinridge
Sellers, Peter
  The Magic Christian
Serrault, Michel
  La Cage aux Folles
Shearer, Norma
  The Women
Sondergaard, Gale
  The Mark of Zorro
  A Night in Paradise
Spain, Fay
  Dragstrip Girl
  Hercules and the
    Captive Women
Stanwyck, Barbara
  Baby Face
Starr, Ringo
  The Magic
    Christian
Steel, Alan
  Hercules Against the
    Moon Men
Sterling, Jan
  High School
    Confidential

Stewart, James
  Ziegfeld Girl
Stole, Mink
  Cry-Baby
  Desperate Living
  Female Trouble
  Hairspray
  Mondo Trasho
  Multiple Maniacs
  Pink Flamingos
  Polyester
Swanson, Gloria
  Sunset Boulevard
Talbot, Lyle
  Glen or Glenda?
  Jail Bait
Tamblyn, Russ
  High School
    Confidential!
  Samson and
    Delilah
Tamiroff, Akim
  Queen Christina
Tani, Yuko
  Samson and the Seven
    Miracles of the
    World
Taylor, Elizabeth
  Suddenly, Last
    Summer
Taylor, Rod
  Colossus and the
    Amazon Queen
Thompson, Shawn
  Hairspray
Tierney, Gene
  Laura
Tognazzi, Ugo
  La Cage aux Folles
Tucker, Sophie
  Thoroughbreds Don't
    Cry
Turner, Lana
  The Prodigal
  Ziegfeld Girl
Tuttle, Lurene
  Sincerely Yours
  Untamed Youth
Tyler, Tom
  The Adventures of
    Captain Marvel
Tyrrell, Susan
  Cry-Baby
Valentino, Rudolph
  The Son of the
    Sheik

Van Doren, Mamie
  College Confidential
  High School
    Confidential!
  Untamed Youth
Veidt, Conrad
  The Thief of Bagdad
  A Woman's Face
Vickers, Yvette
  I, Mobster
Village People
  Can't Stop the Music
von Stroheim, Erich
  Sunset Boulevard
Warner, H. B.
  Lost Horizon
Wayne, John
  Baby Face
Webb, Clifton
  Laura
  Sitting Pretty
Welch, Raquel
  The Magic Christian
  Myra Breckinridge
West, Mae
  I'm No Angel
  My Little Chickadee
  Myra Breckinridge
  Sextette
  She Done Him Wrong
Wilby, James
  Maurice
Wilcoxon, Henry
  Samson and Delilah
Williams, Guy
  Damon and Pythias
Williams, Wendy O.
  Reform School Girls
Winchell, Walter
  College Confidential
Winwood, Estelle
  Dead Ringer
Wong, Anna May
  Shanghai Express
Wood, Edward D.
  Glen or Glenda?
Wood, Natalie
  Rebel Without a Cause
Woodlawn, Holly
  Trash
Young, Gig
  Old Acquaintance
Young, Robert
  Sitting Pretty
Zucco, George
  A Woman's Face

ALPHABETICAL LIST OF AUTHOR PAUL ROEN'S
10 FAVORITE CAMP/CULT FILMS IN THIS BOOK

1. All About Eve
2. The Gang's All Here
3. Hairspray
4. Johnny Guitar
5. Jubilee Trail
6. Myra Breckinridge
7. Some Like It Hot
8. A Star Is Born
9. Sunset Boulevard
10. What Ever Happened to Baby Jane?

ALPHABETICAL LIST OF
EDITOR/PUBLISHER WINSTON LEYLAND'S
10 FAVORITE CAMP/CULT FILMS IN THIS BOOK

1. All About Eve *Bette at her best and bitchiest.*
2. Beyond the Forest *Gay men penned up in Bible-belt small towns can empathize with Bette/Rosa Moline's obsession to lam out for the big, wicked city.*
3. Cobra Woman *Maria Montez at her slinkiest and Sabu in his chicken years.*
4. Gilda *Rita Hayworth at her sexiest; a film with many gay innuendos.*
5. Glen or Glenda? *Must be seen to be believed! Surely the campiest film in this book.*
6. The Maltese Falcon *After 100 + viewings I still get something new from it each time. Sidney Greenstreet, Mary Astor, Elisha Cook Jr., Peter Lorre are magnificent, as is Bogie.*
7. Maurice *Not camp but fast becoming an archetypal gay cult film.*
8. Mildred Pierce *Joan suffering at her glossiest, with a marvelous supporting cast.*
9. Mr. Skeffington *The perils of aging with Bette in top form. Gays can relate! Some camp elements but primarily cult.*
10. What Ever Happened to Baby Jane? *Joan and Bette pull out all the stops!*

Five runners up: The Anniversary; Mandingo; Queen Christina; Samson & Delilah; Sunset Boulevard.

BOOKS FROM LEYLAND PUBLICATIONS / G.S PRESS

ABOUT THE AUTHOR

Paul Roen (born 1948) lives in the woods near Two Harbors, Minnesota. Film reviews by Paul Roen appeared in the 1970s magazine *Castle of Frankenstein*. He reviews theatrical films for a Duluth, Minnesota radio station as a part-time avocation, and has about a thousand classic movies on tape. This is his first book.